Nurit Peled-Elhanan is Lecturer in Language Education in the Faculty of Education at the Hebrew University of Jerusalem. A co-recipient of the 2001 Sakharov Prize for Human Rights and the Freedom of Thought, awarded by the European Parliament, she has written extensively on Israeli education, and is a regular speaker and writer both in Europe and in the USA on matters concerning the Israeli occupation and its effects on both Israelis and Palestinians. She is a member of the Israeli-Palestinian Bereaved Parents for Peace, and one of the founders of the Russell Tribunal on Palestine 2009.

Palestine in Israeli School Books

IDEOLOGY *and* PROPAGANDA *in* EDUCATION

Nurit Peled-Elhanan

I.B.TAURIS
LONDON • NEW YORK • OXFORD • NEW DELHI • SYDNEY

I.B. TAURIS
Bloomsbury Publishing Plc
50 Bedford Square, London, WC1B 3DP, UK
1385 Broadway, New York, NY 10018, USA

BLOOMSBURY, I.B. TAURIS and the I.B. Tauris logo are
trademarks of Bloomsbury Publishing Plc

First published in hardback in 2012
Reprinted 2019 (twice)

A catalogue record for this book is available from the British Library.

ISBN: PB: 978 1 78076 505 1

Typeset by Newgen Publishers, Chennai

To find out more about our authors and books visit
www.bloomsbury.com and sign up for our newsletters.

The human psyche has two great sicknesses: the urge to carry vendetta across generations and the tendency to fasten group labels on people rather than see them as individuals.

Richard Dawkins

CONTENTS

PREFACE

> History is never said or read innocently for it is always for someone.
>
> (Jenkins, 1991: 86)

In Israel, school books are written for youngsters who will be drafted into joining compulsory military service at 18 years of age and carry out the Israeli policy of occupation in the Palestinian territories.

The concern of the present study is not to describe Israeli education as a whole but rather to focus on one specific question: how are Palestine and the Palestinians against whom these young Israelis will potentially be required to use force, portrayed in school books?

My special interest in school books stems from the conviction I share with other researchers, both in Israel and in other countries, that in spite of all other sources of information, school books remain powerful means by which the state shapes forms of perception, of categorization, of interpretation and of memory, that serve to determine personal and national identities. This is true especially in nations such as Israel where 'history, memory, [personal identity] and nation enjoy an intimate communion' (Nora, 1996: 5).

Four years ago, a student of mine, Tal Sela, wrote a preface to his term-paper which consisted of the analysis of Israeli history textbooks:

> On the 5th of September 1997 I found myself in Lebanon, on a rescuing mission. All my friends were in the battle, 12 soldiers

> were killed ... A year later I was in deep depression. Sad and morose. I decided to consult a psychologist. After a few sessions [...] I could reorganize my thoughts. Then I understood that the mental crisis I had was in fact a moral crisis, a crisis of consciousness. What I actually felt was frustration, shame and anger.
>
> How could I be so gullible and let myself be duped? How can I explain that a man of peace exposes himself to such a morbid experience of his own free will? Today, I saw an officer put tight handcuffs on a taxi driver because he failed to obey the soldiers' order to park here and not there. 'We told him a thousand times' the soldiers said. The man was lying on the ground in the worst heat of the summer, thirsty, for hours on end. His friend was luckier: He had to stand on his feet, in a cell, without handcuffs.
>
> What pushes these young Israeli boys to play the role of supreme judges until they lose all judgment? In my opinion it is the 'Grand Zionist Narrative' which serves, explicitly as well as implicitly, as a collective conscience to the whole Israeli society. This grand narrative is the system of values that makes us belong to this particular collective.

This book presents a critical study of one aspect of this narrative as it is reproduced in school books of three disciplines: history, geography and civic studies. It consists of an analysis of the visual and verbal texts that represent the 'others' of Zionist Jews, namely Palestinians – both the citizens of Israel and the non-citizens who have been living under a military regime in the occupied Palestinian territories since 1967.

The study is guided by my own reading. The philosopher Michael Waltzer notes that 'critics are not disembodied hermetic individuals, but interested members of specific societies and social groups with specific points of view' (Waltzer, 1987: 43). This view is shared by literary critics, philosophers and discourse analysts who see the act of reading as a personal 'meaning-making,' whereby the reader is 'filling elements with content and making sense of these elements' (Kress, 2003: 38). The 'sense' is never entirely dictated by the writer, as Renaissance French philosopher Michel de Montaigne had already observed, '*La parole est moitié à celui qui parle moitié à celui qui écoute*' (Montaigne, Essais III).[1]

My own reading and the intertextual connections that I found in the textbooks I analyzed are the basis of my interpretation. Literary scholar Samoyault (2003: 68) explains that in the act of reading the reader is solicited by the intertext on four levels: her memory and her culture; her inventiveness and her playful spirit. All four levels are required to explore the possibilities offered by the multimodal, multi generic and non-linear reading of school book texts because school books are 'intertexts' by their nature: they both refer to other texts and transform texts of different genres (Kress, 2003: 140). The intertextual connections found in the school books analyzed here are informed by my knowledge of Israeli political, cultural, social and educational discourses, and my ideological stance which is what Reisigl and Wodak describe as 'empathic with the victims of discrimination' (2001: 35).

INTRODUCTION

A JEWISH ETHNOCRACY IN THE MIDDLE EAST

In spite of Israel's success to advertise its regime as a Democracy, it is often defined by researchers as either an 'Ethnocracy' or as an 'ethnic Democracy.' This is because ethnicity[1] and not citizenship is the main determinant for the allocation of rights, power and resources in Israel. Jews who are citizens of other countries and Jewish settlers who live beyond the official border of the state have full citizenship rights while Arab citizens inside the state's borders don't, and Palestinians from the occupied West Bank are listed 'state-less.'

Israeli education also propagates the idea of Israel as a democracy – the only democracy in the Middle East – while reinforcing its existence as an Ethnocracy. Israel is defined in all school books, as in the general political and socio-cultural discourse, as the state of the Jews wherever they dwell and not as the state of its citizens.

Ethnocracies, according to Oren Yiftachel (2006), have some democratic features, such as periodic elections, freedom of religion, legislation, relative freedom of media and communication, and they extend significant though partial human and civil rights to minorities. The structure of ethnocracies is based on ethno-territorial domination manifest in control of the dominant ethnic group over land and settlements, the armed forces, capital flow, constitution and public culture (Yiftachel, 2006).

Like other ethnocracies Israel facilitates an undemocratic expansion of the dominant Jewish 'ethno-nation' into Palestinian lands both within and outside the official borders of the state. This expansion is presented in Israeli school books as abiding by Zionist vision and principles and by Israel's need for land and security. These matters will be discussed in chapter 2.

Smooha defines Israel as an ethnic democracy:

> It is a democracy which is propelled by an ideology or a movement of ethnic nationalism that declares a certain population as a nation sharing a common descent, a common language and a common culture. It also claims ownership of a certain territory that it considers its exclusive homeland ... It is a diminished type of democracy for it takes the ethnic nation, not the citizenry, as the corner-stone of the state [...] In Israel the Jews appropriate the state and make it a tool to advance their national security, demography, public space, culture and interests. At the same time this democracy extends various kinds of [individual] rights to 1 million Palestinian-Arab citizens (16 per cent of the population) who are perceived as a threat (Smooha, 1997: 210).

Since some of the important features listed above, such as common language and common culture and history, were hardly available to the modern Jewish-Israeli nation, they had to be manufactured by education, literature and the media, for the purpose of building a collective homogenous memory and identity. Hence an important task of Israeli school books has always been to reproduce a narrative that would connect the Jewish students to their 'origins' in the Land of Israel. Israeli school books have always presented Israeli Jews as the home-coming indigenes. These 'indigenized' Jews are perceived in Israeli discourse as modern Westerners who are the direct descendants of the biblical Hebrews – the children of Israel.

School Books between History and Memory

It is hard to think of a more extended and massive effort to create and control collective memory than that mounted by modern states, especially through their education system (Wertsch, 2002: 172).

The present study is not written by a historian but by a discourse-analyst. It does not seek to verify the facts that are presented in Israeli textbooks but to study their discourse, namely their rhetoric, and the semiotic means by which they convey their messages.

The particular discourse of history books and textbooks has been the object of study of historians, sociologists, psychologists and discourse analysts. One topic of interest is whether school books are the producers and reproducers of collective memory or the agents of historical inquiry. According to Wertsch (2002: 69) state-sponsored narratives are not meant to be logically or scientifically right, or to engage students in historical inquiry, but to form a strong collective identity. Hence, although the official histories are sometimes proven scientifically wrong, the collective memory they enhance is stronger in forming collective identity and loyalty, for memory has a stronger hold on people's mind than history.

Wertsch (2002: 69) observes that nations, being imagined communities and not 'a natural, God-given way of classifying men [...] require major effort and increasing vigilance in the matter of identity' for their creation and maintenance. Although 'states are certainly not the only entities that try to purvey collective memory in the modern world, [...] they are unrivaled in the power and resources they have devoted to this effort.' One of the main channels for perpetuating national narratives is formal education. Wertsch and other researchers of textbooks (see Wertsch, 2002: 10) argue that the main task of school books is to construct a continuous national narrative or collective memories in order to construe and consolidate the national identity for all citizens or at least of those who constitute the dominant group. This observation is undoubtedly true for Israel, where neither the Jewish students who constitute the 'majority' nor the Palestinian-Israeli students who constitute the 'minority,' are taught the Palestinian national narrative, and all learn the Zionist one (see Nasser and Nasser, 2008).

School books serve as what Nora termed *lieux de mémoire* or realms of memory (Nora, 1996). Nora explains that 'works of history become lieux de memoire only when they reshape memory in some fundamental way or epitomize a revision of memory for pedagogical purposes' (1996: 17). What turns school books into 'realms of memory' is their function 'to inhibit forgetting, to fix a state of things, to immortalize death and to materialize the immaterial – all in order to capture the maximum possible meaning with the fewest possible signs' (Nora, 1996: 15).

Nora, like other historians maintains there is a great difference between history and collective memory. Nora argues that in fact history, being a-mythical, is perpetually suspicious of memory which is based on myths. Unlike memory, history welcomes disagreement, change and controversy as part of the ongoing historical interpretation (Nora, 1996: 8–9). That makes history the main enemy of collective memory and its true mission – to destroy it (Nora, 1996: 9), or rather to change the '*lieux de memoires* into *lieux d'histoire*' (Nora, 1984: 14–15). Nora further argues that collective memory is dictatorial, unself-conscious, commanding and retains from the past only what still lives and is capable of living in the consciousness of the group and of keeping the memory alive.

Halbwachs (1992), like Nora, maintains that history begins where memory ends, is extinct or decomposed. Halbwachs explains that history, unlike memory, tends to be more distanced from any particular perspective and to reflect loyalty to no particular social framework; the fundamental difference between memory and history is that history examines all versions and tries to make sense of the differences. By contrast, memory is contextual, depending on a special group in a special place. This is the reason why history couldn't be a sort of universal memory. Being an intellectual and secular artifact, history calls for analysis and criticism. At the heart of history is a critical discourse that is antithetical to memory whose primary aim, especially in the case of collective memory, is not understanding the past but construing a 'usable past' that would justify 'our' way while de-legitimating 'their' way. The main goal of collective memory is to distinguish the group from other groups, be they out-groups or 'enemies.' As Allport (1958) already explained, all groups develop a way of living with characteristic codes and beliefs, standards and 'enemies' to suit their own adaptive needs. These codes and beliefs are the ingredients of collective memory and national narratives. One of these ingredients is hostility toward out-groups which 'helps strengthen our sense of belonging', (Allport, 1958: 171) although, as Wertsch makes clear, it is not required. Allport (1958: 171) maintains that the opposite tendencies seem to mark the tolerant person; but official national accounts, especially in new states, cannot be tolerant, for they require 'the outright rejection' of all other accounts and 'the generation of something completely different' (Wertsch, 2002: 88). Official narratives draw sharp lines between stark opposites – black and white, good and evil, true children of the land and untrue children of the land (Halbwachs, 1997). Such accounts are most typical of ethnocracies such as Israel because 'the ethnocratic public space is formulated around a set of cultural and religious symbols, representations, traditions and practices which tend to reinforce the narratives of the dominant ethno-national group, while silencing, degrading or ridiculing contesting cultures or perspectives' (Yiftachel, 2006: 37). As for Israel, Confino (2007a) argues that Israelis in general are neither able nor willing to look at their past relationships with the Palestinians critically because this past constitutes a crucial contemporary political problem.

The Palestinian-Israeli conflict is what Bar-Tal (2001) termed intractable conflict. Bekerman and Zembylas (p.135–137 in press) who studied both the Greek-Turkish conflict in Cyprus and the Israeli-Palestinian one in the context of mixed schools, explain, that the narrative of collective memories relating to intractable conflicts provides a black and white picture, which enables 'parsimonious, fast, unequivocal and simple understanding of the history of the conflict. This narrative which dominates school textbooks and pedagogical practices, is presented as the history of the society.'

Bekerman and Zembylas argue that 'in terms of particular contents, the societal beliefs of collective memory touch on at least four important themes in terms of the perception of the conflict and its management. First, they justify the outbreak of the conflict and the course of its development. Second, the societal beliefs of collective memory of intractable conflict present a positive image of the in-group. Third, the societal beliefs of collective memory delegitimize the opponent. Fourth, the beliefs of collective memory present one's own society as the victim of the opponent. This view is formed over a long period of violence as a result of the society's sufferings and losses and even sometimes viewed as "chosen trauma."'

Studying the vicissitudes of collective memory in Soviet and post-Soviet Russia, Wertsch (2002) came to the conclusion that it is often quite difficult to categorize any official accounts of the past, reproduced in textbooks, as either memory or history, for they include elements of both. In a way, 'official histories occupy a middle ground between religious texts and documentation' (Wertsch, 2002: 71). Like religious collectives, states often seek to produce texts in which 'the force of the word is strong enough to supersede differences between the participants [and] weld them for a time at least into a unit' (Stock, 1990: 150 in Wertsch, 2002: 28).

Podeh (2002: 5), who studied Israeli school books from 1950 until 2000, claims that school books are not agents of history but rather 'agents of memory whose aim is to ensure the transmission of certain "approved knowledge" to the younger generation.' Podeh maintains that in construing the collective memory, Israeli textbooks play a dual role: on the one hand, they provide a sense of continuity between past and present, transmitting accepted historical narratives; on the other, they alter and rewrite the past in order to suit contemporary needs. 'Since [...] the state controls the educational apparatus, it can shape the nation's collective memory by determining what is to be included and what excluded from the curricula and from textbooks. Such a course of action opens the way for the manipulation of the past in order to mold the present and the future' (Podeh, 2000: 1).

Studies show that Israeli school books aim to inculcate the collective memory created by Zionism which 'constitutes an entirely novel Jewish collective memory.' (Zrubavel, 2002). Israeli school books of history, geography, civics, literature and even science and grammar, promulgate in one way or another the Zionist grand narrative, made according to Zrubavel (2002: 115–116) of two dichotomist parts: the narrative of decline from the 'golden age' of antiquity through 'exile' to its culmination in the Holocaust and a narrative of progress beginning with the Zionist return to the Land of Israel as an act leading toward national redemption. This narrative includes both the denial of 2000 years of Jewish life in 'exile' and the denial of any meaningful life in Palestine during the same period.

The Zionist narrative inculcated in Israeli schools relates a continuous struggle of the Jews against non-Jewish conquerors, usurpers of the land and persecutors.

In their recent history school book, Naveh et al. 2009 reproduce this narrative of continuity as follows:

> The holidays and memorial days of Israel were molded as a continuous struggle of the Jewish people for its very existence, according to the familiar pattern of the Jews as few and good, struggling against the Goyim (non-Jews) who are numerous and bad. In Hanuka – the Makabbin against the ancient Greek, on Adar 11th – Trumpeldor and the defenders of Tel-Hai (1904) against a gang of Arab 'plunderers,' in Purim – The Jew Mordechai and his niece – Queen Esther – against wicked Haman, in Passover – Moses and the children of Israel are struggling to free themselves from slavery against Pharoe and the Egyptians, on Holocaust Day – the rebels of Warsaw Ghetto against the Nazi Germans, on memorial day and Independence Day – the combatants of 1948 against the armies of the Arab states in their masses, and on 33 Ba'Omer – the {ancient} Jewish fundamentalists against the Romans. All these contexts are mixed together to create an artificial defining narrative, which construes the collective memory of the Jewish citizens of Israel. The fundamental idea is the continuity of Jewish destiny and the salvation brought about by the sole forces of the Jewish people. Thus, the war in 1948 has been conceived as the settling of the old historical score, and the fighters of 1948 as the direct descendants of the Makkabim. (p.308)

In this grand narrative of return and redemption, the hero is the 'New Jew' who returned to reclaim his homeland and retrieve it from the Arab invaders. If I may add a personal note here, when I was growing up in 1950–60, every year on 15 of Shvat (Tree Day according to Jewish tradition), we used to go out with our class to plant trees in the forests planted by the Jewish National Fund, as Israeli-Jewish children are still doing today, and we were told we were restoring the glorious biblical forests the Arab invaders destroyed with their herds while 'we' were away.

The reproduction of this type of national narrative in school books is discussed in many studies of state-sponsored histories. Tyack (2003: 40) argues that national narratives involve 'a peculiar mix of inspirational heroes and the flat facts that young citizens are supposed to believe in' and their goal is to inculcate collective memory grounded in state approved civic truth. This calls, as Podeh maintains, for the manipulation of the past, which works in favor of the cult of continuity and the need to construe 'a usable past.'

The Cult of Continuity

Israeli mainstream education, using the Bible as an authoritative historical source, and helped by Israeli-Jewish archeology, which is meant first and foremost to prove the validity and truth of biblical stories and to assert Jewish ancient presence and dominance in the Land of Israel/Palestine,[2] perpetuates what Nora calls 'the cult of continuity.' This cult gives a nation 'the certainty of knowing to whom and to what we are indebted for being what we are' (1996: 12). Nora explains that from this cult came the important notion of 'origins,' which is 'that secularized version of myth' that gives a society, 'in the process of nationalist secularization its idea and need for the sacred' (ibid.). The cult of continuity is meant to justify 'our' ways and 'make us venerate ourselves.' As Nora explains, 'the grander France's origins were, the more they magnified the grandeur of the French' (ibid.). But whereas for the French this notion characterizes the spirit of the nineteenth century (and the Third République), in Israel it characterizes present-day reality and practices. According to the Israeli-Zionist narrative, Jewish Israelis, who have come from the remotest corners of the world, with nothing in common except their ancestors' religion, practiced differently by every ethnic group, constitute a natural nation from the dawn of history. One example of this cult is the current massive campaign titled 'Judea and Samaria are the story of every Jew,' which is being promoted by the Council for Jewish Towns in Judea and Samaria through its new organization, Judea and Samaria Public Relations Council. In this campaign, stories of 'our biblical ancestors' are directly connected to the illegal Jewish settlements in the West Bank, with the aim of reaching out to secular left-wing Jews and convincing them of 'our historical rights' to the Land of Palestine. Huge posters showing settlers' children dressed in biblical clothing tell the biblical story associated with every settlement in the occupied Palestinian territories. For example: A little boy on a ladder impersonates Jacob and his dream in Beth-El; Efrata is the site where the matriarch Rachel died, etc. The rational of this campaign was articulated on 4 October 2008, by the head of the campaign, Mr. Segev, who declared on Channel 7 – *Jewish News*: 'Particularly now, with the loss of faith in leadership, it's important to present our values and say without apologizing: Judea and Samaria are ours, they are part of the story of every Jew.'

As was mentioned above, the cult of Jewish continuity in the land of Israel/Palestine also includes obliterating all signs of Palestinian continuous existence on the land. Regarding this obliteration literary scholar Ariel Hirschfeld comments[3] that the Zionist creed 'know your homeland' means forgetting 2000 years of civilization on this land and seeing present Jewish life in Israel as a direct continuation of the biblical kingdom of Judea. Indeed, the 2000 years of Jewish 'absence' from the land, whose negation is one of the most important Zionist tenets, are literally bracketed in school books, as will be shown in chapter 2. This negation is twofold, for it conceals the historical life-world both of the Jews in 'exile' and of Palestine without its native Jews (Piterberg, 2001). According to the myth of continuity, the land, too, was condemned to a sort of exile as long as there was no Jewish sovereignty over it: 'It lacked any meaningful or authentic history, awaiting redemption with the return of the Jews' (Piterberg, 2001: 32). Piterberg explains that the known Zionist slogan, 'a land without a people to a people without a land,' does not mean the land was literally empty but that it was empty of its historic custodians and populated by insignificant intruders. This notion may be at the base of the statement made by Firer of the Truman Institute for Peace, in her analysis of Israeli school books of History: 'The sovereign state of Israel was *re-established* in 1948' (Firer, 2004: 22, emphasis added). Such a statement assumes that the current state of Israel is a direct successor of another, ancient 'state of Israel' or rather, kingdom. Even the historian Bar Navi, considered by researchers such as Firer and Podeh as one of the most progressive writers of history textbooks, still calls the Palestinian city of Hebron 'our Ancestors' city,' as the Jewish settlers label it in order to justify its colonization and the expulsion of its Palestinian inhabitants from their homes and shops (*The 20th*). As Nora points out, 'When we look at the past we take violent possession of what we know is no longer ours' (1996: 12).

Although collective memory often makes claims to stability and constancy, it appears that one of its few constant attributes is that it undergoes change (Wertsch, 2002: 173). Wertsch shows in his study of Russian textbooks in the former USSR and after its dismantlement, that it is not uncommon for the official account to be presented as immutable even when it is not (ibid.: 45). This is because the changes are slow and not always felt by the group. School books are a perfect example of such changes for they are what Kress calls 'momentary congealing of semiosis' (Kress, 2000: 152), which means in Kress' words 'bringing semiosis [or meaning-making] to a temporary stand still in textual form' (Kress, 2000: 141). This semiosis may change from one government to another though the basic narrative remains intact. Therefore, as studies show, school books are temporary texts in essence and in fact. They undergo frequent – though not always radical – changes and transformations.[4] Similarly to 'real' history books, they may be described as 'products [that] correspond to a range of power bases that exist at any given moment and which structure and distribute the meanings of histories along a dominant-marginal spectrum' (Jenkins, 1991: 26). Israeli school books, though they have a common ideological ground, reflect political controversies and the frequently changing power relations in the state. They are re-published almost annually in new versions, which claim to be 'up to date' both scientifically and pedagogically. Being up to date means presenting the current interpretation of reality. The constant 'updating' of school books is also one of the qualities that make them function as 'realms of memory' for although it is true that their function is to 'fix' memory,

Nora argues that 'functionally works of history thrive because of their capacity to change, their ability to resurrect old meanings and generate new ones along with new and unforeseeable connections' (Nora, 1996: 15).

Two recent instances are the indictment of two history textbooks: *World of Changes* (Yaakobi et al. 2001) and *Nationality: Building a State in the Middle East* (Domka et al. 2009), both published by Labour ministries of education and banned by their right-wing successors. Domka et al. (2009) was republished with minor changes that were apparently very important to this government but may seems less important to others; one of these changes was the replacement of 'ethnic cleansing' regarding the Palestinian exodus in 1948, with 'organized expulsion.' The other changes will be discussed later on.

The official narrative produced in Israeli school books has undergone some changes during the first 50 years of their existence. Podeh (2002: 61) calls these changes radical but at the same time he tones down his optimism by stating that 'the fact that the old Zionist narrative is still found in some textbooks shows that their transformation has not yet been completed.' Podeh summarizes the developments in Israeli history school books regarding the attitude towards Palestinians as follows: in the first period of Israeli textbooks (1950s–60s), 'the historical narrative was replete with bias, prejudice, errors, misrepresentations and even deliberate omissions. Arabs were portrayed in stereotypical terms that in turn reinforced a distorted image in Israel society.' The excuse for that is that textbooks were designed to serve the goals of 'a newly emerging society' that needed to construct a collective memory and consolidate itself while being 'haunted by a sense of isolation and a siege mentality.' Podeh adds that 'the fact that school textbooks were in the past prejudiced and thereby contributed to the escalation of the conflict failed to penetrate the consciousness of large sectors of Israeli society.' By the mid-1970s, new interpretations of Zionist history started to claim their rightful place and reproduced – during the third generation of textbooks (i.e. 1980–90) – more critical and informed historical narrative which constituted 'an important step forward.' However, Podeh observes that even the most progressive books of the third generation have always supported 'set curricula aimed at imbuing Israeli citizens with a love of the fatherland and enhancing their faith in the just cause of the State.'

Podeh's conclusion is that 'students should ideally receive a more comprehensive analysis of Arab-Israeli relations, as well as complementary information on Arab history and culture' (2002: 29).

The Creation of a Usable Past

A 'usable past' is 'an account of events that can be harnessed for some purpose in the present' (Wertsch, 2002: 45).

Wertsch emphasizes the fact, that although they never totally lack accuracy, collective memories are not obligated to represent the past accurately as much as they are obligated to recreate a 'usable past'; the creation of a usable past is the main criterion school books are assessed by along with their capacity to harness this usable past to some purpose in the present, especially to the creation of coherent group and individual identities (Wertsch, 2002: 33). This, Wertsch argues, may lead to sacrificing accuracy and objectivity (ibid.).

The two criteria – accuracy and a usable past – are not mutually exclusive, and they may come together in what Lotman called functional dualism (quoted in Wertsch, 2002: 31). Lotman explains that like any narrative, collective memory has both referential and dialogic functions: the referential function tends to provide the foundation for discussions about accuracy, while the dialogic function is associated with the contestation and negotiation involved in creating a usable past. Although both the referential and dialogic functions of narratives can provide impetus for change in official history, it is the negotiation with a usable past that is responsible for changes in the narrative according to the demands of the present. The driving force behind public memory is not accurate representation of the past, rather it has to do with serving the interests of the present and the future (Wertsch, 2002: 33). In his study of Russian history school books, Wertsch demonstrates how the negotiation with a usable past seems to change with the demands of the new Russian reality after the dismantlement of the USSR.

Regarding Israel, Confino contends that the aim of public memory has to do with presenting 'an image of the past based on the subjectivity of the present' (Confino, 2007a).

Following the line of the above theories, one may conclude that the Israeli-Zionist narrative, which may be seen by some historians (i.e. Piterberg, 2001) as fraudulent and misleading, should not be assessed solely for its historical truth but also for its ability to create a usable past for the sake of group coherence and national identity. Since in Israel 'history,' 'geography' and present-day practices of colonization are closely tied together, the 'usable past' recreated in school books and the (mis)representation of the geo-political reality of the region may often be viewed as justification of or as commentary on current circumstances, living personalities and present-day policies. For instance, in an article from 29 July 2010, the writer Fogleman compares the recently revealed expulsion of Syrian farmers from the Golan Heights in 1967 to the expulsion of Palestinians from Lydda and Ramla in 1948. Under the heading 'The Birth of a Narrative' the writer shows how the narrative regarding the 1967 expulsion was modeled after the narrative of 1948; in both narratives the inhabitants 'fled' and were not 'expelled,' but both narratives have been proven wrong. By shattering the narratives reproduced in school books and in today's media the article criticizes or doubts the credibility of living personalities who participated in either expulsion and are still holding public offices.[5]

To sum, researchers of various disciplines believe that school books fill the educational role of agents of memory more than that of disciplinary agents (Tyack, 2000; Podeh, 2002; Wertsch, 2002). Since the authors of textbooks are not always professional researchers in the discipline but rather, as Bernstein put it, 'working in the field of recontextualization,' they obey educational dictums more than disciplinary rules and conventions. Therefore, as Coffin argues in her study of secondary school history in Australia, 'at stake is the disciplinary politics of truth' (1997: 201).

The Discourse of Identity

'Nations are made up of individuals whose patriotism is not unalterable datum but undergoes a long formative period proceeding initially from an elemental awareness of belonging to a greater whole' (Hroch, 1985: 13).

As was mentioned above, the most common reasons to develop a national narrative with a usable past have to do with claims of identity (Wertsch, 2002).

Allport (1958) observed that one fundamental role of education is to assure that the group's preferences be every individual's preference, its enemies his or her enemies.

Group identity has been prevalent in Western societies since the nineteenth century. As Nora explains, 'The concept of identity [...] has gone from being an individual and subjective notion to a collective, quasi-formal and objective one. Identity, like memory, is a form of *duty*. I am asked to become what I am: a Corsican, a Jew, a worker, an Algerian, a Black. It is at this level of obligation that the decisive tie is formed between memory and social identity. [...] The two terms have become all but synonymous' (1996: 10).

In Israel, where Jewish personal and national identities are almost completely interfused and Jewish-Israeli identity is almost symbiotic with the collective national memory,[6] Jewish citizens, to use Nora's expression, tend to define themselves 'from without,' as group members. For example, when asked to define themselves, students in my class, in a course about multiculturalism and racism in Israel, would usually say: I am Jewish, Israeli, Zionist, in this or in any different order. Arab students usually state they are Arab or Palestinian with an Israeli identity card.[7] Very few students – especially newcomers and particularly women – would identify themselves by individual criteria such as 'I am a mother and a wife, I love poetry, I am an optimist / generous,' etc.

However, in Israel, as is typical of conflictual societies, and especially since the Jewish ethno-nation is a mixture of people from all over the world with hardly anything in common, questions of collective and individual identities are still 'passionately' debated and often become heated arguments and even history wars (Zrubabel, 2002). Such is the case of the repeated argument about 'who is a Jew' which has never subsided and which causes serious ruptures in the Israeli political arena and in the relationships of Israel with the Jewish Diaspora.[8] Questions of loyalty and the right to citizenship and immigration are closely related to the question of Jewish identity and are constantly debated as well, especially now when a new Law of Citizenship, approved on the 29 March 2011 by the knesset, is opposed to by anti-racist movements all over the world.[9]

These debates show to what extent the discourse of identity, like the discourse of collective memory, is also the discourse of difference, inclusion and exclusion. The construal of national memory and identity includes strategies of denying other memories and other identities that seem threatening. When these memories and identities surge up in defiance at all the means to erase or suppress them, they are conceived as obstacles that must be eliminated. Nora warns in fact, that 'the real problem raised by the sacred aura with which {collective} memory has now been invested is to know how, why and at what moment the otherwise positive principle of emancipation and liberation on which it is based backfires and becomes a form of closure, a ground for exclusion and an instrument of war. To claim the right to memory is, at bottom, to call for justice. In the effects it has had, however, it has often become a call to murder' (1996: 10).

As was noted above, one of the aims of the Israeli-Zionist narrative, as of every phase of the Zionist project, is to create a homogeneous identity to all the Jewish ethnicities in Israel (The most popular slogan of Israeli politicians is: One nation – One heart!), while attempting to erase – both physically and spiritually – traces of a continuous Palestinian life on the land, so that both Israeli and Palestinian memory of it would die (Piterberg, 2001; Algazi, 2007).[10] Israeli authorities have always stood guard against the teaching of Palestinian history or the *Nakba*, even in Arab schools (Nasser and Nasser, 2008) – a prohibition that has recently been formulated as a law (The '*Nakba* Law'), following the mentioning of the *Nakba* in the Arab-Israeli version of *Living Together in Israel* (a booklet of Geography and civics for third grade in the Arab sector) in 2007 and the May 2008 Supreme Court ruling in favor of the Islamic movement's commemoration of the *Nakba* in Israel.[11] The law forbids public mourning on Israel's Independence Day or general mourning for the establishment of the

State of Israel as a Jewish state. As explained by the Israel Democracy Institute,

> The so-called '*Nakba Law*' aims to prevent public commemoration of the catastrophe — or 'Nakba' in Arabic — that befell the Arab population of Palestine during the Arab-Israeli war of 1948 which enabled the establishment of the State of Israel.[12]

The bill, approved by the Israeli Knesset on the 23 March 2011, authorizes the finance minister 'to decrease the budget for bodies receiving government funding if they allow marking Israeli-Jewish Independence Day and the founding of Israel with mourning ceremonies' (ibid.). Obviously, those who fear the commemoration of Palestinian 'Shoa' as Bar-Navi (1998) calls it in his textbook *The 20th*, understand that the need of people and nations to mourn, which is so ingrained in Jewish tradition,[13] has to do with 'identity claims [...] the desire to foster patriotism and the need to erase the sting of defeat and redeem a lost cause' (Wertsch, 2002: 31). The '*Nakba* law' expresses the fear prevailing in Israel, of teaching Palestinian children their own narrative lest they be given cause to grieve and would indeed try to 'redeem' their lost cause.[14] Israeli authorities and especially the educational authorities feel that admitting the *Nakba* will destroy Israel as a Jewish state and will give the Palestinian citizens reason to rebel.[15]

This policy is typical of Ethnocratic regimes that construe historical narratives about the dominant ethno-nation as the rightful owner of the territory, while 'the Other's history, place and political aspirations are presented as a menacing package to be rejected thoroughly' (Yiftachel, 2006: 19).

The Palestinian citizens of Israel do not have their relative share or rather any share at all in any report that concerns them in the textbooks studied here; they are practically absent from the texts, except as negative phenomena: a primitive lot which is a developmental burden or a security and demographic threat (see chapter 1). In geography school books, the tendency to erase Palestinian life from the Israeli scene is realized by omitting the international border of Israel – the green line – from maps, by depicting the occupied West

Bank – renamed Judea and Samaria – as part of Israel though it has never been officially annexed to the state, and by presenting illegal colonies such as Ariel or Alon Shvut as equal to Tel Aviv or Jerusalem, while omitting Palestinian cities and even mixed cities within Israel such as Acre or Nazareth (see chapter 2). Thus, Israeli school books realize Nora's observation (1996: 12) that 'the whole dynamic of our relation to the past [and in Israel's case to the present] is shaped by the subtle interplay between the inaccessible and the nonexistent.'

Reading Israeli School Books

The Nature of School Books

Basil Bernstein (1996: 39–41) argues that the transformation of knowledge into pedagogic communication is made by the pedagogic device which, just like the language device, has rules which are not ideologically free. These rules 'regulate the pedagogic communication which the device makes possible. Such pedagogic communication acts selectively on the meaning potential, namely on the potential discourse that is available to be pedagogized' (1996: 42). The rules fall into three categories:

1) Distributive rules whose function is to regulate the relationships between power, social groups, forms of consciousness and forms of educational practice.
2) Recontextualizing rules that regulate the formation of specific pedagogic discourse. These rules not only regulate the 'what' of teaching but mostly the 'how,' which derives from the theory of instruction that determines, in addition to the sequence, the pacing and the rate of expected acquisition, the semiotic means by which the subject matter is presented to the students.
3) Evaluative rules whose purpose is 'to transmit criteria [and] produce a ruler for consciousness.' (1996: 46)

Like all other educational texts in which knowledge is transformed, collective memory, distributed especially through narratives (Wertsch, 2002: 171), is reproduced in school books according to the pedagogical rules of recontextualization. In other words, disciplinary content is transformed in school books in order to inculcate the desired narratives and educational values. This transformation is done through the mediation of various semiotic resources, which include besides narratives, strategies of argumentation, mythic structures (Wertsch, 1994) and visuals (Van Leeuwen, 1992).

As Theo Van Leeuwen (2007: 96) makes clear, 'What exactly gets transformed depends on the interests, goals and values of the context into which the practice is recontextualized.' Transformation is defined by Hodge and Kress (1993: 10) as 'permissible tampering,' which involves 'deleting, substituting, combining or reordering a syntagm and its elements.' Hence, 'transformations are not "innocent". They serve two functions: economy and distortion, which are often so inextricably mixed that even the speaker cannot separate them' (ibid.).

Historian Hayden White (1978: 56) argues that the facts in all history books 'are constituted rather than given' and the writers 'choose, sever and carve selected facts for narrative purposes'. This is all the more true about school books. However, the duty of the historian, which is not necessarily the duty of the writer of textbooks, is to try and represent the world truthfully and honestly, 'to criticize, loudly and bravely, erroneous thoughts about the past, wrong conceptions and prejudice, no matter how close to his heart they are, or how well-meaning they once were' (Confino, 2007b). By contrast, the writer of history textbooks is not obligated to provide a 'better insight into the ways in which people in the past used to construct their world and their beliefs' (ibid.). His or her selections are intrinsic, not to the logic of the discipline but rather, to what Bernstein terms the 'regulative pedagogic discourse,' which is a social discourse that regulates the activities of the school (Bernstein, 1996: 49).

Since transformation or the recontextualization of disciplinary texts to education is based on social, pedagogical and disciplinary considerations, school books can be considered as *hypertexts* both of the dominant socio-political *hypotext* and of their respective disciplinary *hypotexts*; Hypertextuality and Hypotextuality are employed here in the sense used by Genette (1982: 12–14). Hypertextuality according to Genette is any relation a certain Text B has with a previous Text A from which it is derived or on which it is 'grafted.' Genette explains that this derivation can have many forms: Text B may not even mention Text A but cannot exist without it, for it is its transformation.

Though they vary in the way they teach the disciplines,[16] Israeli school books serve as relays of the Zionist ideology and its explicit message about the historic rights of the Jews to the Land of Israel/Palestine. This is the primary condition for their authorization by the Ministry of Education. Therefore Israeli school books are considered by many researchers first of all as hypertexts of the Zionist hypotext and secondly of their respective disciplinary hypotexts (Bar-Gal, 1993a; 2003; Firer, 1985; Podeh, 2002).

Bernstein (1996: 47) argues that in the process of recontextualization, discourses are being dislocated, relocated and refocused according to pedagogic principles. Hence the discourses of textbooks are never identical with their disciplinary discourses. In Israeli school books, the boundaries between the disciplinary text and the political, prophetic or military ones are quite frequently fuzzy. The discourses of history and geography are both mixed with political, ideological, military, historical, verbal and visual scientific discourses, reinforced by biblical prophecies, patriotic songs and heroic poetry. Consequently there is a peculiar mix of genres, modes and messages, both verbal and visual, which is quite unique to these school books. This mix as we shall see later, is designed to immortalize Jewish dominance through its presentation as legitimate from the dawn of civilization.

Wertsch (2002: 70) observes that the importance of history instruction in the formation of national identity 'snaps into focus' especially during times of transition and turmoil; in the case of Israel, so is the instruction of geography, because, according to the Zionist narrative, 'the Land of Israel is the only site on which the nation's destiny could be fulfilled' (Piterberg, 2001: 31). Geographer Bar-Gal observes that Zionism has 'recognized at the very outset the importance of teaching territorial identity' (Bar-Gal, 1993b: 421) and that Israeli Geography curricula has always 'emphasized the national goals as the principal goals' (Bar-Gal, 2000: 169); the aim of geography teaching has always been to teach that 'an historical event, the resurrection of the Jewish nation, had an impact on the landscape' (Bar-Gal, 1993a: 60). Therefore, while history school books reproduce and legitimate the Jewish-Israeli national narrative, geography studies are meant first and foremost to teach how to 'know and love our country,' (Bar-Gal, 2003), hail the Zionist achievements in agriculture and in settlement.

Tyack (1999 quoted in Wertsch, 2002: 71) observes that national narratives use geography to introduce ideas about 'natural' boundaries of nation states. Indeed, as we shall see in chapter 2, Israeli geography textbooks present on all their maps the 'greater land of Israel' of which the present state of Israel is just a small (and temporary) part, justifying it by biblical quotes regarding the Promised Land. Geography school books highlight the glorious mythological past of the Hebrews while concealing the geo-political reality of the present, that seems to Israeli curriculum planners an 'accidental consequence of cease fire commands which paralyzed military momentum' (Bar-Gal, 1993a: 125).

The Ideological Common Ground of Israeli School Books

In Israeli education the Zionist hypotext is the ideological common ground against which all facts are verified and on which all narratives are 'carved.' A common ground is necessary for any form of social communication and interaction. As Fairclough (2003: 55) explains 'the capacity to exercise social power or domination and hegemony includes the capacity to shape to some significant degree the nature and content of this "common ground."' Every common ground, says Fairclough, is construed of 'shared assumptions' which are presented as given and irrefutable. These assumptions or convictions are never submitted to discussion but rather, presented as 'known' and agreed upon. The shared assumptions of Israeli school books regarding Palestinian Arabs are as follows:

1) Assumptions about what exists:
   a) Jewish historical rights to the Land of Israel.
   b) Arab threat and hatred and world Anti-Semitism.
   c) The 'Arabs' have 21 countries and we have only one.
2) Propositional assumptions: what can or will be the case:

   a) Palestinian citizens constitute a demographic problem which can expand into a 'demographic threat' unless controlled.
   b) Palestinians in the occupied territories are a constant threat and must be controlled otherwise they would slaughter us.
3) Value assumptions: What is good and desirable? (Or what ought to be):
   A Jewish state, Jewish majority, Israeli control.

These convictions stem from the Jewish collective memory summarized by Daniel Bar–Tal and Rafi Nets–Zehngut in their study *Emotions in Conflict: Correlates of Fear and Hope in the Israeli-Jewish Society*:[17]

> By and large, the Israeli collective memory is deeply marked by the hostile approach of the world towards the Jews. Jewish history shows that from the destruction of the Second Temple and the beginning of the forced exile in the Roman era, through the Middle Ages, the Reformation, and the Industrial Revolution until the present Jews, in almost every place they lived, have consistently and continuously been subject to what is now called anti-Semitism. Through this long history they experienced persecution, libel, social taxation, restriction, forced conversion, expulsion, and pogroms. [...] As a result, [...] Jewish tradition finds anti-Semitism to be the norm, the natural response of the non-Jew. [...] Israeli society can therefore be characterized by its siege mentality, which is based on a prevailing belief according to which Jewish society is alone in a hostile world. [...] This perception constitutes a significant part of the Israeli ethos [...] and as such it obviously affects the perception of the Israeli-Arab conflict and its resolution. Studies for example showed that Jews in Israel who hold this type of memory tend to reject peaceful resolution of the conflict which suggests two states to two nations.

Fairclough notes that 'socially shared representations, especially the evaluative ones, provide the grounds for the judgments about what is right and what is wrong' (ibid.). In Israeli school books they serve as legitimation to every practice that helps maximize Jewish control over the contested multiethnic territory, which has always been declared Israel's main goal (Yiftachel, 2006).

The School Books used in the Study

The sample of school books was chosen according to the popularity of the books among teachers.[18] Ten history school books were chosen for the present study; six geography school books and one school book of civic studies which was written for both Jewish and Arab Israeli high schools. The books were published in the years 1996–2009, after the Oslo Peace Agreement between Israel and the Palestinian National Authorities, and all but one have been used during this time in mainstream secular elementary, middle or high school. Three of the history books – *The 20th (1998), Modern Times II* (1999) and *Building a State in the Middle East* (2009) – were written or co-written by well-known historians, Professor Eli Bar Navi and Professor Eyal Naveh. These books were appraised by researchers as more progressive than others for presenting more complicated narratives than the usual simplistic tale of the redemption of the Land and the just wars as well as for foregrounding critical perspectives. (Podeh, 2002; Firer, 2004). Two other history books – *Journey into the Past* for grades 8 and 9 and its version for grades 11 and 12, *The Age of Horror and Hope* – were written and published within the Centre for Educational Technologies which is the main producer of school materials for mainstream schools in Israel. *World of Changes*, was published by the Ministry of Education in 1999 and pulped in 2001 by a subsequent minister, mainly on the charge that it attributed greater importance to global forces, historical structures and political powers than to Zionist national ethos such as the Jewish yearning for Zion in 2000 years of 'exile,' the return of the Jews to their legitimate homeland and the idea of Redemption through Zionism.[19] Two history books, published in 2004 (*50 Years of Wars and Hopes*) and 2006 (*The Face of the 20th*) by private publishing houses with adaptations to the newly revised curriculum, were most recommended by the Ministry of Education until 2010 for high school and for matriculation. Though none of the books is overtly connected with a political party or ideology, these two books are more right-wing oriented and unlike the others, concentrate almost exclusively upon the military achievements of Israel and hardly touch on matters of culture, society, science etc.

Two history school books were published in 2009, one written by Naveh et al. and the other by Domka et al. both with the same name: *Nationality: Building a State in the Middle East.* These books were written during a labour ministry and one of them (Domka et al. 2009) was pulped immediately after publication, with the change of government. Unlike *World of Changes* its indictment was not subsequent to a committee deliberation; following a complaint by a history teacher in Tel-Hay teachers college, who heard it included a quote from Walid Halidi stating there was an ethnic cleansing of Palestine in 1948, the minister of education Gideon Saar ordered the book to be collected off the shelves; its later authorized version omitted Halidi altogether and replaced 'ethnic cleansing' with 'an organized expulsion' (p.107). It also replaced Halidi – as the representative of the Palestinian version – with the Israeli historian Benny Morris (p.109).

Most books will be referred to by an abbreviated form:

1) *The 20th Century* (1998): The 20th;
2) *Modern Times II* (1999): MTII;
3) *World of Changes* (2001): WOC;
4) *Journey into the Past* (1999): JIP;
5) *The Age of Horror and Hope* (2001): AHH;
6) *50 Years of Wars and Hopes* (2004): 50 Years;
7) *The Face of the 20th* (2006): Face;
8) *Being Citizens in Israel* (2001): BCI;
9) Naveh et al. (2009): *Nationality in Israel and the Nations: Building a State in the Middle East*
10) Domka et al. (2009): *Nationality – Building a State in the Middle East.*

The last two books will be referred to by their authors' names because of their similar titles.

The six geography school books studied here have all been used in Israeli schools during the study. All books declare they are compatible with the current national curriculum and all but one were authorized by the Ministry of Education. The books will be referred to by an abbreviated form:

1) Aharony. Y., and Sagi T. (2003). *The Geography of the Land of Israel: A Geography Textbook for Grades 11-12.* Tel Aviv: Lilach Publishers. (GLI)
2) Fine, T., Segev, M., and Lavi, R. (2002). *Israel: The Man and the Space: Selected Chapters in Geography.* Tel Aviv: The Centre for Educational Technologies Publishers. (IMS)
3) Rap, E., and Fine, T. (1996/1998). *People in Space: A Geography Textbook for 9th Grade.* Tel Aviv: The Centre for Educational Technologies Publishers. (PIS)
4) Rap, E., and Shilony-Tzvieli, I. (1998). *Settlements in Space: Chapters in the Geography of Settlements in the World.* Tel Aviv: The Centre for Educational Technologies Publishers. (SIS)
5) Segev, M., and Fine, Z. (2007). *People and Settlements.* Tel Aviv: The Centre for Educational Technologies. (PAS)
6) Vaadya, D., Ulman, H., and Mimoni, Z. (1994/1996). *The Mediterranean Countries for 5th Grade.* Tel Aviv: Maalot Publishers. (TMC)

Four of these books were published by the Centre for Educational Technologies (*People in Space, Israel Man and Space, Settlements in Space* and *People and Settlements*) and are declared as school books for Jewish, Druze and Arab schools. One was published by the Ministry of Education (*The Mediterranean Countries*) and one (*Geography of the Land of Israel*) by the same private publisher that published the 2004 and the 2006 history books. This geography textbook, although it claims to be compatible with the national curriculum and is taught in schools, does not have the official authorization stamp of the Ministry of Education.

The Nature of Israeli School Books

As was mentioned before, school books are 'intertexts' for they both refer to other texts and transform texts of different genres. The result is multimodal, multigeneric texts that 'operate both transgenerically (work to obliterate the traces of its prior textual origins) and intragenerically (work to affirm the stability of textual types)' (Kress, 2000: 140). In Israeli school books of history, every page or double-spread offers transgenerically the political or social canonical narrative, where the traces of the original texts such as quotes from opinion essays of favored leaders and military men, or even the personal opinion of the writer himself, are often presented as fact. In addition each page presents strongly framed and coloured 'windows' which contain historical 'sources' of all kinds, such as testimonies about events, official and personal documents, selected writings and statistical data. Sometimes, under the guise of 'sources' the writer expresses his/her own views in these 'windows.' Although the 'windows' are located at the margins of the editorial texts and therefore as marginal to the main narrative, their salience – through colour and frame – often makes them the first items to be read. Consequently these 'windows' may determine the reading path of the entire page or double-spread and with it the interpretation or meaning-making of the editorial text. As the analysis will show, these salient windows are often used rhetorically either to reinforce the official narrative or to foreground the writer's own interpretations and critique.

The composition of the page or double-spread may suggest various reading paths and intertextual connections; as meanings are not made by writers alone, school book texts, which are a collage and bricolage of different modes and different genres, are what Kress calls 'a constantly shifting flow' (Kress, 2000: 54), whose meanings are constantly made by readers through the changing intertextual connections they make.

Recontextualization, intertextuality, transformation of prior texts and different sorts of 'congealing of semiosis,' raise some questions about the nature of the text itself (Kress, 2000: 137): one question is, what kinds of meaning-making are created in every text? Related questions are, do we read one or several texts? What are the text boundaries? As Kress explains, 'The boundaries of the text are not necessarily the boundaries of the genre,' which means that a text may display a mix of genres and interact with different texts and genres.

Methodology

The analysis follows the principles of social semiotic enquiry and uses methods of multimodal and discourse analysis. It considers the page or the double-spread as one semiotic unit that has meaning beyond or apart from the meaning of any of its parts. As Lemke (1998: 283) explains, 'Meanings are not fixed and additive (the word meaning plus the picture meaning), but multiplicative (word meaning modified by image context, image meaning modified by textual context), making a whole far greater than the sum of its parts.'

The present study examines the verbal text – discourses, genres and style – as well as the visuals and layout and the relationships between the different elements on the page, the double-spread, the chapter or the whole book.

The following overview of the principles of social semiotic enquiry and of the methods of multimodal analysis is presented in direct and indirect quotes from the works of Kress and Van Leeuwen, who have studied school books from a social semiotic perspective and applied multimodal methods of analysis.[20]

The social semiotic approach is convenient for the analysis of textbooks because it is 'not a pure theory or a self contained field [...] it does not offer ready-made answers but rather provides ideas to formulate questions about human meaning making through sign making. [...] Social Semiotics only comes to its own when it is applied to specific instances and specific problems and it always requires immersing oneself not just in semiotic concepts and methods as such but also in some other field [...]. Interdisciplinarity is an absolutely essential feature for a social semiotic analysis' (Van Leeuwen, 2005: 2).

The basic assumption of social semiotics is that meanings are made in signs or sign-complexes in distinct ways in specific modes, none of which is arbitrary (Kress, 1993). In social semiotic enquiry no sign is treated as a pre-given entity but as motivated by interests, perspectives, values and positions of the sign maker regarding the message and the recipients of the message because signs are made to function in communication (Kress, 2003). Signs reflect ideology and are affected by use, namely by their history in a given culture. Reading and interpretation also reflect the interests and beliefs of the interpreter within a certain culture and history.

The social semiotic study investigates how semiotic resources are used in specific historical, cultural and institutional contexts and how people talk about them in these contexts – plan them, teach them, justify them, critique them etc. (Van Leeuwen, 2005).

Language is one system of semiotic resources; it is not just a set of rules for producing correct sentences but an inexhaustible resource for making meaning (Halliday, 1978: 192). Every semiotic resource, linguistic or other, has a function in the structure of the text, and each part contributes to the whole by its position and function and is interpreted as functional with respect to the whole (Halliday, 1985: xiii). Hence, order in language and placement in images or multimodal texts that combine verbal and visual chunks have meaning.

However, Van Leeuwen reminds us that in all societies there are 'semiotic regimes' (2005: 53), differential kinds of rules for the use of semiotic resources. These rules may receive their legitimation from impersonal authority such as tradition, scriptures, laws or ideology, but they all need agents to implement them, and therefore there is always room for personal interpretation. The choice of different parts of a narrative or images and their ordering on the page result from a combination of convention and personal interest of the producers of texts.

Within the semiotic regimes, the use of semiotic resources is not free for all. Those who have the power also control the semiotic resources. Those who are dominated cannot participate freely in the 'language game' or the 'semiotic game' and may be punished for using semiotic resources to create their own new signs. For instance, until the Oslo Accords in 1993, Israel routinely inflicted severe punishments upon Palestinians who raised their home-made flags to proclaim their nationality, and Israelis were forbidden to wear a broach that combined Israeli-Palestinian flags as a sign of reconciliation.

Any fully functioning semiotic resource must have the potential to meet three demands (Kress, 2003: 65): to represent states of affairs in the world (ideational function), to represent or establish relations between reader and writer, speaker and listener (interpersonal function) and to represent all this as a message-entity namely as text which is internally coherent and coheres with its environment (textual function). 'Different semiotic modes such as image, writing or vocal modes, can realize the same roles by different means through different observable forms' (Van Leeuwen, 2005: 75).

The present study investigates the semiotic resources used in the representation of Palestinians in Israeli textbooks. Studying these representations in the context of conflict and occupation may allow some insight into educational and social ideologies and interests.

Social-Semiotic Analysis

Social semiotic analysis addresses four major aspects: discourse, genre, modality and style (Van Leeuwen, 2005: 37).

1) *Discourse* is the way semiotic resources are used to construct representations of what is going on in the world.
2) *Modality* is the way people use semiotic resources to create the truth or reality values of their statements, to communicate whether they are to be taken as fact or fiction, proven truth or conjectures etc.
3) *Genre* refers to aspects of the organization of the text.
4) *Style* is the way people use semiotic resources to perform genres and express their identities and values in doing so.

'Only looking at all these together can give a multimodal complete picture' (Van Leeuwen, 2005: 92). Following is an elaboration of some questions regarding discourse, genres and modality.

Discourse

Discourse is, as Foucault has amply demonstrated, 'a socially constructed knowledge of some aspect of reality which can be drawn upon when that aspect of reality has to be represented' (Van Leeuwen, 2005: 94). Discourse describes the organization of content from a particular institutional point of view, as in legal discourse or religious discourse, scientific, military or political discourse.

Discourses are plural: there are several ways of knowing, and there can be different discourses, different ways of making sense of the same thing, which include and exclude different things, and serve different interests (Van Leeuwen, 2005: 95). Van Leeuwen gives as example the American discourse of war in its representation of 'special operation,' which usually leaves out or backgrounds aerial bombardment or civilian casualties, concentrating on Elite soldiers and sophisticated equipment and technology, and on superior combat skills, which usually stress the speed and efficiency of the 'forces.' Israeli discourse of war does show aerial bombardments but conceals their civilian casualties as much as possible. Both American and Israeli discourses of war tend to present the enemy as a 'despotic warlord' such as Saddam Hussein or Ahmadinejad, tyrant or super-terrorist such as Bin Laden, Nasrallah or Haniyeh, 'leading ill disciplined, dirty, hairy, and ill equipped men' (ibid.) or mobs, incited by all sorts of fundamentalist propaganda.

These examples are variants of the discourse of war; other variants may be the 'war on terror' discourse which presents the combative actions of usually poorer and weaker groups without uniform as 'evil,' while the combative actions of the powerful and sophisticated 'Forces' are depicted as just 'reaction.' The same 'terrorist acts,' when discussed in the framework of the discourse of 'freedom fighting' or 'resistance' are conceived as appropriate responses to the terror inflicted on poor defenseless groups by the super-powers.

The most dominant discourse in Israel with regard to the occupation of Palestine is the discourse of 'security' which legitimates aspects of Israeli behaviour towards Palestinians that are denounced in the framework of the discourse of human rights. In Israeli textbooks, acts of terror and weapon-smuggling committed by Jewish underground forces and gangs such as the Hagana, the Irgun-Etzel and Lehi (the Stern Gang) against British occupation and against the Palestinian resistance to Zionism before the establishment of Israel, are glorified within the discourse of Jewish emancipation and redemption, while the same acts committed by Palestinians against Israeli occupation are presented in criminal terms. Lately there has been some objection to this duality from educators and school principals following the Ministry of Education Circular published in 2009 announcing a special program on the subject of 'Oley Hagardom' (Jewish guerilla fighters from the Etzel and the Stern Gang who were hanged by the British for terrorist activities). High school principals objected to this program, which glorifies Jewish 'terrorists' and includes a writing competition for years 8–9 titled 'In Their Death They Decreed us Life.' The main argument against this program was that these actions cannot be glorified when performed by Jews while being denounced when performed by non-Jews.[21]

Discourses are finite. They contain a certain number of statements. Once I know a discourse a single part of it can trigger the rest (Van Leeuwen, 2005: 97). Van Leeuwen brings the example of the discourse of Heart-at-risk which immediately evokes obesity, smoking etc. In Israel, there is a distinct 'anti-Arab' discourse in which the label 'Arab' evokes dirty masses of incited people, terrorism and primitiveness, the oppression of women, over-multiplication and fundamentalism. In Israeli popular discourse, Arab taste, Arab colours, Arab work, Arab music and Arab odors, all connote negative values. Here are some edifying examples of that discourse. On 16 June 2009, Israeli minister of internal security – Yitzhak Aharonovitch – met undercover police agents during a tour in the crime-ridden old central bus station in Tel Aviv. One of them excused himself saying: 'Sorry, but I am rather dirty,' to which the minister responded, laughing: 'Dirty? You look like a regular Arabush.' 'Arabush' when referring to Arabs is equal to 'nigger' in referring to black people in American or British discourse.

Aharonovitch later apologized for the remark, saying that it did not reflect his worldview. A spokesman for the public security minister also issued a response, saying that 'in a moment of jest, and using common slang, the minister said what he said, not intending to hurt anyone. If this or that person were offended, that was not his intention.' Being part of 'jest' and 'common slang' shows how deeply ingrained these racist expressions are in Israeli everyday discourse. Visiting Lod (former Palestinian city Lydda cleansed in 1948 and repopulated with Jewish immigrants mostly from Arab countries), minister Aharonovitch said the city looked horrible 'like the refugee camp in Jabalia (Gaza).' Then he added: 'I can see the problems: Arabs, junkies and prostitutes everywhere.' A Jewish inhabitant complained to the minister, saying:

'When Israelis sit together and "cousins" come along, the police stay out. And they come in masses. It is so unpleasant.'[22] Note that by 'Israelis' he meant Jewish Israelis, ignoring the fact that the 'cousins' – namely the Palestinian-Arabs, are Israeli citizens as well. This is typical of Israeli-Jewish discourse in which Palestinian-Israelis are held as lesser citizens, more similar to the Palestinian non-citizens in the occupied territories than to Jewish citizens. This discourse reflects the reality, in which Palestinian citizens are never granted the same rights as Jewish citizens, in any aspect of their life. When Palestinians citizens revolt against their own discrimination, or against injustice done to other Palestinians, they are treated with much less tolerance than their Jewish co-demonstrators, as happened in October 2000 and in October 2010 in Um El Fahem and during the 2008 raids on Gaza. To this day the state has not acted against the policemen who killed 13 persons in the demonstrations in Um El Fahem in 2000.[23]

The 'anti-Arab' discourse is mostly anti-Muslim and seldom refers to Christian Arabs although a great number of Israeli-Palestinians are Christian; but the term 'Christian' belongs to another, more positive, discourse, which evokes Western civilization, development, liberalism, beauty, good manners and wealth.[24] An edifying example of the attitude towards Palestinian Christians is given in Nitzan (2009), *The Rarity of Military Rape in the Israeli-Palestinian Conflict*, where soldiers are quoted talking about their sexual fantasies regarding Palestinian women:

> It is quite simple isn't it? They are unattractive, absolutely. There are some pretty ones but not on the level of... I don't remember ever fantasizing on a (Muslim) Arab girl. (p.170–171)

Nitzan explains that Muslim women don't match the criteria of Western beauty. They are described by the soldiers as too big, ungroomed, incarnating rustic simplicity, poverty and primitivism; they are 'irrelevant as women, as mates, not even as imaginary ones' (p.172). However, 'along with their apparent repulsion from the "Haja" (religious Muslim woman) the soldiers meet another type of women, young, beautiful, well-groomed and maybe even educated and good conversationalists. These women are conceived as a surprising phenomenon, outstanding, as described by Major Shay: "The first time I came to a Palestinian town like Jericho [...] they dress like Israeli women, not this black outfit and the Hijab [...] and they look quite good, surprisingly. They go to university, they study, and they are quite pretty, even very pretty [...] the Arabs who live there are Christian and they have money [...] they look Western and [...] suddenly it's like Wow, is that what an Arab woman looks like?"'(p.177).

Needless to note that many Muslim girls do not wear Hijab or black dresses, and even those who do, lead 'modern' life; a very high percentage of them (with or without Hijab) complete their graduate studies in Israeli and Palestinian universities; but facts could never beat myth.[25] Rabinowitz, in a survey of peace-and-reconciliation encounters between Jewish and Palestinian-Arab youth in Israel notes, that even constant positive encounters with Palestinian doctors or basketball coaches, 'fail to swing real changes in the attitudes and stances of the Israeli partners, or otherwise enhance the Israelis' willingness to see beyond the circumstances of this particular encounter. Stereotypes are perhaps moderated, but other aspects of Israelis' world view remain intact' (Rabinowitz, 2001: 78).

Discourses have a history and this history gives them meaning. Secular Zionism for instance has always used and is still using ancient and sacred terms for earthly practices: Jewish immigration to Israel is termed 'Aliya' which meant originally pilgrimage to the Temple and to Jerusalem in ancient times; our times were termed by General Moshe Dayan 'the Third Temple'; the state of Israel is Zion, Jewish colonialism is spoken of in apocalyptic terms, expansion and confiscation of Palestinian lands are termed the Redemption of Zion. All these expressions in the use of secular Zionism give it what Nora termed 'a sacred aura' and endow it with sacred validity that legitimates it beyond human conventions of morality and law. Scholars of Jewish thought, such as Leibovitch and Sholem warned against this use of sacred or ancient words in Modern Hebrew. Leibovitch, whose article 'After Qibya' will be discussed in chapter 4, warned that the sanctification of the earthly was paving the way to fascism. Sholem was adamant in his criticism of Zionist leaders and especially of the first prime minister David Ben

Gurion whom he held 'responsible for the unrestrained use of the messianic proverb, 'such as Athchalta de-Geula (Beginning of Redemption) regarding the establishment of the state of Israel, endowing Zionism and the state of Israel with a messianic character incompatible with both Jewish orthodox and Zionist secular thought.'[26] Sholem feared the terrible revenge of the ancient words:

> After having sworn the ancient names day after day, we cannot push their powers away anymore. We have woken them and they will rise, since we have sworn them so powerfully. [...] every word that was created not from the void but from the 'good old treasure' is full to its rim with gun powder [...]. The revivers of the Hebrew language did not believe in Dooms Day, which nevertheless they have decreed us in their acts. Let us wish their vanity, that has led us to this apocalyptic way, will not be our perdition.[27]

Discourses have social distribution. As was mentioned before, different contexts use different discourses to talk about the same thing and semiotic regimes determine what discourse can be used by whom and where. The question of the present enquiry is, what kinds of discourses are used to represent Palestinians in the context of Israeli Jewish schools, for students who are about to join the army and carry on the Israeli policy of occupation in the West Bank and Gaza Strip.

Discourses are almost always legitimatory, for they are about why we do things, and are about the practices and the ideas and values attached to them. 'Hence they don't only reflect but transform practices so as to safeguard the interests at stake in a given social context' (Van Leeuwen, 2005: 104). In Israel the discourses of security and redemption legitimate practices of oppression, discrimination and assassination and transform them into practices of defense, 'deterrence' and retaliation. The most recent example is the eviction of Palestinian families from Sheikh Jarakh in East Jerusalem, viewed within the Jewish-Israeli discourse of 'Redemption' as legitimate, for it serves the goal of the 'unification' of the capital under Israeli rule namely its Judaization; in different, more democratic contexts such actions would be considered outrageous and illegitimate. Equally, the construction of the separation wall and the ongoing siege on Gaza are legitimated by Israeli discourse of security though they are illegitimate by any other standards.

This discrepancy was addressed, during the raid on Gaza 2009, by Foreign Minister Zipi Livni who using the discourse of war against terror spoke of the 'legitimate rights of Israel with respect to international law' in a conference whose participants included senior legal officials and public figures. Referring to world criticism of Israeli policy, the foreign minister said she was

> ready to receive the criticism of the international community in every matter, but {I} want the evaluation to be legitimate. { ... } It is incumbent upon the international community to make a distinction between a situation in which terror organizations willingly attack civilians and a situation in which a state acts against terror organizations and sometimes accidentally harms civilians. { ... } We share the values of the free world, but there is a tremendous gap between the true values of the state of Israel and its image in the world.

Livni further noted that the 'legitimacy of Israel is derived from its core principles as a Jewish and democratic state,'[28] namely both from Jewish norms and rules and from the founding principles of democracy.

The discourse of the 'war on terror' justifies many of Israel's actions against Palestinians and their supporters, especially what is called 'focused prevention' which means targeted assassination of people who seem or known to be suspicious. This discourse was used right after the attack on the flotilla Marmara in June 2010, when Israeli media announced that most of the killed passengers[29] were actually members of extreme Islamic groups, which are perceived as the most dangerous enemies of Israel (and the West). One such declaration was the following:

> According to a report of the {Israeli} Centre for the Legacy of Intelligence and Terror all killed passengers were members of

> extreme Islamic organizations in Turkey and about half of them declared to their relatives their wish to die as *shahids* (martyrs). There were no human rights activists among the dead, either from Arab or Western countries.[30]

And more recently still:

> A French judge: I knew Turkish group behind Gaza flotilla had terror ties in 1996: Jean-Louis Bruguière, who fights global terror groups and those who finance them, says the IHH is a terrorist group, not a charity.[31]

These revelations were meant to appease the 'beautiful souls' who thought the IDF attack on the flotilla Marmara outside Israel's territorial waters was not justified. Israeli norms allow eliminating terrorists and potential terrorists without trial. As we shall see in chapter 4, this discourse also uses the biblical expression 'kill whosoever sets out to kill you' in its modern interpretation of 'deterrence' and 'retaliation.'

Van Leeuwen notes that there are three kinds of ideas or attitudes we need to examine while studying discourse:

1) Evaluations of the actions or things involved. Evaluation is an expression of attitude. Evaluative expressions, in Halliday's words, serve as 'the speaker's ongoing intrusion into the speech situation,' and affect the whole stretch of discourse like 'a continuing motif or colouring' (1979: 66). Evaluation may be realized through various linguistic and discursive means, that show how people judge, appreciate, disapprove, abhor etc. and enable writers and speakers to share their emotions, taste and normative assessments with their intended or ideal audience (Martin and White, 2005). The means of evaluation, such as appraisals, are discourse and genre-specific (Coffin, 2006). Appraisals will be discussed extensively in chapter 4, regarding the legitimation of massacres.
2) Purpose: Different discourses attach different purposes to the same action: the same deeds can be described as purposeful actions meant to emancipate the Jewish people, to redeem the

'Promised Land' and liberate Jerusalem, or alternatively, to ethnic-cleanse Palestine.[32]

3) Legitimations: Reasons why particular things should be done or were done in particular ways by particular people. Legitimation in discourse will also be elaborated in chapter 4.

These three attitudes and their analysis may help answer the question any social semiotic analysis asks: 'how does a discourse transform reality into a version of this reality?' (Van Leeuwen, 2005: 106).

Van Leeuwen suggests that the way to find out how this happens is: 1.) to inventorize the elements of the social practice. 2.) Look how they are transformed by discourse.

However, in the analysis of texts we change the direction: we try to infer from the text the circumstances and the social practices, beliefs and interests that engendered it.

Modality

Modality is a way of describing how writers increase and decrease the force of their assertions and how they sharpen or blur the semantic categorizations with which they operate (Martin and White, 2005: 13–14). Fairclough (2003: 219) defines Modality as 'the relationship the sentence or clause sets up between author and representations.' Modality indicates how the author's voice positions itself with respect to other voices and other positions, and as Hodge and Kress point out 'linguistic resources of modality also [...] allow people to downgrade the truths of others'. For instance, 'some say the Arabs were expelled, some say they fled. Both explanations are nothing but myths' (*The 20th*, p.195). Authoritative texts such as school books can use the modality resources of language to impose a view of truth that is hard to counter. This, as Van Leeuwen reminds us, is a pretty unavoidable part of academic writing. An example from the present study can be: 'Perhaps the feud may have been settled without bloodshed, but the prime minister wanted to have a deterring act' (*The 20th*, p. 198). However, Modality does not tell us how true the information is but as how true is it represented, how true the sign maker wanted it to appear (Van Leeuwen, 2005: 160). Since truth is not 'either/or' modality allows degrees of truth and also kinds of truth (Halliday 1985). Fairclough distinguishes between two sorts or modality: the first – deontic modality – indicates what authors commit themselves to in terms of truth or necessity. This is the modality of necessity and obligation. The other type of modality is epistemic modality or the modality of probabilities. While deontic modality is always high, probability can be high, median or low (Martin and White, 2005: 13–14).

Genre

Genre is one of three significant factors in the constitution of the text, in addition to discourse and mode. The category of genre is essential in all attempts to understand text whatever its modal constitution: spoken, written, musical or plastic, for 'there is no text or textual element that is not generically formed' (Kress, 2003: 93). Today most researchers adopt the Bakhtinian conception of genre (1984: 157) in which genre has a culturally and historically situated logic as well as social purposes. Bakhtin (1986) maintained that language is always socially and generically formed, and we always encounter language as genre. Interactions have conventional, generic shapes and these shapes have meaning and purpose. From the first cues we know what genre we are in and that helps us to convey and understand meanings. Therefore 'errors in genre are often seen as errors of behaviour' (Kress, 2003: 85).

One feature of genre is site. The transformation of reality into a version of this reality is only realized in texts that appear in special sites, for instance a school book, a directory, a journal, the Bible, and this site gives the text many of its qualities (De Beaugrande, 1997). One can never mistake a school book for anything else because the differences between a history school book and a history book for experts or a history book for the general public are apparent from the front cover. School books bear, in addition to the title, the Ministry of Education authorization stamp and the age group for which they are intended; however, the name of the author is often omitted from the front cover of textbooks. By not advertising the names of their authors the books create the impression that these writers are only messengers or mediators between the bare facts and the readers and not propagators of ideology or of an ideological point of view. In non-school books there is no indication of age group; they are not subject to authorization, but the name of the author and his or her professional credits are the main items of information on both the front and the back covers. Other differences are to be found in the structure of the book, of every chapter and of every page where one sees questions, suggestions for further reading etc. These generic differences that are typical of site, affect the way the texts inside the books are written, read, kept, remembered, appreciated and believed.

Since social actions take place in fields of power, genres are the expression of power relationships. To participate fully in social life one needs to be able to produce fully adequate genres (Kress, 2003: 85). However, genres are not considered by Social Semiotics as stable forms or vessels into which one pours content. Rather, they are semiotic resources or templates for performing communicative acts (Van Leeuwen, 2005: 128). Therefore genres are very versatile and as Kress asserts, 'most texts are hybridization of genres and blending of categories' (2003: 76). This hybridization determines the organization of the text, which is very important for its interpretation. The event may have different meanings according to its different modes of organization in text. As Lotman explains, 'the very fact of transforming an event into text raises the degree of its organization' (Lotman, 1990: 221–222). School books, which are inevitably mix-genres, organize reality differently according to subject matter, age group and educational purposes.

Most Genres, as we shall see later on, unfold in stages (Martin, 1993) that normally appear in certain order. The change of this order usually has rhetorical purposes or 'implicature' (Grice, 1989). Any given stage can be realized by several alternative modes, visual or verbal, and a given stage can itself be multimodal.

Genres are realized in texts, for communication always happens as text. For social semiotics text is the result of social action (Halliday, 1978); it reflects the social circumstances that produced it (Kress, 1996). Hence, by analyzing a text we can infer the social circumstances of its production, i.e. who acts in relation to whom and for what purpose. Text, as an organizing unit of events and relationships, structures meaning, communication, and through it creates understanding (Wertsch, 2002: 14).

In light of these observations, the questions to be asked in text analysis are: who is involved, with what purpose, what roles they have, what power and in what environments? (Kress, 2003: 48). The expression of these social matters gives one kind of shape or genre to text.

The Multimodal Genre: Writing and Images in Textbooks

Genre is not a linguistic category but rather, a category that realizes and expresses social meanings (Van Leeuwen, 2005: 74). Generic meanings can be realized in images, in font types, in colour and in the type of paper they are written on (ibid.: 105). Moreover, genres are not defined by the same criteria in all modes (science, literature, music, film). Van Leeuwen shows that even in a single mode such as film, genre definitions have different criteria, such as place (westerns), content (detective stories), form (musicals) or the film's truth claims (documentaries). Some genres are defined by their function or in terms of what they do, i.e. appeal, legitimation, persuasion, explanation etc. (Van Leeuwen, 2005a: 74).

School books must be defined by their function for it is their function that determines their *raison d'être* and therefore their generic and discursive qualities.

The multimodal genre or text is usually made of language and images. The relationships between text and image are defined by Barthes as either *anchorage* or *relay* (1977: 39). In anchorage words elucidate pictures. As Van Leeuwen puts it, 'The text directs the reader through the signifieds of the image, causing him to avoid some and receive others,' and 'remote-controls him towards the meaning chosen in advance' (Van Leeuwen, 2005: 229). One example from the present study is a photograph of a flooded street defined by its caption as 'The Palestinian Problem' (*The 20th*). Nothing in the photograph itself could have told the viewer that he or she is watching 'the Palestinian problem' for although it shows a problem – an environmental one at that – there is nothing 'Palestinian' about the image – neither Palestinian people nor Palestinian landscape or houses are shown, only a flooded street in a poor neighbourhood that could be anywhere in the world.

In relay, 'Text and image stand in complementary relationship and are both fragments of a more general syntagm to which each contributes its own distinct information' (Van Leeuwen 2005: 229). Images can extend words and vice versa, through similarity – similar content in words and image – through contrast or through complement. For instance, in both *The 20th* and *MTII* there is a photograph of a man running with a wounded girl in his arms. The circumstances of the event are detailed in the caption. The caption specifies who the people are – an Israeli soldier rescuing his sister from her school that became a battle zone after the students were taken hostages by Palestinians and Israeli forces attacked the place in an attempt to rescue the children. The verbal and visual parts in this case are complementary – words and image are 'fragments of a more general syntagm' and form a single text. The text tells the general story of the attack but the image shows its final step: the rescue. Images frequently serve as elaborations, adding more details about place, action and object-signs such as clothes or tools. For instance, when a heading in the geography textbook *PIS* says 'traditional life in the non-Jewish population' it is the photograph of the 'primitive farmer' that tells us exactly who the 'non-Jewish' population is and what 'traditional' means in this context.

Integration: Text and picture can be integrated into one another or overlap. Some texts in Israeli school books are written against a background of photographs such as soldiers coming or going to war, a historic event such as the declaration of the state, a symbolic image such as the flag, or against the background of ideologically drawn maps of Israel. Images and verbal texts appear on the background of these defining texts; for instance in *AHH* (p.289) Arafat – fully armed and in uniform – speaking in the UN, is bursting out of a text about the PLO; pictures of dead and wounded, of politicians and battle ships are depicted on the background of a soldier's personal diary. Such backgrounds serve as cohesive devices that connect together all the elements of the layout – as a whole and its parts, as elaboration and specification – and give them meaning as one semiotic unit.

Though words and images may be parts of the same message, 'the world narrated is different from the world displayed' (Kress, 2003:

2). Van Leeuwen argues that over the past two or three decades, the status of language has been in decline and today image acquires status and becomes controlled, taught and codified like a language (Van Leeuwen, 2005). Kress emphasizes that since mode, whether image or writing, is a culturally and socially fashioned resource for representation and communication, meaning is differently realized in different modes. Every mode has different material aspects; it bears everywhere the stamp of past cultural work (Kress, 2003: 45) and the stamp of regularities of organization, that is to say, every mode has its lexicon, grammar and syntax, just like language (Kress and Van Leeuwen 2006).

Since we have, in the words of De-Saussure, a sort of dictionary of signs imprinted on everyone's brain, these signs and their cultural meanings have become automatic, so they are frequently considered as rules of nature instead of cultural conventions. A very common example is the significance of colours.[33] In multicultural classrooms teachers often treat the significance of colours as 'natural' while children from different cultures see colours differently (Peled-Elhanan, 2008). Colour as a semiotic mode will be discussed in chapter 2.

Kress explains that meanings can be realized in any mode but they are also mode specific (2003: 106). So we have to attend to what is mode specific and what is not, and why. In multimodal texts such as school books, information can be carried in one mode more than in others. The motivation to use one mode or another is their aptness, or their being 'best fit' for the occasion. For instance, the pulped book *World of Changes* is the only school book that presents a map depicting the escape routes of Palestinian refugees in 1948. These routes are not specified in the verbal text but are marked on the map by fire-coloured arrows, which express with an immediacy that cannot be created in writing the circumstances of the flight.

In textbooks meanings are realized by writing and images and in different combinations of these two modes. Kress (2003: 69) details the differences: writing is time-based whereas image is space-based. Writing is governed by the logic of sequence or linearity: first and second are inescapably hierarchic. Image is governed by the logic of space and simultaneity. It depicts elements in spatially organized arrangements: placing something in the centre means that all other things are marginal. Being above means being superior, given our position in space (head in the sky and feet on the ground). Hence the meaning relations on the page are bottom equals grounded or earthly, namely empirical or real, and top means not of this earth, ideal, abstract, theoretical or divine.

The relationships between left and right on the page or in a single image are these of 'given' and 'new' like in verbal syntax:

> For something to be given means it is presented as something the viewer already knows, as familiar and agreed-upon point of departure for the message. For something to be New means it is presented as something not yet known [...] hence as something the viewer should pay more attention to. (Van Leeuwen, 1992: 37)

In English, the information on the left of the page would be what the writer would like us to see as given, known, accepted or as the starting point of the message, while the information on the right would be what the writer wants us to treat as new. In Hebrew, since the directionality of writing is from right to left, the order is reversed so that the right side of the page or the image is the starting point of the message or the given part and the left side is where we are heading or will get to. These points will be elaborated much more in chapter 3.

Another difference between writing and images specified by Kress is that in writing, the commitment is to naming relations and classifications: 'The cell has...,' 'this man is...' and nothing has meaning unless it is named (Kress, 2003: 43). In picture the commitment is to location – this is where it goes – and to shape – this is what it looks like. In writing we lexicalize movement. Image does not need verbs or precise description of relations, all these are shown through layout, colour and perspective (Kress, 2003).

The question regarding the relations between writing and images is, what it is we want to mean, and what modes and genres are best for realizing this meaning. Related questions are: do we read images as we read text? How do different modes realize different meanings? How do images represent social relations and social interaction? How does each mode express values and interest? (Kress, 2003: 105–106).

Reading paths as access to knowledge in the multimodal text

Multimodal texts, such as school books, open the question of directionality and the question of 'point' (Kress, 2003: 157): what elements are to be read together? Whereas in reading verbal texts (the world as told) there is a distinct and strict 'reading path' I must follow in order to make sense of the writing – from left to right in English and from right to left in Hebrew; from the top of the page to its bottom in both languages – multimodal reading enables reading as design (the world as shown) which means it does not constraint the viewer to a pre-established reading path, rather the viewer is following a to-be-constructed path of reading. Reading images focuses on ordering and arrangements which endow the images with new meanings. Therefore reading images is harder given the pre-established reading path of the written page. The reader is much more active in constructing the reading path of a multimodal text, which is actually established according to principles of relevance to the reader. Shape, size and colour may determine the reading path of the whole page, which may be different for different readers. In order to read the multimodal text one must know about the constituents of image as we know about the constituents of sentences. The significance of elements depends upon their placement in the layout of the page or double-spread, which is a framed space. These principles are utterly different from ordinary reading.

To follow different reading paths is to construct completely different readings, epistemologically speaking: 'What seems to be the same kind of text calls for different readings of what is really a different text.' Therefore the analysis of textbooks must take place at two levels: 1.) verbal and visual analysis of the text components and 2.) study of the pathways it allows. One must remember however, as Kress notes, that 'the power lies with the reader to remake the text more than with the writer' (Kress, 2003: 164–165).

Analysis of Multimodal Texts

Multimodal analysis is the only one that can encompass the full range of signs and significations of textbooks. Kress assumes (2003: 159) that, in reading and understanding the multimodal text, we perform a few consecutive steps: First we would see there are 'blocks' of writing and image, and then we would decide which are the dominant modes; we would integrate the non-dominant with the dominant or treat them as equal and read them conjointly. Then we would decide what function every mode has, both on the structural level – are they complementary to each other or is one supplementary to the other – and in terms of their specialized meaning-role – does writing have the role of pedagogic framing, and image that of representing curricular content? As we shall see, many Israeli textbooks are quite consistent in the distribution of labor between text and image. One of the questions that came up in the present study was: which mode is used for critique or demystification, and which mode is employed for mythization?

School Books as Multimodal Texts

50 Years (2004) and *Face* (2006) lack colour and have significantly less photographs, sources, maps or graphs than the other books. In that they resemble textbooks of the 1950s–60s, which consisted solely of text and imposed one single reading path on their readers. All the other books – geography and history alike, are multimodal, namely contain texts and visuals of all sorts and offer various reading paths.

Earlier studies about Israeli school books do not focus on the multimodal nature of school books and concentrate on content analysis. Content analysis usually considers images as illustrations to verbal reports. Firer (2004: 58) remarks that photographs contribute to the 'text appeal' of the book. In her view, some photographs depicting the Israeli-Palestinian conflict have an illustrative function, while others are more elaborative and 'confront the readers with damage and destruction Arab bombs caused to Israeli life.' Content analysis avoids critical discourse analysis and therefore touches very lightly on questions of rhetoric, genre, modality or style.

Examples of multimodal analysis that will be brought up later on, show that strategies of discourse and multimodal analysis can enhance meanings beyond the single sentence, the single paragraph or the single image, meanings that are different from those reached by content analysis alone.

The Importance of this Study

Coffin (1997: 211) argues that 'Success in school history is dependent on a student's control of the lexicogrammatical resources and text structures that realize the arguing genres.' I would argue, following Kress and Van Leeuwen, that success in school history, geography, science and other subject matters also depends on the student's control of multimodal resources and structures.

Kress recommends the study of texts that are not overtly ideological, but rather 'the mundane text [which] is as ideologically saturated as a text which wears its ideological constitution overtly' (1993: 174). School books are not overtly ideological. For teachers and students they possess the authority of unbiased truth, being presented as objective neutral reports of 'the bare facts' and scientific data. However school books around the world have been proven to be ideological and authoritative,[34] and to obey rules of recontextualization, distribution and evaluation dictated by the state or by dominant groups.[35] They represent, verbally as well as visually, ideologies that are 'representations which can be shown to contribute to social relations of power and domination' (Fairclough, 2003: 9). The importance of revealing their ideological undertones lies in the fact that even students who may never read a book for pleasure or for general instruction must read their textbooks in order to pass their matriculation exams. A majority of Israeli students, being deprived of any meaningful contact with their Palestinian neighbors, receive most of the information about them through school and school material. Since they are drafted into the army immediately after graduating from high school and are sent to carry out the Israeli policy in the Palestinian occupied territories, a critical reading of their textbooks may have crucial importance for them and their teachers who, as Weinburg proved, usually do not look for subtexts because they do not think subtexts exist (Weinburg, 2001: 77). According to Weinburg, students normally 'overlook or not know how to seek the features that are designed to shape their perceptions or make them view events in a particular way.' They do not interrogate the text, but accept its overt narrative as the ultimate or even 'divine' truth (Weinburg, 2001: 77–78).

Weinburg's study (2001: 76) shows that 'for students, reading history was not a process of puzzling about author's intentions or situating texts in a social world but of gathering information.' But, as Bernstein argues (1996: 39), 'Pedagogic communication is often viewed as a carrier, a relay for ideological messages and for external power relations.' As Jenkins maintains, 'History does not correspond to the reality of things in the past' (Jenkins, 1991: xiii) but teachers and students are not aware of what Barthes called 'the effect of the real' (1967) or the bias created by writers' interpretations. They ignore the fact that in school books, as in any other history book, 'the choices of plot structure and the choice of paradigms of explanations [are] products of [...] an interpretive decision: a moral or ideological decision' (White, 1978: 67).

This is all the more true of geography textbooks, for students expect these scientific books to be neutral, objective and factual. Even experienced teachers claim they treat the textbooks as 'information' and not as ideological accounts. When confronted with the complexity of the multimodal representations, teachers claim they have not acquired the tools to read such texts[36] and that they had been 'blind' to their undertones. This 'blindness' must be addressed in order for teachers and students to be able to read school texts and be empowered by the knowledge they acquire.

History, according to Jenkins, is a 'field of force' [...] a field that variously includes and excludes, centres and marginalizes views [...] in ways and in degrees that react to powers of those forwarding them.' (Jenkins, 1991: 85–86). This is all the more true about history and geography school books, especially in a state such as Israel, where history and geography are so tightly linked together. Jenkins concludes that 'knowing this might empower the knower.' In order to know how to read school books and be empowered by this knowledge, students and teachers need explicit instruction in the multimodal ways whereby these texts convey their messages; otherwise they are left outside the ideological controversies and manipulations that engender the texts. By withholding such instruction educators may seem as 'willfully obliterating the communicative needs of their readers' (Kress, 1993: 184). The present study tries to offer an introduction to such an instruction, which seems essential in multicultural countries such as Israel where critical reading of the official narrative is still considered unpatriotic if not an act of outright treason (Firer, 2004).

Final introductory note: all the extracts from the school books were translated by me. However, they were all checked by a professional Hebrew–English translator as well.

1

THE REPRESENTATION OF PALESTINIANS IN ISRAELI SCHOOL BOOKS

> Israel never sought to achieve equal citizenship between Palestinian Arabs and Jews, nor did it seek the consent of its Arab citizens for the forceful ideological imposition of a Jewish state. (Yiftachel, 2006: 93)

Many Israeli textbooks not only discard and silence the Palestinian version of History but as Podeh (2002) found, they often manipulate the past in a way that entails the use of stereotypes and prejudice in describing the (Palestinian) 'other.' Stereotypes serve prejudice and 'foster delegitimization – categorization of groups into extreme negative social categories which are excluded from human groups that are considered as acting within the limits of acceptable norms and/or values' (Podeh, 2003). Oren and Bar-Tal (2007) found that common means used in school books for this delegitimization are dehumanization, outcasting, negative trait characterization, use of political labels and group comparison.

However, both Podeh and Bar-Tal refer only to explicit verbal delegitimation, especially through evaluation, while neglecting almost entirely other rhetoric devices and visual means. The following chapters will concentrate on the visual discourse and the rhetoric devices as well.

Podeh and other researchers define the views that dominate school books in Israel as prejudiced and ethnocentric and therefore differentiated from racism, but the socio-cognitive approach adopted by many researchers of racism today does not distinguish between ethnicism, racism and adjacent forms of discrimination and consider them to be 'fuzzy and overlapping concepts.' Wodak and Reisigl contend that 'Ideological articulations such as racism, nationalism, sexism, ethnicism, verge on one another, are connected and overlap.' These articulations are meant first and foremost 'to protect the interests of the dominant in-group' (Reisigl and Wodak, 2001: 21). All the above 'isms' reinforce the de-legitimation of 'others' mainly through exclusion and classifications, by which control over conceptions of reality is achieved (Hodge and Kress, 1993: 63). Regarding exclusion I will only mention at this point that none of the textbooks studied here includes, whether verbally or visually, any positive cultural or social aspect of Palestinian life-world: neither literature nor poetry, neither history nor agriculture, neither art nor architecture, neither customs nor traditions are ever mentioned. None of the books contain photographs of Palestinian human beings and all represent them in racist icons or demeaning classificatory images such as terrorists, refugees and primitive farmers – the three 'problems' they constitute for Israel.

Classification of Palestinians in Israeli Textbooks

> Categories engender meaning upon the world like paths in the forest that give order to our life-space. And like such paths they tend to resist change. (Allport, 1958: 171)

The classification of people or of 'social actors' is used 'whenever actors are referred to in terms of the major categories by means of which a given society or institution differentiates between classes of people: age, gender, provenance, class, wealth, race, ethnicity, religion, sexual orientation etc.' (Van Leeuwen, 2008: 42). These differentiations help constitute what Van Dijk (1997) terms the language of self-presentation and other-presentation. A major feature of the language of self-presentation and other-presentation is manifest in Israeli textbooks in the ethnic classification which differentiates between the Israelis or Jews[1] and the 'Non-Jews' who are the 'Arabs.' This dichotomy, characteristic of racist discourse (Reisigl and Wodak, 2001), has always seemed to Israeli educators 'essential for maintaining a distinct Jewish-Israeli identity and for sustaining the ability to compete successfully with the Arabs' (Podeh, 2000: 2). As Allport (1958: 171) maintained, 'It is characteristic of the prejudiced mentality that it forms in all areas of experience categories that are monopolistic, undifferentiated, two-valued and rigid.'

The distinction between Jews and non-Jews helps establish the Jewish in-group not only as dominant but as more real – for it has a distinct name – and to marginalize and subjugate the Palestinian citizens as an out-group which is defined only negatively as non-in-group. As we shall see in the following chapters, the differentiation between Jews as the dominant in-group and non-Jews as the marginal out-group of Israeli society pervades all areas of investigation. Even in matters that do not touch upon national or ethnic matters, such as industry, agriculture or the professions, textbooks – following the social and political discourse – divide the Israeli life-world ethnically, into Jewish and 'non-Jewish' or 'Arab.' This distinction is used in geography books to connote the difference between progress and backwardness, and illustrate on maps, graphs and diagrams the incompletion of the Zionist project of the 'Judaization' of the Land. For instance in the Geography textbook *Settlements in Space* (p.59) a map of 'rural areas in Israel' depicts the Jewish settlements in blue and the Arab villages in red. The text below the map defines the Jewish settlement as: kibbutz, moshav, [Jewish] community settlement etc. while the Arab villages are only defined as 'Arab,' and that, in spite of the fact that there are several kinds of Arab villages in Israel (Katz and Grossman, 1993). In civics 'the Non-Jewish/Arab sector' connotes the centrality of the Jewish citizens and the marginality of the Palestinian 'minority,' and in History books it immediately connotes the distinction between right and wrong versions: the Jewish narrative is the right one while the Arab narrative is the wrong one. In terms of modality, the Israeli versions of events are stated as objective facts, while the Palestinian-Arab versions are stated as possibility, realized in openings such as

'According to the Arab version.' Here are two examples from school books that are considered by researchers more progressive:

1) 'In the Arab sector the Kaffer Kassem massacre became the symbol of the evils of oppression' (*The 20th*, 1998: 121).
2) 'Dier Yassin became a myth in the Palestinian narrative [...] and created a horrifying negative image of the Jewish conqueror in the eyes of Israel's Arabs' (Naveh et al. 2009: 112–113).

Immediately after this statement the book provides a definition of 'myth,' explaining that 'myth is a story that becomes a meaningful symbol in the life of a nation, based on reality but at the same time distorts it. Narrative [is] the story of the people as the people perceives and tells it.'

As we shall see later, Israeli actions are usually presented in history books as right morally, according to universal and Jewish norms, while Palestinian actions are presented as whimsical or vicious. Israel 'reacts to Arab hostility,' performs 'operations' in their midst, and executes 'punitive deterring actions' against Palestinian terror, while the 'Arabs' murder Israelis, commit terror actions against Israel, take revenge and use what they call their suffering in anti-Israeli propaganda.

What's in a Name?

> Things don't have meaning unless they are named. (Kress, 2003: 43)

As Firer (2004: 63) has already noted, the label 'Palestinian' is hardly ever used in school books for naming the Palestinian occupied territories or the Palestinians themselves. In Israeli social, political and educational discourse Palestinian citizens are called by the demeaning label 'Israel's Arabs.' The Palestinians in the occupied territories are labeled, in addition to 'Arabs,' either Pales(h)tinaiim (in Hebrew) or Palestinim according to the speakers' or writer's political inclinations. Usually the left-wing oriented voices would call them Palestinim, which is equal to Palestinians, or in the Arabic pronunciation Falastinians as they call themselves. The right-wing oriented voices would call them Arabs or Pales(h)tinaiim, which is closer to Philistines and can be translated as 'Philistinians.' Therefore I will translate it as such from now on. Historically, the Palestinians are people who come from Palestina, or Syria Palestinae as the Romans named it, the land of the Philistines. Palestina was the name used by the Greek, the Romans and then by the Europeans and was the official name used by the British during their Mandate on the region. It refers to the whole land of southern Syria and not only to the portion of today's Palestine, and was homeland to all the people, including the Hebrews, who lived there. Professor Shimon Shamir (2005) explains that the Jews living in Palestina were called Pals(h)tinaiim, and not necessarily the Arabs. For instance those who volunteered to the British Army during the Second World War were called Pales(h)tinaiim, and Golda Meir herself said once 'I am also Pales(h)tinaiit,' meaning that her origins were from the ancient land of Palestina and that on her identity card – issued during the British Mandate, Palestina was marked as her home. Hence, the two-state solution, says Shamir, would mean having a Jewish state – Israel and a Palestinian state on the land of Palestina.[2]

Palestinians (pronounced Falastinians) and Palestine (Falastin) are the names the Palestinian national movement chose for their land and their people at the beginning of the twentieth century, thus distinguishing themselves from the British label, from the Philistines and from the Hebrews, and ridding themselves of all the other connotations of Palestina.

Even though the books studied here were published subsequent to the Oslo agreement which included the mutual recognition of the Israeli and the Palestinian nations, they do not respect the name Palestinians call themselves by – Falastinians. The more left-wing books call them Arabs, Israel's Arabs and Palestinians alternately, while the right-wing books call them Arabs, Israel's Arabs and on rare occasions Pales(h)tinaiim which is usually reserved for terrorists. The label Arabs enhances the idea Israel has always tried to convey, that the Palestinians are not a nation by themselves but are part of another, much bigger nation outside Israel – the Arabs. In that they are similar to Israeli-Jews who are part of the bigger Jewish people, most of whom reside outside Israel. The only difference between Palestinians and Israeli Jews, according to Israeli conception, is that the Jewish people have only one state – Israel, while the 'Arabs' can settle in any of the 21 different states they have. Therefore any Jew who comes to Israel is granted instant citizenship, while Palestinians cannot be granted citizenship at all.

Served by this perception, Israeli policy has always been to implicitly (or indeed, sometimes explicitly) 'encourage' Palestinians to leave their homes and settle in other Arab countries. A significant example is a declaration made by Zipi Livni while she was the Minister of Foreign Affairs:

> The national solution of Israel's Arabs is elsewhere: In order to maintain a Jewish-Democratic state we must constitute two nation-states with clear red-lines. Once this happens, I will be able to come to the Palestinian citizens of Israel, whom we label Israel's Arabs, and tell them that their national solution is elsewhere (*Haaretz*, 10 December 2008).

This is a rare occasion in which a prominent leader suggests to substitute 'Israel's Arabs' with 'Palestinian citizens of Israel.' However, the reason for this shift is aligned with the old intentions and goals. Livni uses the label Palestinians for the same reason the school books use the label Arabs, namely to indicate that these people, though they are the citizens of the state of Israel, do not belong where they actually live and work, and where they have lived for generations. Livni is reiterating the ever-persistent idea of transferring them to the (still non-existent) neighbouring state of Palestine. This speech is worth mentioning here because Livni spoke to high school students in Tel Aviv, on the eve of their conscription.

In most of the books studied here the label 'Palestinian' is mainly reserved for terrorists. For instance, 'The calm in Lebanon did not last [...] Lebanon's independence was at stake again when in the years 1968–69 Palestinian terrorist organizations, headed by the PLO, settled in Lebanon and started to act from its territory against Israel' (*AHH,* p.288). Or: 'After the 1967 war the presence of Palestinian terrorist organizations increased in Jordan and they created a state within a state. From these territories they set out to commit terrorist acts in the Jordan valley, without the king's permission' (ibid.: 284). Both *Face*, and *50 Years* emphasize the fact that the Palestinian refugees were a source of trouble and insecurity to all the countries they dwelt in, such as Lebanon and Jordan. On page 378 in *Face* there is a whole sub-chapter entitled 'The Palestinian factor threatens the integrity and unity of Lebanon,' and on page 382 there is a similar sub chapter about Jordan. In *50 Years* The Palestinian non-terrorists, called 'The Arabs of the Territories,' are only mentioned as cheap labor and a threat to Israeli agriculture, or as 'infiltrators' who come from Jordan and Egypt to commit terror acts in Israel. The chapter ends with a photograph of fully armed, masked people wearing kaffiyah on a vehicle. This is the only photograph of Palestinians in the whole book, placed at the bottom centre, as if concluding the report. The caption explains these are 'armed Philistinians patrolling the streets of Amman during the conflict between the Jordanian army and the Philistinians.' In these books, as in books of the 1950s–90s 'the Palestinians are perceived as a factor that constantly inflames and escalates the conflict' (Firer, 2004: 64).

Palestinians who are not terrorists are usually called Arabs: 'The Arab countries did not come to terms with the consequences of the [Israeli] War of Independence and, although they signed the cease-fire agreements, they demanded that Israel returns to the partition borders and reinstates the Arab refugees in their homes' (*JIP,* p.309). Or: 'As a result of the fall of the Arab countries, vast areas where a million Arabs dwelt were annexed to Israel' (*AHH,* p.337). Only when the peace agreement between Israel and the PLO is mentioned, does *JIP* state explicitly, 'Israel recognized the PLO as the sole representative of the Palestinian people' (*p.*332).

While *50 Years* and *Face*, with their right-wing orientation, use the labels Pales(h)tinaiim which is equal to 'Philistinians,' and 'Arabs,' Naveh et al. (2009) and Domka et al. 2009, with their left-wing orientation use 'Arabs' and 'Palestinians' alternately. In Naveh et al. (2009) we find in one sub-chapter 'the reasons for the departure of Israel's Arabs,' the name 'Arab' five times, and the name 'Palestinians' twice, when referring to the same people. By contrast, when this book reports about the *Nakba* the ratio is opposite: 'Palestinians' is used four times, and 'Arab' only once (pp.142–143). In Domka et al. (2009) one sees the same tendency. Regarding the 1953 'infiltrations' of Palestinian refugees who tried to come back to their fields and homes, the book uses in the same paragraph the word 'Arab' three times and the word 'Palestinians' twice (pp.158–159).

The civics textbook *Being Citizens in Israel: A Jewish Democratic State* devotes substantial paper time to Palestinian views and events; it details the discriminatory acts against the Palestinian citizens, names the conflict 'the Israeli-Palestinian Conflict' and not 'The Jewish-Arab Conflict' as it is usually named and mentions – unlike most other books – the fact that in 1993 the PLO erased from its charter the entries that called for a destruction of Israel and the denial of its right to exist (p.337). However, it calls pre-Israel Palestina 'Mandatory Israel' and alternates between Arabs and Palestinians quite randomly without any apparent logic, using the label Arab much more frequently. For instance a chapter called 'The National Split [in Israel]' opens with the following statement (parenthesis in the original text):

> In order to understand the essence of the national split one has to know the characteristics of the Arab society. [...] In 1948 [...] lived in mandatory Israel (Palestine as it is called by the Arabs) nearly two million people. Two thirds of them were Palestinian Arabs and one third Jews. [...] Following an expulsion and a massive flight of Arabs during the war, only 160,000 Palestinian Arabs remained within the borders of the state of Israel, 10% of the Palestinian Arabs who had lived there until then (p.279).

From this point on, the label Palestinian is rarely mentioned and the Palestinian citizens are called 'Arabs,' 'Arab minority' or 'Israel's Arabs.' In the two or three pages of this chapter that use the label 'Palestinians' (pp.279–280), we find the label 'Arabs' attached to Palestinian citizens or refugees 25 times against 4 occurrences of the label 'Palestinians.' In one paragraph of 12 lines I found one occurrence of 'Palestinians,' four 'Arabs' and two 'Israel's Arabs,' all referring to the same group of people, or as they are called 'population' or 'sector.' An example of this is the following sentence:

> The reality imposed on the Arabs in Israel as a result of their turning into a minority in the state that subjugates them, while being in conflict with the rest of their Palestinian people, heightened their political awareness etc. (p.281).

'Arabs' is often used as a generic label to indicate all the native non-Jews. The geography book *Israel: Man and Space* names all the minorities in Israel: One example is found on p.12:

> The Arab Population: Within this group there are several religious groups and several ethnic groups: Muslims, Christians, Druze, Bedouins and Circassians. But since most of them are Arab they shall be referred to henceforth as Arabs.

In this book the label Palestinians is reserved for ill-paid 'foreign workers':

> Some of the foreign workers are Palestinians from areas controlled by the Palestinian Authority etc. (p.12).

Presenting the Palestinian areas as 'controlled by the Palestinian authority' instead of as their native land and the people who live there as foreign workers emphasises the idea that the Palestinians do not belong where they have lived for centuries.

The only book that uses the label Palestinians consistently is *World of Changes* which was interdicted. This book labels the conflict 'the Zionist-Palestinian conflict' and the 1948 war a civil war instead of the war of independence; it is the only book that calls the pre-Israel territory 'Palestina' as it was actually called instead of Mandatory Israel as it is called in other school books. It presents the two adversary sides symmetrically and gives almost equal weight to their arguments and their national claims (this will be discussed further in chapter 3). Furthermore, *World of Changes* is the only book in this study where the Palestinian occupied territories are named the West Bank and not Judea and Samaria or the Western Land of Israel as in *50 Years* and other books; destroyed Palestinian villages are mentioned by their original names and even 1948 Eilat is called by its Arabic name Um-Rash-Rash as it was called at the time.

Since the position of the present study is that no sign is neutral and every sign is motivated by interests and ideology, the mixture of labels is perceived as motivated not only by disrespect for the name the Palestinian people have chosen for themselves but also by the perception that it doesn't matter what they call themselves, for 'us' they are merely Arabs. This perception nourishes the arguments used in Israeli popular and political discourse for barring the return of the Palestinian refugees, along with the argument that Arabs should not be allowed to return to Israel after many Jews were expelled from Arab countries such as Morocco, Iraq and Syria.

The Use of Racist Discourse

Verbal Racism

According to Bar-Tal and Nets-Zehngut's study mentioned earlier, *The Israeli-Jewish collective memory regarding the Israeli-Arab/Palestinian conflict*, 'Israeli Jewish consciousness is characterized by [...] blind patriotism, belligerence, self-righteousness, dehumanization of the Palestinians and insensitivity to their suffering.'[3] Regarding the dehumanization of Palestinians these findings are not different from findings in other surveys, that have been conducted for the last 30 years or so; for instance, the survey of Zemach (1980) indicated 'a stereotypical tendency among Israeli youngsters to view all Arabs, anywhere within the state of Israel and beyond, as a menacing and ill-intentioned collective. It also exposed a worrying level of support for legal and administrative measures which, if ever implemented, would curb the freedom of Palestinian citizens of Israel, limiting their civil and even human rights' (quoted in Rabinowitz, 2001: 65).

A survey led by the Maagar-Mohot institute in Tel Aviv University, headed by Professor Yitzhak Katz, revealed in February 2010, that

50 per cent of Israeli-Jewish high school students believe Palestinian citizens should not be granted equal civil rights and 56 per cent believe they should not be allowed to be elected to the Knesset. The survey emphasizes the significant relation between these positions and Jewish religiosity. For instance 82 per cent of the religious students and 39 per cent of the secular ones believed Palestinian citizens should be denied civil rights. Similarly, 82 per cent of the religious students and 47 per cent of the secular ones believe Palestinian citizens should not be allowed to be elected to the Knesset.[4] The argument of the present study is that these attitudes are the product of Israeli education and that Israeli mainstream school book texts manifest what Reisigl and Wodak (2001: 24) term, following Van-Dijk, 'elite racism,' which is the 'racism reproduced in elite discourses, such as papers, school books, academic discourse, political speeches and parliamentary debates – the racism which is then implemented and enacted in other social fields,' such as the army.

As was already mentioned Podeh (2002: 61) argues that in the first period of Israeli textbooks (1950–60), 'the historical narrative was replete with bias and prejudice'.

As for more recent books, both Podeh (2002) and Firer (2004) claim that, in the textbooks of the 1990s, the 'Arabs' are no longer described in stereotypical terms and that on the whole, these textbooks seem to present a balanced picture of the Arab-Israeli conflict. Firer (2004: 75) claims that 'as political correctness has reached Israel it is no longer appropriate to use blunt, discriminatory language in textbooks,' and then adds that in the years 1967–90 'the stereotypes of Arabs and Palestinians almost disappear' (ibid.: 92). However, the analysis applied in my study reveals that in the major school books from 1996–2010, including the ones Firer and Podeh praise for being more balanced and less dogmatic, Palestinians are still represented – visually and verbally – either in racist stereotypical ways or not at all, namely either as 'impersonalized' negative element or as 'a blind spot,' excluded from where they should have been, from where one can guess their existence, like a missing book on the library shelf.

In books for the very young (years 1–4), the Palestinians, either the citizens of Israel or the Palestinians in the occupied territories, hardly exist. One cannot find them in any drawing, photographs or major verbal texts, either factual or fictional. In anthologies there is almost no trace of their literature or poetry, children songs, proverbs or folk tales, and there is hardly any trace of their existence in factual books about the state of Israel.

In other school books the discourse relating to Palestinians responds to all the criteria of racist discourse as defined by sociologists and discourse analysts such as Allport (1958), Van Leeuwen (2001), Essed (1991), Van Dijk (1997) and Reisigl and Wodak (2001). Essed argues that racism as ideology is present in everyday activities and serves 'to cement and unify, namely to preserve the ideological unity of the dominant group. It includes a whole range of concepts, ideas, images and intuitions that provide the framework of interpretation and meaning for racial thought in society, whether systematically organized in academic discourse or in casual every day, commonsense thinking' (p.44).

Racism, according to Essed, whether as ideology or as everyday practice is 'the expression or activation of group power' (p.37) and consists of shared social representations of others. Essed explains that 'social representation is a general term for a socially shared structure of cognitions, such as beliefs, knowledge, opinions, attitudes, purposes and emotions' (p.44). She does not distinguish between personal and institutional racism for 'racial or ethnic beliefs or opinions expressed by individual dominant group members are not relevant as personal opinions but as reflections of socially shared representations of racial and ethnic groups' (p.44).

From this point of view, authorized Israeli textbooks describing the Palestinians in ways that are typical of racist representation i.e. as primitive, subservient, deviant, criminal or evil, and as a problem-to-be-solved,[5] should not be treated merely as a reflection of the writers' personal opinions but as a reflection of a large swathe of the official Israeli attitude towards the Palestinians as a whole.

Racism, which is a social process, is recurrently reinforced and reproduced through a complex of attitudes (prejudice) and actions (discrimination). As Essed explains, '[...] the acquisition, use, and transformation of ethnic prejudice are social processes in which in-group preference is confirmed discursively' (1991: 45). Prejudice, according to Essed is not just antipathy. It is a social representation compounded of in- and out-group differentiations. The assumed differences are evaluated as negative in relation to in-group norms, values, traditions or goals and are subsequently attributed to racial or ethnic characteristics of the out-group. These negative evaluations are 'generalizations based on insufficient or biased representations that are constituent elements of an ideology rationalizing and reinforcing existing systems of racial and ethnic inequality' (ibid.).

Israeli geography school books often rationalize and reinforce the systems of discrimination, land confiscation, and lack of infra-structure in the Arab villages (chapter 2).

For example, since Palestinian-Arabs can seldom obtain permit to build and expand, either on municipal or personal land, the houses or annexations they manage to build for their children are treated by Israel as illegal and are immediately demolished.[6] *GLI* justifies this practice and reinforces it as follows:

> **Illegal Construction in the Arab villages**: Most of illegal houses are built on municipal land and agricultural lands that belong by the Israeli law to the state. Illegal building is also a result of wishing to evade payment for licence. (*The Geography of the Land of Israel*: 199)

But as Yiftachel (2006: 133, 143, 166) explains,

> 'Territorial Judaization facilitates unequal allocation of land [...] rezoning and redevelopments for the benefit of the dominant groups.' Although 'the Arabs make up 20% of the population they have only 3.5% of the land [...]. Over a half of land owners were expropriated by the state after 1948 and more than 500 Jewish settlements were built on these lands. [...] Since its establishment the state has built over 700 Jewish localities and 0 Arab localities [...]. Although the Arab population had grown six fold by 2006, the land under its control had halved. This situation creates virtual ghettoisation of Arabs.'

The Palestinian citizens lost both their personal property and their collective territorial assets and interests because nearly all their land has been proclaimed state land.

Geography school books often rationalize the 'forced stability' of the Palestinian citizens and the fact that they have not become as 'modern' as the Israeli sector by depicting them as clannish; one of the repeatedly mentioned features of Arab clannish mentality is the 'unwillingness' of the Palestinian-Arab citizens to allocate land for public use:

> **Management of land use in the Arab sector**: In the Jewish sector there is no objection to allocate some of the private lands for public building. In the Arab sector there is an expectation that all public services and needs be provided from the land reservoir of the state. (*GLI*: 303)

'The land reservoir of the state' to be sure is made of the lands that have been confiscated from the Palestinian citizens. Yiftachel (2006: 145) explains the idea behind turning Arab confiscated lands into 'state-lands':

> Settler states often regard native land as public land that can be disposed of by governments without the natives' approval or even knowledge. As a result the natives become trespassers on their own land. Even if the state recognizes native possession it is usually conceived to be only at the whim of a sovereign and may be revoked at any time.

As we shall see in chapter 2: the geography of hostility and exclusion, the Geography textbooks studied here discredit Palestinian agriculture as non-developed or un-modern (*PIS*). This description conceals the Israeli system of inequality which compels the Palestinian citizens to do with much fewer resources, less funds, water and land than their Jewish co-citizens.

Israeli policy against granting the Palestinian refugees the right of return is justified by describing their exodus, whether through expulsion or flight from Jewish aggression, as 'panicked escape' in which they 'abandoned' their homes, often to the astonishment of Israeli people and leaders. Palestinian non-citizens in the occupied territories are often depicted as terrorists, and this depiction reinforces the policy, presented in school books as an agreed-upon necessity, of constant control, restriction of movement and even extra-judicial assassinations.

As will be made clear in the following chapters, the basic tenets of prejudice listed by Essed are compatible with Israeli attitude towards Palestinian Arab citizens and non-citizens as it is reflected in the school books. These are:

1.) A feeling of superiority, which in Israeli social discourse and textbooks is expressed by the narrative of (Jewish-Western) progress. In this narrative the Jews are the representatives of the West and hence of progress, while the non-Jews or Arabs represent the Orient and hence backwardness. Though discarded by modern geographers and anthropologists (Page, 2003), this colonialist perception of progressive westerns civilizing the backward indigenous population of the East, still persists in geography school books (see chapter 2), in Israeli literature (Zrubavel, 2002) and media, as described by historian and journalist Tom Segev (*Haaretz*, 28 December 2008):

> This is the basic assumption of the Zionist project since its onset: we are the representatives of enlightenment and progress, rational sophistication and morality, and the Arabs are a primitive rabble, tempestuous and violent, ignorant boys who should be tamed and educated by our wisdom, and this, needless to say, by the 'stick-and-carrot' method as the donkey-driver treats his donkey.

2.) Perception of the subordinate race as intrinsically different and alien. This perception is tightly connected to the first one and is expressed in Israeli school books in classifications and in generalized observations such as 'The Arab society is traditional and objects to changes by its nature, reluctant to adopt novelties. [...] Modernization seems dangerous to them' (*Geography of the Land of Israel*: 303).

3.) A feeling of propriety claim to certain areas of privilege and advantage, which in Israel pertain to land, to emigration rights exclusively given to Jews by the 'law of return' hailed in all school books, to budgets and municipal services, to national identity and to cultural dominance. In school books this feeling is most apparent in the repeated statement about the exclusive Jewish rights on the entire Land of Israel/Palestine, expressed both verbally and in the maps which depict Palestinian lands as part of the state of Israel although they have never been annexed by law.

4.) Fear and suspicion that the subordinate race covets the prerogatives of the dominant race. In the Israeli context this fear relates to personal and municipal expansion, professional and political advancement, national and cultural rights and the commemoration of the Palestinian catastrophe – the *Nakba* – on Jewish Independence Day. One example of this fear is the general response to the document called 'The Future vision of the Palestinian Arab Citizens of Israel' published in 2006 by the National Committee of the Heads of Arab Local Authorities in Israel, a document in which the Arab citizens demanded far-reaching changes in several areas of citizenship, that would lead to equality with the Jewish population. The changes pertain to the following domains:

1) The legal status of the Palestinian Arabs in Israel
2) Land and housing
3) Economic development
4) Social development
5) Strategic vision for Arab Education
6) Arab Palestinian culture in Israel
7) Institutions and political work

The document which addresses all the crucial aspects of prejudice and discrimination against the Palestinian citizens and demands to rectify them, alarmed both right and left wings of the political arena.[7] This fear has been resolved by allocating all the above privileges, rights and services, by law, almost exclusively to army veterans (Druze and Bedouin veterans notwithstanding) namely to Jews only. In school books, this fear is manifest in the exclusion of the history, the culture and all the social facts of nearly 20 per cent of the population from the curriculum, and the depiction of these citizens as a marginal, backward, hostile and disturbing 'element,' despite Israeli efforts to modernize them.

Another aspect of this fear is the fear that the Palestinians would be considered as victims or even consider themselves as victims, as is evident from the aforementioned *Nakba* law. Israeli journalists for instance, do not call Palestinian casualties victims; there are hardly any photos of their sufferings either in the media or in school books and almost no expression of empathy on the part of journalists, politicians or educators regarding their dire circumstances. In the school books, most of the reports about Palestinian death are devoid – as in the media – of what La Capra (2001: 125) calls 'empathic unsettlement,' which should be 'the response of even secondary witnesses (including historians) to traumatic events which must involve empathic unsettlement that should register in one's very mode of address,' that entails 'being responsive to the traumatic experience of others.' (p.41) In the Israeli context such empathic unsettlement regarding Palestinian victims during the *Nakba* or in the following years, would risk to de-legitimate the Israeli-Zionist narrative and the legitimated wrong done to the Palestinians and is therefore impossible.

Exclusion and marginalization are typical of racist heterophobic behaviour (Memmi, 1999). But as Van Dijk (1997) notes, in order to legitimate their racist behaviour, dominant groups who exclude and marginalize 'minorities' will not refer openly to their own interests but claim their actions are for the common good or even good for the dominated. Van Dijk concludes, 'a group needs to show that its basic principles are just and those of the other are wrong. Ours are general, universal and apply to everyone; our actions are within the general moral order, which means they constitute the commonsense' (1997: 258).

One example is the quote from the speech by former Israeli foreign minister Zipi Livni mentioned above (*The Jerusalem Post* 26 March 2008).

In this speech, as in others during the raids on Gaza in 2009, Livni tried to persuade the Palestinians as well as the world in general that whatever Israel is doing is compatible with universal norms. Zipi Livni, like other politicians, recruited universal values and principles while 'using and abusing the rhetoric of survival and security and at the same time denying the relevance of the same security and survival considerations for the Palestinians' (Yiftachel, 2006: 67). In this speech, as in reports about massacres in Israeli school books (chapter 4), the legitimating discourse of security and protection conceals the hostility and excuses the brutality by the argument that Israel does whatever is required to 'protect its citizens from terror.'[8]

Strategies of Negative Representation

Van Dijk (1984: 40) enumerates the categories used to rationalize prejudice against minority groups, labeling them the '7 Ds of discrimination': dominance, differentiation, distance, diffusion, diversion, depersonalization or destruction and daily discrimination. Reisigl and Wodak (2001: 22) specify that 'these categories serve in various ways to legitimate and enact the distinction of the "other" for example by dominating the minority groups, by excluding them from social activities and even by destroying and murdering them.'

The discursive means by which these forms of discrimination are expressed in Israeli school book match Van Leeuwen's (2008) strategies of representing social actors negatively; these strategies include exclusion, suppression and backgrounding of social actors, genericization, collectivization, functionalization and impersonalization. Here are some examples:

Impersonalization

'Reference to people by means of a negative quality assigned to them, often realized in an abstract noun that does not include the semantic feature "+human," for instance as a problem' (Van Leeuwen, 2008: 46).

In addition to being defined by association as non-entity (non-Jews), Palestinians are often referred to as 'the Palestinian problem.' This expression, repeatedly used in the school books written by Eli Bar-Navi, who is considered a progressive writer (Podeh, 2002 and Firer, 2004) is in fact an expression that was salient in the ultra-right-wing ideology and propaganda of Meir Kahana.[9] Labeling a nation 'a problem' is disturbing and even more so finding it in a Jewish textbook only 60 years after the Jews were called 'The Jewish problem.' And indeed, labeling the Palestinian people a 'problem,' (sometimes even a poisonous problem as in Bar-Navi, 1998: 184) signals not only their social exclusion from the main stream society but goes one step further and leads – as was the case of Jews and other unwanted groups in racist Europe – to the legitimation of their elimination. As Allport explains (1958: 171), and as Israeli reality demonstrates time and again, verbal indoctrination and negative other-representation can infect people's minds to such a degree that they recur to physical attacks quite easily. Allport explains that since 'the victim group has long been typed, people have begun to lose the power to think of the members of the out-group as individuals.' Israeli high school students, who are about to become soldiers, are taught that the very existence of Palestinians in our midst is a problem that must be solved. For example, in the history school book *The 20th* (p.249) Professor Bar-Navi explains that annexing the Palestinian occupied territories to the state of Israel would create 'an absurd situation where the Jews would be a minority in their own land,' and this, he adds, would turn 'the Zionist dream into a South African nightmare.' The historian, wrote these words while Nelson Mandela was the president of South Africa. However, in his view South Africa is still a nightmare for the white population with whom he equates the Israeli Jews.

Genericization

Whenever Palestinians are mentioned in the history, geography and civics books studied here, it is always as a collective, either generically: 'The Arabs are...' or through what Van Leeuwen terms a 'singularizing synecdoche' (2005) i.e. 'The Arab is...', or through 'indetermination', by approximate numbers and indeterminate quantities (i.e. most... some). The reference to people by quantities is what Van Leeuwen (2008: 38) defines as Aggregation: 'A linguistic treatment of persons as numbers and statistics by means of definite or indefinite quantities.' The impression created by these kinds of reference to Palestinians, whether dead or alive, alongside the lack of photographs or reports about Palestinian individuals and Palestinian life-world, is that they are all alike and exist only in packs or masses, like cattle. Even their death in massacres or wars is reported like the death of animals, by approximate numbers or quantities; in several reports about the Dier Yassin massacre we find the following:

> 245 corpses were counted in the village – men, women and children.

The 20th 1998: 184 (11–12 grades)

The number of casualties is not clear and it ranges between 100 and 254.

Journey into the Past 2001: 284 (8–9 grades)

In the course of the battle that developed on the ground, between 100 and 250 persons were killed, including women and children.

Fifty Years of Wars and Hopes 2004: 180 (10–11 grades)

In summing up the consequences of wars Israeli history books give exact figures of Israeli losses such as '6,000 killed, of which 4,500 soldiers and 1,500 civilians, and more than 30,000 wounded' (Hagiladi and Kassem, 2007: 20). However, Palestinian losses are usually described in estimated quantities. In Hagiladi and Kassem we read 'there were many casualties, many villages were destroyed and hundreds of thousands Palestinians became refugees' (ibid.). Hagiladi and Kassem's book, which is not a school book, presents the two narratives – the Israeli one and the Palestinian one – side by side, and still, each version uses 'aggregation' with regard to the other group's losses. This may point to a common trait of these two national narratives – not to exhibit any empathy or empathic unsettlement while reporting the death of 'our enemies.'

Aggregation eliminates the possibility to see these 'corpses' as individual human beings, and their elimination as a human tragedy, especially when, as Ruth Firer notes in her study of Israeli textbooks until the late 1990s, no photos of suffering Palestinians and Arabs can be found.

Van Leeuwen and Jaworski (2002: 258) found a similar attitude in Western media reports about Palestinian or pro-Palestinian victims of Israeli aggression. They observe that 'western audiences are invited to feel the agony of Israeli [victims while] Palestinian deaths are rarely made so graphic or memorable: they are anonymous people, counted as numbers, bodies aloft among depersonalized funeral crowds.'

This stance also dominates the negotiations between Israel and the Palestinian Authority regarding the exchange of prisoners, which transform thousands of Palestinian captives, all 5,777 of them, including 216 minors and 45 children,[10] into a faceless 'price' Israel has to pay in return for one particular Israeli captured soldier (called 'child') who has a name and a face, a family and a biography.

The Palestinian collective never receives any positive attributes or any affective or cognitive verbs, which implies that these people never think rationally or feel anything. As a rule, Arabs and Palestinians don't do much in Israeli school books except for lurking, attacking in all sorts of ways and multiplying (e.g. *PAS:* 78). The few transitive verbs I came across regarding this unanimous group of people included 'poison,' 'attack,' 'refuse,' 'evade tax payment' and 'thank Israel for the progress it has brought into their life' (*SIS:* 60).

Functionalization

'Functionalization occurs when social actors are referred to in terms of an activity, in terms of something they do' (Van Leeuwen, 2008: 42). Van Leeuwen explains that in stories people are 'functionalized' when they remain '... nameless characters [who] fulfill only passing, functional roles, and do not become points of identification for the reader or listener' (ibid.: 40).

An edifying example of functionalization is found in the geography book *SIS* (p.63) in a report about the Jewish religious village Bnei-Reem. The village is praised for combining modern technology with Jewish tradition, a combination made possible initially thanks to 'an Arab family who dwelled in the 'area'. This family served as ' "Sabbath Goy"[11] and would open and close the irrigation system [on the Sabbath]. But today, modern technology enables them to do it without human touch, with the help of a Sabbath clock which operates the machines.'

Since the book does not mention that Bnei Reem was built on the ruins of the Palestinian village al-Masmiyya al-Kabira, that was cleansed and destroyed in 1948, with the exception of its two schools and several houses, and whose 2923 inhabitants were driven out, we don't know why this one family stayed on after the others had gone or where exactly the family 'dwelled.' Had the text offered any details about this 'functionalized' family, it should have also mentioned that the 'terrorist infiltrators' who 'harassed' the village, frightened the cows and demoralized the people to the point of leaving (p.64) were none other than its original inhabitants who came at harvest time to gather their crop and take revenge.

By 'functionalizing' these people and by treating them as if they were a tool, the book teaches the students that not everyone deserves a history or an individual identity. Some people only have functions in other people's story, such as 'Sabbath Goy'; on being replaced by machines they become non-existent.

Demonization

Contrary to the conclusions drawn by Podeh and Firer, explicit means of demonization are not absent from the 1994–2010 books. In the books of Bar Navi, especially praised by Podeh and Firer for their political correctness, we find the most blatant comparisons of Palestinians with Nazis or the Devil. For instance: 'The Prime-Minister saw in Arafat the embodiment of Hitler' (*The 20th:* 252). 'Arafat was considered as the personification of Satan and the PLO as a clan of murderers' (ibid.: 257). 'The action in Lebanon seemed to [Prime Minister Menahem Begin] as a salvation war that would save Israel from a second Auschwitz' (p.251).[12] These comparisons are mostly extravocalised, namely brought as direct or indirect quotes from authoritative leaders of the state, and therefore possess the authority of truth which is never contradicted by the writer.

Discrimination as Naturalization, Existentialization and Self-Directed Phenomenon

In Israeli textbooks, as in the media and in the general political and social discourse, discrimination of Palestinians is very often described as their natural situation, and their misfortunes as their 'lot' (*The 20th* 1998: 195), the result of their own doing (*PIS:* 110) or of unfavorable circumstances that are presented in one of the following fashions (coined by Van Leeuwen, 2008: 67):

1) In terms of 'existentialization' or 'naturalization' – where human action is represented as something that 'simply exists,' natural and outside temporal boundaries. For instance: 'The population in the

refugee camps is growing fast and conditions of life are very hard, the rate of unemployment is high, the houses are crowded and poor and the standard of health services, education and hygiene is low' (*PIS*, 1998: 110). The verb 'is' helps present Palestinians' dire situation as constant, stagnant, out of time and devoid of human agency or cause.

2) As a self-directed phenomenon that acts independently of human social actors:

> Although Israel came victorious out of the survival-war that was forced upon her, the Palestinian problem would poison for more than a generation the relationships of Israel with the Arab world and with the international community (*MTII*: 239).

Or: 'Immigration has no role in the increase of Arab population' (*PIS*: 109). Both the 'Palestinian problem' and 'immigration' are presented in these quotes as free agents that act on their own. 'The Palestinian problem' to be sure is not the problem the Palestinians have as a result of Israeli aggression but the problem the Palestinians constitute for the Israelis themselves who are afflicted with this poisoning 'trouble.' In a similar fashion, the phrase about the lack of Arab immigration doesn't give any reason for this phenomenon but presents 'immigration' as a free agent. This phrasing conceals the whole problem of Palestinian refugees and their debated right of return. In the same line the phrase 'their lands are diminishing' (*SIS:* 59) disguises a whole system of land confiscation (detailed in Yiftachel, 2006) presented as a natural or self-directed phenomenon.

Podeh (2000: 1) tries to align the verbal racist representations in Israeli textbooks with other Western school books, claiming that 'many studies in the West have demonstrated that ethnocentric views and myths, stereotypes and prejudices often pervade history textbooks. The case of Israel is no exception.' Podeh further argues (ibid.: 2) that 'it is common knowledge that textbooks in social sciences and humanities do not merely convey an objective body of information, but are responsible for conveying to youth what adults believe they should know about their own culture as well as that of other societies.' According to the school books studied here, what adults in Israel believe Israeli youth should know about their Palestinian neighbours is tightly connected with these adults' conviction that Palestinians should be eliminated or at least excluded, marginalized, segregated and controlled.

Visual Racism

Van Leeuwen argues (2008: 137) that the consideration of images 'should have the pride of place in any inquiry into racist discourse. We need to show that images do more than just show what is, we need to make their racist sense explicit.'

Van Leeuwen calls our attention to the fact that visual racism can be denied much more easily than verbal racism and dismissed as 'in the eyes of the beholder' (ibid.). That is why he recommends for the critics of racism 'to attend to the visual racism in apparently "innocent" and "entertainment" contexts rather than to more blatant forms of racism' (2008: 147).

Van Leeuwen asks two questions regarding the relationships between the image and the viewer (p.142) that have to do with the options and the choices the 'language of images' gives us to depict people. The first is, how are people depicted as 'others'? And as a follow to this question, when depicted, what do these people do?

Van Leeuwen counts five different strategies for visually representing people as 'others,' all of which can be found in the school books studied here:

1) The strategy of exclusion, not representing people at all in contexts where in reality they are present.
2) Depicting people as the agents of actions which are held in low esteem or regarded as subservient, deviant, criminal or evil.
3) Showing people as homogeneous groups and thereby denying them individual characteristics and differences.
4) The strategy of negative cultural connotations.
5) The strategy of negative racial stereotyping.

The first strategy is the most widespread in Israeli school books, namely not to show Palestinians at all, to ignore these people and the contexts in which they live and work. The second strategy is to show them engaged in negative or problematic actions: terrorism, being refugees, working their fields with primitive tools etc. A particular aspect of the representation of Palestinians is that they are usually engaged in activities of which we cannot see the goal: the photographs do not show either where the refugees came from or where they are heading; they are placed in no-places that can easily be in Afghanistan or Iraq or any other arid landscape. Similarly, we cannot tell from the images where the nomad is leading his camel or what the stones of terrorist children are aimed at. This intransitivity of images contributes to their being 'phenomena,' or objects frozen in time and out of context rather than individuals who perform human action or reaction at a specific point in time and space.

For example in *MTII* there are only two photographs of Palestinians, one of face-covered Palestinian children throwing stones 'at our forces' (p.321) but the forces – jeeps or tanks – revealed in the Palestinian reproduction of this photograph – are not shown probably because showing them would turn the picture into 'little Davids against Goliath' and would obviously miss the point of depicting these children as terrorists.

The other photograph is of 'refugees' (p.267) placed in a nameless street and looking like nothing but 'refugees,' overloaded with babies and bundles. The caption of this photograph says: 'A Palestinian family that had to leave their village in the 1948 war,' and then adds, 'The victory of Israel in the war of Independence was a tragedy to Israel's Arabs, which was carved in the collective Arab memory as "El-Nakba".' The nameless family, who had to 'abandon' their nameless village, is but a symbol for all other refugees and an embodiment of their tragedy.

Regarding the third strategy, people can be depicted either specifically or generically. Van Leeuwen (2008: 143–144) emphasizes that 'this is of evident importance to the study of racist discourse. Are we talking about a specific Jew or black or about Jews and blacks? Moving from one to another is always moving from specific judgment to prejudice and racism. Depiction can be concentrated on what makes a person unique or a certain social type.' Van Leeuwen found for instance that during the Gulf War Allied soldiers were depicted as individuals while Iraqi soldiers were always depicted in groups. This implies that 'they are all the same, and that you cannot tell them apart.' (ibid.)

As was already mentioned, Palestinians are always depicted as a collective or as types of primitive farmers (*PIS*), nomads (*GLI*), refugees (*JIP, AHH*) and terrorists (*The 20th, 50 Years*). The stereotypical images representing Palestinian refugees, farmers or masked terrorists, located in no-places, nameless and timeless, are objectified, presented as 'an object to be scrutinized' (Van Leeuwen, 2008: 46). These representations turn them into universal 'problems,' or rather the embodiment of the 'problems' or 'threats' they constitute for the Israelis: 'Asiatic' backwardness, terrorism and the refugee 'problem' which as Bar Navi (*The 20th* 1998) tells the students, stains Israel's image in the eyes of the world and 'poisons' its relationships with other nations, or as Domka et al. (p.158) describe it 'has remained as a menacing sword that threatens the very existence of the state of Israel.'

People can be categorized visually as well as verbally in terms of negative 'cultural' or 'biological' characteristics or any combination of those. Usually these characteristics are exaggerated and work through connotation: they connote negative or positive values and associations attached to a particular socio-cultural group. Van Leeuwen explains that biological categorization of people implies that these

Figure 1 (*GLI*: 303): 'The Arabs refuse to live in high buildings and insist on living in one-storey land-ridden houses'.

characteristics are 'in the blood' (146). But cultural characterization can also be presented as 'in the blood', for instance, 'The Arab society is traditional and objects to changes by its nature, reluctant to adopt novelties [...]. The Arabs refuse to live in high buildings and insist on living in one-storey land-ridden houses.' (Figure 1, *GLI*: 303). These statements portray the 'Arabs' – all millions of them – as possessing by nature or by heredity these 'negative' qualities. This particular text is attached to a caricature of an Israeli 'Arab' wearing Ali-Baba pants and shoes, kaffiyah, a moustache and followed by a camel. Since this image hardly represents any real Arab it symbolizes all Arabs, as they are seen in Israeli eyes.

The iconic 'Arab' in the cartoon is what Groupe μ (1992: 132) calls an icon of an icon, imported into Israeli school book from European illustrations of books such as *The Arabian Nights*; it receives its features not from the 'model' itself but from the producer's imaginary model and represents an imagined 'Arab' in a context where real Arabs live and work. It is presented to Jewish Israeli students who live next door to their Arab co-citizens but may go through life without ever meeting them face to face.

The oval frame of the caricature forms an enclosure which is 'a closed system which taken as a whole behaves as a center of energy [and] fences off [its image] from the environment. [...] Its function as an enclosure is most uncompromisingly expressed when its shape is circular' (Arnheim, 1988: 56, 62). In this icon the Arab is separated from the modern house in an irreversible way. The camel – the object-sign of the primitive nomad, is partly in the frame but it is turning its behind to the modern house which obviously cannot contain it.

Van Leeuwen emphasizes that cartoons are less factual than photographs and therefore express opinion, not fact (2008: 167). He summarizes the motivation for cartoon-like presentations:

> Cartoons are general without being abstract. Represent people as types rather than as tokens. All Turks have moustaches and all Arabs have camels. This reality is replacing the reality of naturalism and individualism. (Van Leeuwen, 2000: 349)

Another Palestinian 'type' is the 'Oxfam image' (term coined by Hicks, 1980: 31) of the primitive farmer who follows a primitive plough pulled by oxen or donkeys (see chapter 2 for a detailed analysis of this photograph). The primitive plough, as Van Leeuwen notes, is included in the taxonomy of racist representations and connotes backwardness, under-development and a non-Westernized society. It is used in an Israeli Geography school book (*PIS*) as illustration of the verbal statements about Palestinian 'traditional' and un-modern way of life. Thus, 'the naturalistic image authenticates the "scientific" analysis' (Van Leeuwen, 2000: 349). Since no other Palestinians are ever shown in this school book, the icons that connote backwardness represent the whole Palestinian population. Yet as Van Leeuwen (2001: 97) explains following Barthes, these connotative meanings are based on 'very broad and diffuse concepts which condense everything associated with these represented people into a single entity [...]. These meanings are ideological meanings, serving to legitimate the status quo and the interests of those in power' (ibid.).

An important question Van Leeuwen asks regarding visual representations of 'others' is, how do the depicted people relate to the viewer?

Kress and Van Leeuwen (1996/2006) distinguish three dimensions in these relationships: the social distance between the viewer and the people represented in the picture, the social interaction between them and the social relation between them. These three factors are translated to distance, angle and gaze, and they must always be in every picture, for one cannot decide to photograph without making choices in these three aspects.

> The gradation and multiple combinations these dimensions allow, can realize many ways of depicting people as 'others.' The same image parameters can be used to show the exclusion, the keeping-at-a-distance of people in order to accuse and critique, or to ourselves exclude and keep at distance members of our own school class, our own community, our own country etc. as in the case of school textbooks. (Van Leeuwen, 2008: 141)

In the school books studied here there are three strategies of depicting Palestinians as 'others.' '*distanciation* – representing people as far-away strangers, "foreigners" alien to us; *disempowerment* – representing people as "below" us, and *objectivation* –representing people as objects for our scrutiny rather than as individuals that may engage our attention and empathy' (Van Leeuwen, 2008: 141).

Distance indicates closeness. We keep our distance from strangers, but we 'work closely' or talk face to face with someone we like. Hence, in pictures, people shown from a 'long shot' are presented as strangers, and those shown in close-up photographs seem more like 'one of us.' According to Van Leeuwen 'this kind of differential use of distance, is common in school books dealing with questions of immigration, developing countries and so on' (Van Leeuwen, 2008: 138).

Palestinians, when depicted, are usually shown from a long distance, which makes them alien to the Israeli viewers. When the viewers are school children they learn to keep their distance from this kind of people.

On the other hand Israelis or Jews, whether citizens or refugees, are always depicted from a short distance, as familiar and close (as will be shown in chapter 2).

Disempowerment has to do with social relations, expressed in vertical and horizontal angles, which determine whether we look at the person from above or from below, eye to eye or from the side. All these angles represent power relations. Palestinian people and places are usually below our gaze, so that we look down at them (as discussed in chapter 2).

Objectivation has to do with gaze: here 'the crucial factor is whether or not depicted people look at the viewer' and how (Van Leeuwen, 2008: 140). If they do not look at us they are 'offered to our gaze as a spectacle for our dispassionate scrutiny' (ibid.). Such are most photographs of indigenes, 'refugees' and immigrants in Australian and Dutch school books studied by Kress and Van Leeuwen (1996) and Van Leeuwen (1992), where the depicted people become an object to behold and examine. We look at them as 'voyeurs' rather than as interactants (Van Leeuwen, 2008: 141). When figures in photographs do look at us it means they engage us in a closer relationship and even 'demand' something of us; this 'something' may be guessed from their expression and from the context. For instance the only close shot of a

Figure 2 Palestinian refugees class in Jordan: *World of Changes*, p.164.
Courtesy of Maalot Publishers. Source: Hulton Getty/A.S.A.P

Palestinian in the books studied here is a photograph of Palestinian refugee children in Jordan, presented in the pulped school book *World of Changes*: one girl looks directly into the camera and hence into our eyes. As an Israeli who knows the context of the photograph and the circumstances of this child, her gaze leaves me pretty shaken and uncomfortable, but I cannot run away from it (Figure 2).

The Expulsion of Palestinians

In order to assess the progress of Israeli education according to its recognition of the past, Podeh compared the way textbooks from 1950s to the late 1990s dealt with the problem of Palestinian refugees. Podeh summarizes the developments in Israeli school books of history regarding the attitude towards Palestinians as follows:

> In the first two generations the texts blamed the Arab leadership for the plight of the refugees. The expressions used to describe the Arab departure were identical: 'flight,' 'abandon,' 'exit,' 'desert,' 'vacate,' and so on. (2002: 79)

However, Podeh adds, 'the first seeds of change were visible in the second generation of textbooks that first appeared in the mid-1970s. This change reflected developments in Israeli society, which in turn led to the introduction of new history curricula. New interpretations of Zionist history also played a part in this transformation.' Podeh explains that 'the fact that school textbooks were in the past prejudiced and thereby contributed to the escalation of the conflict failed to penetrate the consciousness of large sectors of Israeli society. In this respect, the historical narrative presented by the third-generation textbooks (i.e. 1980–90) constitutes an important step forward.' This third generation, witnessed the publication of textbooks which differed substantially from previous textbooks and mentioned, albeit briefly and rather vaguely, that 'during the battles many of the country's Arabs were expelled' (2002: 79).

Podeh argues that such a change in the narrative may 'facilitate the reconciliation process between Israelis and Arabs.' Yet since changes in textbooks are often the product of social and political developments, 'further changes may await the fourth generation of textbooks' (2002: 88).

Most of the books I examined constitute the fourth generation Podeh anticipated. In both right and left-wing school books the Zionist hypotext is unaltered and is still compatible with the Israeli socio-political discourse that has prevailed since 1948.

Although the goal of having an Arab-free land is never spelled out explicitly, either in the public discourse or in school books, the crucial need to Jewify the country and keep a Jewish majority is. As Confino (2007a) explains it:

> The goal of the Jews was not to kill Arabs systematically, but to establish, as much as possible, a state with as few Arabs as possible, and this by means of expulsion, by frightening them away, and by preventing them from coming back through the complete destruction of their villages and by closing the borders.

None of the books studied here conceals the fact that there was some official expulsion[13]; however none of them states there was a plan of ethnic cleansing. The exodus is attributed to the failings of Palestinian leadership, the lack of Arab help and to the natural outcomes of the war, which made Palestinians 'abandon' their villages and cities.[14] All the books studied here present this Exodus as one of the positive consequences of the 1948 war. The achievement of 'emptying the land of its Arabs' is woven into the texts, especially into the reports about massacres of Palestinians which are, as we shall see in chapter 4, legitimated mostly by their outcome.

One example is found in *JIP* and its version for older students, *AHH* which provides this rather opaque statement:

> The uprooting of the 600,000 Arabs from their homes was a direct result of the war and not the fruit of a pre-plan of either Jews or Arabs [...] However, the expulsion of Lod and Ramla received the authorization of the political echelon (*AHH*: 313–314).[15]

The authority of the 'political echelons' is used to legitimate the expulsion or at least to present it as a necessary evil. In that it is compatible with statements about present day extrajudicial assassinations and other forms of aggression against Palestinians. For instance a report, about a 10-year-old Palestinian boy who was shot in Naalin while trying to push away the soldiers from his brother, in a rally against the Apartheid wall, ended with the words: 'The IDF says the shooting was done according to regulations,' (*Haaretz*, 1 September 2008) and that, in the Israeli discourse of legitimation, is enough to exonerate the shooters. *AHH* and *JIP* mention the ethnic cleansing of 1967 as well stating that 350,000 Palestinians escaped to Jordan from the territories Israel conquered during the 1967 war, without any specification. In *The 20th* and *MTII* Bar Navi and Naveh call the refugee problem 'painful' and 'a horrible human tragedy' (*The 20th*: 194). These authors insist on labeling 'tragedy' all the catastrophes inflicted on the Palestinians by Israel. Tragedy, being an act of fate, wherein human beings are no more than agents, diminishes human responsibility. However in *The 20th* Bar Navi quotes Morris (1991) regarding 'some 369 abandoned villages' whose 100,000 inhabitants were expelled, without specifying either names or locations and without providing a map. He further explains that the villagers were cleansed for reasons of security: 'The villagers were expelled after the battles were over, for the purpose of "cleaning" the border areas of hostile elements' (*The 20th*: 195). Nevertheless he dismisses both Israeli and Palestinian versions regarding the ethnic cleansing, as 'pure myths,' though the arguments supporting his thesis are somewhat deficient: 'The reason for the panicked flight of the Arabs can be summed up in one word: WAR.' (*The 20th*: 195). These books reiterate the argument that there was no planned cleansing on the part of the Israeli leadership.[16]

Naveh et al. (2009) and Domka et al. (2009) admit there were cases of expulsion and both juxtapose two Israeli views regarding the refugee problem. Domka et al. state very clearly the Israeli policy of 'barring the return' of the Palestinian refugees, and the policy of 'reprisals' in the 1950s against Palestinians' return that resulted from it. They emphasize as *The 20th* does, that most 'infiltrators' were farmers who came back to work their fields and harvest but that Israel suspected there might be some spies among them (since they were all men!) and therefore reacted harshly (pp.158–159).

Naveh et al. (2009) write about the 'departure of Israel's Arabs' and enumerate the advantages of this exodus for the Jews (in security, land appropriation and housing), emphasizing that this exodus determined the Jewish character of Israel, while mentioning the fact that the Palestinians lost the state they could have had. The book indicates that expulsion and the Dier Yassin massacre were two of the reasons for the Palestinians' escape and then juxtaposes two views of two Israeli historians while adding in a special 'window' the personal story of a Palestinian woman from Jaffa who recalls the forced 'departure' of her parents. However, it is worth noting here that Jaffa was attacked and cleansed by the Irgun-Etzel – the dissident guerrilla organization – and not by the official forces of the Hagana. Finally this book blames the Arab states for not integrating the refugees in their countries and for eternalizing their dire situation (pp.144–145). The chapter ends with questions regarding Minister Sharet's reasons for not allowing the return of the refugees. One of these questions is:

> Following the Second World War there were millions of refugees all across Europe who were forced to leave their homes but they had rehabilitated themselves. Why, in your opinion, the Palestinians did not take care to rehabilitate themselves? Why didn't the Arab states help them?

This question creates a reading position that legitimates Israel's policy regarding the Palestinian refugees, through what Van Leeuwen terms 'conformity to norms': If everybody else does that [and if the Europeans did it to us] why can't we? Besides, if we could rehabilitate ourselves away from our countries of origin, why cannot they? Furthermore, the question presents the Arab countries' duty to rehabilitate and integrate the Palestinians as given, namely as a known and accepted fact. This presupposition reinforces the Israeli perception that the Palestinians belong to the great Arab nation and should be taken care of by their own as the Jewish refugees were taken care of by Israel.

At this point it is worth paying attention to the structure of the reports about the Palestinian 'refugee problem.' Some books deal with the subject of the *Nakba* by using the sub-genre *exposition* (definition by Coffin 2006), in which two versions regarding an event are juxtaposed. As Coffin explains (2006: 78), 'Exposition is an analytical text that puts forward a particular interpretation of the past and then "proves" the validity of the interpretation though a series of arguments and supporting evidence.' Although it includes two competing versions, exposition presents alternative interpretations without discussing or refuting them, thus creating an impression of balance and debate, though they lead the reader to a single point of view (Coffin, 2006: 80). The exposition is usually constructed in a way that one of the versions is overshadowed by the interpretation reinforced by the other, usually at the end of the chapter. Thus, the results of the 1948 war are sometimes presented from two points of view, either one after the other or one against the other on the page or double-spread. Following is the exposition from *The 20th*: 195 (emphasis added):

> *In the Arab consciousness* the 1948 war and its consequences are conceived as 'Shoa.' Not only had the Palestinian Arabs lost the Land but they had turned into a nation of refugees. By contrast, *in the eyes of the Israelis* the flight of the Arabs solved a horrifying demographic problem and even a moderate person such as [the first president] Weitzman spoke about it as 'a miracle.' *And indeed*, very soon it became obvious that Israel was not going to allow the return of the refugees. [...] The Arab leaders chose to use the refugees as a battering ram against Israel. As one UNRWA official said 'the Arab countries do not want to solve the refugee problem. They prefer to keep it as an open wound, as an insult against the UN and as a weapon against Israel. May the refugees live or die, what do the Arab leaders care? (Amman, August 1951)'.

The use this text makes of exposition exemplifies the function of this sub-genre. Not only does the Israeli perspective receive more paper-time and higher value through appraisals and modality, but it has so to speak 'the last word,' the *ultima verba*, first through the words of President Weizman who has the authority of a renowned man of science – hence the authority of truth and objectivity – in addition to his institutional authority as president and his personal authority as an honest, brave and admired leader and then through the closing observation of UNRWA representative. The rhetorical reason that lies behind the decision to quote UNRWA representative – an objective international witness whose function was and still is to help the Palestinian refugees – and let him have the final statement on the matter is quite obvious. As Kress explains, 'Writing is governed by the logic of time and sequence or linearity {and} first and second are inescapably hierarchic' (Kress, 2003: 82); therefore the last word – of the UNRWA observer – which supports the Israeli argument has more weight. Following Lyotard, I would argue that this ending has a 'redeeming function,' it acts 'as if the occurrence, [...] could come to a completion, or as if there were a last word, by virtue of its place' (*The Differend*: 151). The role of Israel regarding the Palestinian refugees of 1948 comes to its term in this text with the observation of the UNRWA official, which constitutes the end of the story as far as Israel is concerned; by having the UNRWA representative shift the blame for the creation of the 'problem' to the Arab countries Israel is exonerated from all responsibility.

The implicit claim of this passage is that the war and its consequences did not necessarily have to be a Shoa for the Palestinians, had it not been for the Arab leaders who created the refugee problem for their own interests. The low modality regarding the catastrophe as existing only 'in the Arab consciousness' is thus accounted for by the extravocalised judgment of the UNRWA observer.

Both *50 Years* and *The Face* dedicate a lot of paper time to convince their readers that Israel had no part in the flight of the Palestinians and that the refugee problem is not 'our' problem. While the other books omit or blur some facts regarding the ethnic cleansing of Palestine, these books revert to the discourse that according to Podeh characterized the school books in the 1950s, handing the students a simplistic victory story instead of a serious historical account. *50 Years* allocates long paper time to the goals and gains of cleansing plan D, all very positive for Israel. In military jargon, the book enumerates eight goals which 'attest to the change in the war doctrine from defense to adopting patterns of regular warfare [...] against a regular enemy, a semi-regular enemy and an irregular enemy, who act from bases outside the Hebrew state' (p.180). The 'Refugee Problem' – discussed in three-and-a half pages – is described as 'the massive flight of the Arabs [...] which the Hagana's Head Quarters and the Zionist leadership did not anticipate and whose motives they found hard to understand' (p.202). The text does not refute the general opinion of most books about the massacre of Dier Yassin being an incentive for this flight, stating that 'it is possible that the rumors about a massacre in Dier Yassin encouraged Philistinians to abandon their dwellings' (ibid.). However, the book asserts, the 'conquest of Dier Yassin did not represent any policy and did not reflect any strategy of the Yishuv institutions or the Hagana Head Quarters' (ibid.).

The book offers, in a sort of exposition, 'the Philistinian version of the massive flight' whose advocates, it emphasizes, are mostly non-Jewish historians but also post-Zionist Jews. This version actually quotes the facts written by Morris (1991) and other modern historians before claiming that 'this interpretation does not stand the test of documentation' (p.202). The book repeats the argument used in the first generations of school books, when military and state archives were not yet accessible, that 'here and there, there were cases of score settling of past feuds that were expressed in the wish to drive away the unwanted neighbours, but these cases were few.' It further cites as fact the story about Prime Minister Ben Gurion who on the 30 April visited the village Salame near Tel Aviv, where he found an old blind lady who was left alone in the village. After inquiring why this old blind granny was left alone 'he was informed by the representatives of the Jewish Agency about the flight.' Ben Gurion asked where had all the Arabs gone? And marked the answer in his notebook. Though 'one representative of the Jewish Agency argued they had an order "from above" to leave,' this argument was 'ill founded and stemmed from the difficulty to explain this phenomenon.' The book goes on to ask: 'What were the reasons for Arab "desertion"?' and offers some possible reasons: fear of anarchy, chaos, economic depression and war.

The text emphasizes Israel's efforts in the last 55 years to convince the world that this problem should be settled in Arab countries and not in Israel, 'that absorbed the Jewish refugees who were expelled from the Arab states.' The final claim of the text is, 'The Arab leaders claim that hostilities cannot be terminated before the refugees are allowed to return to their homes, and that in spite of what happened in Europe' (pp.202–204).

Face (pp.322–323) also dedicates substantial paper time to the Palestinian refugee problem. The book specifies that the 'Arabs' who supported Israel could have stayed, but the others were to be expelled, or allowed to flee (p.318). Then it presents (pp.322–323), at least structurally or rather visually, two points of view, the 'Jewish' one and the 'Arab' one regarding cleansing Plan D. From the Jewish point of view Plan D was a great success. Omitting the massacres this book presents very positively the results of Plan D by bullet points:

- It strengthened the military power of the Jewish community.
- It created a [Jewish] territorial sequence as a 'strategic asset.'
- It had positive effects at the diplomatic level for it convinced the Americans and the Russians that the Jewish community is strong militarily and can fend for itself.

Bullet points are the extreme manifestation of high deontic modality or assertivity. Kress (2003: 16) explains that 'bullet points are, as their name indicates, bullets of information. They are "fired" at us, abrupt and challenging, not meant to be continuous and coherent, not inviting reflection and consideration, not insinuating themselves into our thinking. They are hard and direct and not to be argued with.'

Under the heading 'the Arab point of view' we find a text which reiterates the Israeli interpretation of the Palestinian defeat and the refugee problem. This 'Arab Point of View' starts by stating that 'the expulsion was the lot of both sides' because the Arabs too, 'whenever they conquered a Jewish neighbourhood or city would expel the Jewish inhabitants, as in Gush Etzion and the Jewish quarter in Jerusalem.' Then the 'Arab Point of View' goes on to assert that 'the Arabs brought it upon themselves for they fought the Jews to perdition,' and refused to accept the two-state partition plan offered to them by the UN. 'The war ended in their defeat and in hundreds of thousands refugees who left their homes because of the unwillingness of the Arab-Philistinian public and its leaders to come to an agreement' (p.323).

The troubled reader will have to read the text several times looking for an 'Arab point of view,' before realizing the rhetorical gimmick. The untroubled reader will probably accept it as 'the Arab point of view.'

At the end of the chapter the book dedicates another whole page (p.347) to 'the creation of the problem of Philistinian Refugees.' Here the book elaborates the previous report by specifying that 'in the context of Plan D the territories were sometimes conquered without orders to expel the local Arabs, but part of them fled. Sometimes there was an order to conquer and expel the population. The expulsion was made both directly and indirectly, by the spreading of rumours about the atrocities committed by the Jews. These rumours caused a massive exodus.' The book emphasizes time and again that Israeli citizens were unanimous in their demand to deny the refugees the right of return. When finally the UN decided some refugees must be returned, 'time was against them. The villages were razed to the ground, empty Arab house that remained after the "leveling" received the legal label "abandoned property," and Jewish immigrants were lodged in the "abandoned" areas.'[17]

At this point I must be allowed a personal note. 'Time was against them' is marked by a certain undertone that may not come through in the translation but which I recall from my own days at school during the 1950s–60s, an undertone of joy and triumph. When I was growing up the current popular argument was: 'They deserted their houses and their lands, so we can take hold of them. Finders keepers, losers weepers.' The relevance of this undertone for the present analysis is that it may explain to an outsider the connotation of the verbs 'abandon' or 'desert' that are constantly used in school books to describe the Palestinian exodus. Desertion, 'panicked flight' and 'abandon,' convey negative evaluation of tenacity and capacity (Martin and White, 2005). According to Israeli norms, since the Palestinians abandoned their land they do not deserve to have it back. Abandoning the land also contradicts the Palestinian norm of Sumud, adopted by the Palestinian national movement, which means clinging to the soil of the homeland at all costs. Hence, in addition to the deep insult embodied in verbs such as desert and abandon, Israeli education and public discourse try to convince the young generations of Palestinians that their parents or grandparents have deserted the land, and therefore they have lost the right of return.

The chapter ends with the same statement used in *The 20th* as well: 'The leaders of the Arab countries exploited the problem of Philistinian refugees for their own political needs' (p.348). This similarity shows that ideologically the more progressive critical approach of *The 20th, MTII*, Naveh et al. and Domka et al. and the right-wing nationalistic approach of the *50 Years* and *Face,* are not that far apart.

The civic studies book *BCI* (2001), also used in Arab-Israeli schools, puts the blame for not solving the refugee problem on the Arab countries as well:

> In the course of the war 700,000 Arabs who lived in the land of Israel during the British mandate fled or were expelled. They moved to Arab countries and to Judea, Samaria and Gaza. This is how the Palestinian refugee problem was created in the Arab countries and added a facet to the Israeli-Arab conflict. (p.289)

In conclusion, it seems that Israeli school books of 1994–2009 do not always seek to deny the expulsion of Palestinians, but rather to diminish its measures and to legitimate it. Most books don't only admit there was expulsion but more or less explicitly justify this strategy emphasizing the positive results it had for Israel. These examples prove that the change in attitude should not lie solely in the admission that there was expulsion but in the way this expulsion is viewed.

None of the books except for the pulped *WoC* (p.162), gives any details about the whereabouts of the Palestinian refugees after their expulsion or flight, just as none of them gives any details concerning Palestinian suffering in general, during or after wars and massacres.

WoC, though it also uses the verb 'abandon' regarding Palestinian escape and expulsion, presents a map that depicts by fiery arrows the escape routes of the Palestinians and provides the exact number of people who settled in the different neighbouring Arab states.

Geography textbooks manifest the same stance that Podeh defines as that of the first and second generations of Israeli education. Both *PIS* (1996) and *PAS* (2006) present the Palestinian *Nakba* as the unsolved half of the Jewish and Arab refugee problem in the Middle East, caused by the Israeli-Arab war. This attitude also marks current Israeli political stance, expressed for instance in a report from *Haaretz* on 15 September 2008[18]:

> Prime Minister Ehud Olmert said on Monday he was sorry for the plight of Palestinians and Jews who became refugees as a result of the establishment of the state of Israel: 'I join in expressing sorrow for what happened to the Palestinians and also for what happened to the Jews who were expelled from Arab states.'

PIS (1996: 152–153) presents the problem of Palestinian refugees under a heading: 'Refugees as a result of the Israeli-Arab conflict'. Regarding the Arab refugees 'known by the label "Palestinian refugees",' the book states they escaped during the two wars that the Arabs waged on Israel, abandoning their houses but leaving their belongings behind; using aggregation the book informs us that 'some of them were expelled,' by 'various Israeli factors,' 'some settled in the places where they escaped to, some returned to Israel, and some remained in refugee camps and poor neighbourhoods.' Thus presented, their destiny seems random and given to their choice. The book juxtaposes this problem with the problem of Jewish refugees from Islamic countries who were treated badly in Syria, Iraq, Egypt and other Arab countries and had to leave destitute. But 'contrary to the Arab refugees, who still live in poverty and whose problems have not been solved yet, the problem of Jewish refugees has been solved [...] the state of Israel [...] made great efforts to absorb these refugees etc.' (p.154). *PIS* (1996) shows a graph of refugees all over the world, 1.2 million of *whom* are in areas controlled by Israel, but in its later version, *PAS (2006)*, the bar of Israel is omitted from the graph; instead, the graph presents one bar for Central, Southern and Western Asia and North Africa, where the number of refugees is the highest in the world, without any specification (p.111). *PAS* specifies that the number of 'Arab refugees known by the label of "Palestinian refugees" is controversial. [...] The Arab counties refused to absorb them as citizens with equal rights and that is why to this day many of them live in refugee camps and slums.'

The conclusion from this short overview is that contrary to Podeh's expectations the fourth generation of school books (1998–2010) manifests a regression in the presentation of the problem of Palestinian refugees. If in the 1990s there were books that addressed some of the complexity of the problem, in the books of the second millennium studied here there is an increasing tendency to re-simplify it and recreate a narrative of good guys versus bad guys, that justifies 'our' ways without any reservations. An edifying example from the books studied here is the difference between *MTII* (1999: 273) and Naveh et al. (2009) both co-written by Professor Eyal Naveh. In *MTII* one reads:

> 'The border with Jordan, which had been delineated arbitrarily and separated Arab villagers from their lands, became a real line of fire.' This, the book explains, entailed infiltrations that were mostly 'attempts by villagers to return to their homes [...] only few of them were Fadayun – armed Palestinians sent to carry out intelligence and terrorist activities [...] But Israel refused to acknowledge the difference and her reprisals were harsh.'

In Naveh et al. (2009) the 'villagers' disappear and all the infiltrators become terrorists:

> From 1952 on, there were many cases of infiltration from Jordan for the purpose of robbery and sabotage, and even murder [...] the terrorist acts of the infiltrators created serious anxiety among the citizens if Israel and the state was obligated to react. (pp.202, 204)

While in *MTII*, published in 1999, Israel is depicted as head-strong non-compromising and insensitive, a state which refuses to acknowledge the difference between desperate farmers who want to enjoy the crop of their fields, from which they were separated 'arbitrarily' and terrorists, in Naveh et al. (2009) the actions of Israel are fully legitimated by the norms of war against terror and the protection of citizens. Similarly, Dier Yassin, whose inhabitants were massacred in 1948, is described in *MTII* as 'a friendly village, whose inhabitants signed a non-aggression agreement with the Hagana and kept it meticulously,' but in Naveh et al. (2009: 113) it becomes 'a base for aggressive attacks on Jerusalem.' This change means that even the more progressive writers tend to regress to a portrayal of the Palestinians as nothing but terrorists. This portrayal helps legitimate both the expulsion and the killing (discussed in chapter 4) of the indigenous population according to universal norms and values such as the 'war on terror' and the protection of citizens.

As this overview shows, Israeli school books of the 2000s still insist on denying Israeli responsibility for the *Nakba*, putting the blame for the 'refugee problem' on the Arab countries.

One should bear in mind that the ethnic cleansing of Palestine in 1948 and in 1967 have not yet become history in the Israeli discourse or practice, and the refusal to take responsibility for the Palestinian refugees bears on the contemporary policies of Israel versus the Palestinian population within the borders of the state and in the occupied territories. The ever-present plans for real and 'retroactive' transfer, the expulsion of the Druze villagers from the Golan Heights, the actual ongoing eviction of Palestinians from their homes in East Jerusalem, of Bedouins from the West Bank and the Negev, are all part of the same continuous process of Judaization.[19] As was mentioned earlier, *Face*, published in 2006, mentions several times the unanimous opinion of the Israeli public against accepting even the 65–70,000 refugees the UN suggested as compromise in 1948. This emphasis is no doubt contextualized to present-day debates about the Palestinians' right of return, to which both left and right wing Zionist Israelis are opposed, as is manifest in the above mentioned report from *Haaretz* (15 September 2008) which includes the following declaration of Prime Minister Olmert:

> Under absolutely no circumstances will there be a right of return, but we are prepared to be part of an international mechanism that will work to solve the problem.[20]

Granting the right of return to Palestinian refugees means recognizing the Palestinian version of the *Nakba* and allowing it to exist within Israeli discourse and reality. Such recognition, crucial as it is for peace and reconciliation, is still far from being accepted by Israeli educators, as asserted by Professor Ben-Amos, head of the department of history and the philosophy of education in Tel Aviv's school of education:

> A crucial condition for the progress towards peace with the Palestinians is the recognition not only of what had happened in 1948 but also of the Nakba as a legitimate point of view. The policy of Israeli ministry of education, to deny this point of view puts spokes in the already faltering wheels of the negotiations. [This policy] relies on an archaic simplistic way of history teaching. If we wish our students to be critical thinkers we must teach them that our point of view is not the only one, that there are several points of view – all of which are not less legitimate than ours. (*Haaretz*, 5 October 2010)

Palestinian Nationality

> As the years passed, hatred, alienation, the desire for revenge and the hope of return, all exacerbated by Arab propaganda, fused the refugees into a single nation and transformed the refugee problem into an international problem. (*The 20th*: 244)

Israeli education which literally brackets the 2000 years of Jewish life-world in Diaspora and preaches its denial, all but conceals the 1300 years of Palestinian life on the land of Palestina. These years are mentioned – if ever – very briefly, usually as a claim made by the Palestinians themselves. In the pulped History school book *World of Changes* these 1300 years are summarized in a single sentence (p.98): 'In the seventh century the land passed into Muslim hands and this molded its culture and lifestyle for more than 1300 years.'

All books allocate a considerable paper time to the PLO and its development but they all present Palestinian nationalism as a serious problem for Israel, and Palestinians' wish to return to Palestine or rather to 'our' Land of Israel, as a threat on Israel's very existence.

The bleak description of the rise of Palestinian nationality quoted above is part of a chapter titled 'The Palestinians – From Refugees to a Nation.' Facing this title is a photograph – not of Palestinian refugees as one might expect – but of an Israeli soldier carrying his bleeding sister from a school in Maalot that was seized in 1974 by Palestinians who held the pupils hostages and demanded the release of Palestinian prisoners. The photograph and its relationships with the title and the main text will be discussed at length in chapter 3, but at this point I mention it only in order to contextualize the title and the text that follows it. The objective reader may wonder at the choice of photograph but Israeli readers (such as my university students) see nothing abnormal in it. In their eyes, this picture, depicting terror victims, connotes the concept of 'Palestinian' in Israeli discourse.

As for the main text of this chapter, Podeh (2002: 94–95), who does not mention the photograph, praises it as the most thorough account of the rise of Palestinian nationality until the late 1990s. However, this 'comprehensive and more tolerant analysis' as Podeh values it, manifests a scornful and mocking tone. Bar-Navi starts his account with the following observation:

> When did a Palestinian nation appear, separate and aware of itself? The Palestinians claim that their roots are deeper in the Land than those of the Jews. No wonder: Many peoples hold on to ancient sources and build myths for themselves, which glorify their ancestry and their ancient past [...]. Nations are usually built out of hostility and competition with other nations. Following the massive exodus, in the wanderings of exile and in the pitiful refugee camps, [...] was molded the myth of return to the lost homeland, in a language and in ardent expression that reminds one of the yearnings of the Jews for Zion. And indeed, a sort of

> Palestinian 'Zionism' grew. The longing and the sub-human conditions of exile endowed the land of Israel with an image of Paradise lost.

Genette (1982: 291) calls this type of intertextuality *transposition*, 'the most serious type of transformation,' where a story is planted in another ideological sphere, another time, with other protagonists (e.g. Goethe's *Faust* or Joyce's *Ulysses*). Transposition is characteristic of parody. Here the struggle of Palestinian refugees to return to their homes seems like a mock-Zionism although the Palestinian context is quite different.

The text 'plants' the Jewish myth of 2000 years of 'exile' and wanderings, dreams of return to an ancient father land based on myths of 'a glorious ancestry and ancient past,' mingled with the Judeo-Christian myth of 'Paradise Lost,' in the context of Palestinian Muslims, who are presented as yearning for (our) Israel, not for (their) Palestine. Evidently, this account does not reflect the Palestinian view of their national history. Unlike the Wandering Jews the Palestinians are only a few decades and a few kilometers away from their ravaged land, they do not dream of a messianic redemption or of Paradise lost, but of an actual return to their still-existing homes, fields and orchards. However, the parodic 'Zionization' of Palestinian history serves to ridicule their nationalism and present it as disingenuous. Palestinian nationality is presented here as more fake than authentic, more fantastic than genuine, and more artificial than real.

Ten years after Bar Navi, Domka et al. (2009) treat the Palestinian nationality in quite the same manner, enumerating the factors that 'ignited' Palestinian nationality: the occupation, the radical changes in Palestinian standard of living (thanks to Israel) and the military government 'that was free of the constraints of human rights and had ample means to treat disobedience and protest' (p.182). This, the book explains, resulted in a movement in which 'thousands of young people, especially from the poorer and hopeless classes in the refugee camps in Jordan, Syria and Lebanon, fell into the arms of the rebellious organization that sprang rapidly.'

Naveh et al. (2009), though their book is called *Nationality in Israel and other nations*, dedicate less than half a page to Palestinian nationality. The paragraph starts by specifying the role of the PLO as 'a source of suicide attacks in Israel and as a nucleus of world terror' (p.263). Unlike Domka et al. this book sees the beginnings of Palestinian nationality not in the poor classes but among the rich and educated, who incited the others 'to rebel, to strike, to disobey, to burn tires, throw stones, bar roads etc.'

No other 'national' aspects are mentioned. Hardly anything is said about the history of the Palestinian people, their roots, their culture and their ties to the land of Palestine.

Although the school books in this study present the Palestinian citizens of Israel as Arabs and hence as belonging to the Arab nation, when this linkage is expressed by the Israeli-Palestinian citizens themselves, the following text mentions it as a problem and a threat that 'aggravates the conflict.'[21] For instance:

> Another factor that aggravated the conflict was that Arabs who stayed in Israel have always identified themselves with the Arab nation culturally, socially and historically and seen themselves as part of the Palestinian people who has an affinity to Palestine (this is how the Palestinians call the Land of Israel). (*AHH:* 289. Brackets in the original)

In *50 Years* Arafat is never mentioned but the PLO is mentioned several times, always by the way, as yet another source of 'trouble' with the Arabs. Its establishment is described in a chapter called 'The reasons for the six day war,' (p.260):

> In 1964 tension was created in the region when the Arab states objected to the operation of the Cross-Country National Water Pipe of Israel*. They decided to divert the sources of the river Jordan and establish a joint headquarters to monitor the struggle against Israel, in addition the PLO was founded.

* The Cross-Country National Water Pipe diverts water from the Jordan River and the Sea of Galilee to the Jewish settlements in the Negev Desert.

Before that the PLO is mentioned briefly as a factor that disturbed Jordan (p.229) and Lebanon (p.235), where the Palestinian 'terrorists' created a state within a state and set off a 'whirlpool of conflicts: between the PLO and Israel, the PLO and the Lebanese army, and between the PLO and the Phalanges.' This 'whirlpool,' the book explains, is what dragged Lebanon into a deep crisis from which it has not been able to recover.

Face dedicates a whole paragraph to the establishment of the PLO which is depicted as one of three 'anti-Israeli decisions' taken by the Arab countries (p.408):

1) The diversion of the sources of the river Jordan in order to obstruct the National Cross Country Water Pipe.
2) The establishment of a joint Arab Headquarters.
3) The establishment of the PLO.

The aims of the PLO were, according to this book, to 'liberate Palestine and found a Palestinian state on all the areas of the Land of Israel' (p.410). The mutual recognition of the PLO and Israel is never mentioned.

The Intifada

Since hardly anything is written about the principles or practices of the Israeli occupation, the uprising of the occupied Palestinians seems unfathomed. In most of the school books studied here the intifada is not mentioned at all. The books that mention it describe it (i.e. *MTII:* 289; Naveh, 1994: 255; and Domka et al, 2009: 204) as a sudden event, unexpected and unaccounted for, that contributed however to the acceleration of the peace process between Israel and the Palestinians. How it contributed and why it had erupted is not explained.

Although none of the books specify the reasons for this uprising they elaborate on the great surprise of the IDF and on its lack of means to fight the violent outbursts of the Palestinians. For instance Domka et al. write (p.204):

> The IDF governed Judea, Samaria and Gaza since the Six Days War, and was confronted time and against with hostile actions against its presence and control over these areas. But the scope of the uprising in 1987 surpassed everything the IDF had known before and the high commandment found it difficult to find appropriate solutions. The Palestinian uprising included continuous attacks against civilian and military Israelis, especially in Judea and Samaria and Gaza. The attacks included throwing stones and Molotov bottles, barring roads, stabbing and running over Jews with cars in central bus stations. The IDF's attempts to suppress the Palestinian uprising included siege, checkpoints on the roads, increased presence in Palestinian villages, arrests and punishments to the offenders. The IDF was not prepared, either militarily or psychologically, to warfare against civilian population.

This description portrays the Palestinians as vicious murderers and terrorists while the IDF is portrayed as a civilized, law abiding, responsible and reasonable organization. It never kills, wounds, tortures nor harasses anyone. On the contrary, it takes all the civilized measures to stop the 'disorder': it punishes the offenders, it blocks the way of violence and altogether tries to calm things down. The practical meaning of siege and closure, permanent checkpoints and collective 'punishment' is not made clear.

This kind of description is compatible with media news where Palestinian resistance is always described as out-of-the-blue violent outbursts, connected to nothing that preceded it.

Naveh et al. (2009) dedicate one page to the Intifada, with the same kind of reasoning, specifying that the Palestinians 'provoked' the Israeli soldiers. The IDF did not know how to react and the world, nourished by photographs of soldiers beating up children, was again against us. However, Naveh et al. (2009) give as factors that surged the intifada:

1) Personal and social despair from the poverty, deprivation and humiliation in encounters with Israelis.
2) Understanding that time was against the Palestinian people and that facts are being made on the ground.
3) The wish of the Palestinians living under Israeli rule to push the PLO to a serious negotiation.

What is actually meant by 'deprivation' and 'humiliation' in 'encounters with Israelis' remains completely vague.

Note that the conflict is described as a clash between the Palestinians and the army, not between the Palestinians and Israeli government. The military rule itself is not given to discussion or debate. The books seem to assume reader's understanding and compliance on this subject. All the measures and 'solutions' these books mention are military ones, meant to suppress the revolt; the occupation itself is never contested or described in any detail that can shed light on the real situation of the Palestinians under Israeli military rule.

In conclusion, the books that mention Palestinian nationality concentrate on its threatening aspects for Israel. This negative representation attests to some characteristics of Israeli school books as reproducers of collective memory:

1) They tend to present events 'from a single committed perspective; [and are] impatient with ambiguities' (Novick, 1999: 3–4); their perspective is usually military.
2) They undergo very little change if at all in their view of Palestinian Nationality.
3) In the Israeli-Jewish narrative, as it is reproduced in school books, everything Palestinian can exist only as an obstacle to be overcome or eliminated.

As this short analysis shows, the most recent school books (2009) do not fulfill Podeh's hopes for 'the appearance of a new narrative in history textbooks [...] that may, in the long run, facilitate the reconciliation process between Israelis and Arabs' (2002: 29).

Conclusion

The representation of Palestinians in Israeli history school books has made a full circle, from a prejudiced biased and antagonistic representation in the 1950s to a prejudiced biased and antagonistic representation in the 2000s. In between these two points there were few attempts to recognize the Palestinians as a distinct national entity and take them into account, albeit hesitantly and cautiously (Podeh, 2002). The fact that both right wing and Labour ministries of education have continued to produce and recommend books where Palestinians hardly exist except as terrorists and a demographic threat, may point to a nation-wide consensus regarding the need to inculcate ignorance and hostility towards the subjugated neighbours and the discriminated fellow-citizens.

The fourth generation of textbooks Podeh was waiting for in 2002 manifests the same ideological stance and uses the same rhetorical devices that characterized the first generation of Israeli school books. Podeh (2000: 9) excuses the writers of the first books by saying:

> Since most of the textbook authors came from Eastern Europe or Germany [...] they were not conversant with Middle Eastern customs and were unfamiliar with the region's traditions and language. Consequently, even naturally, they associated Arab violence with the pogroms of Eastern Europe, and regarded the Arabs as a local version of the anti-Semitic goy.

Unfortunately this excuse cannot hold for books written in 2004 or 2009. The fourth generation of school books marks a regression factually as well as ideologically by forsaking historical truth in a much more blatant way than the books of the previous generations, which lacked the ample archival evidence accessible today. What determines the factual content of these books is not archival information but the ideological voice they have to ventriloquate and the 'consciously fraudulent' narrative (Piterberg, 2001: 38) they have to transmit. Even though, as Podeh argues, in the most progressive books of the late 1990s and the beginning of 2000, 'an attempt was made to understand the Arab point of view, especially in discussions of some of the sensitive issues in the history of the conflict,' the texts are based primarily on the Israeli-Zionist narrative, with its military perspective and its convictions regarding the Jewish historical rights on the Land and the need for Jewish supremacy.

2

THE GEOGRAPHY OF HOSTILITY AND EXCLUSION: A MULTIMODAL ANALYSIS

Geography textbooks are what Van Leeuwen defines as multimodal genres (2005a: 80). Their generic structure is multimodally realized through images, graphs, maps and diagrams, layout, colour and verbal chunks.

This chapter examines the multimodal ways in which ideologies are recreated in geography school books in Israel.

Six school books published between 1995–2006, after the Oslo Peace Accords between Israel and the Palestinian Authority and currently used in Jewish mainstream schools in Israel[1] were analyzed for the use they make of visuals such as photographs, maps, graphs, icons and colour in order to recontextualize both disciplinary and political discourses to education. The semiotic analysis of these school books will be supported by observations of social and political geographers.

The argument put forward in this chapter is, that in Israeli geography school books, scientific conventions and principles of visual and verbal representations are compromised by political messages and the commitment of these school books to promote a Jewish territorial and national identity which is largely based on the denial of Palestinian identity. The 'Judaization' of geography, which entails the distortion of geopolitical facts and the concealment of any meaningful life besides the Jewish one may promote hostility and reproduce 'Elite Racism.'[2]

The first section of this chapter discusses the Zionist ideological basis of geographic curricula in Israel and the recruiting of geography to the perpetuation of territorial identity. The second section discusses the verbal and visual representations of Palestinians in geography school books. The third section discusses the cartography of exclusion, namely the ways in which maps distort the geo-political reality of the region and exclude the indigenous population of the land. Next, the chapter discusses the impersonalization of Palestinians by means of stereotypical representation such as racist cartoons, racist icons and demeaning photographs. The final section describes classification images used in Israel's meta-narrative of 'development,' in which progress means the victory of 'Jewishness' over 'Arabness' or the conquest of the Middle East by the West. This section will also discuss colour as a semiotic resource of meaning.

The general question this chapter sets out to answer was best formulated in Van Leeuwen (1996: 35):

> How are social practices transformed into discourses about social practices [...] both in the sense of what means we have for doing so, and in the sense of how we actually do it in specific institutional contexts which have specific relations with the social practices of which they produce representations?

Questions that derive from this general question are formulated in Van Leeuwen (2005: 90):

1) How are semiotic resources used to construct representations of what goes on in the world?
2) How do people use semiotic resources to express their identities and values?

The institutional contexts and social practices addressed in this chapter are school and geography teaching in Israeli mainstream school books. The means by which the books transmit their messages are multimodal. The specific relations they have with the social practices of which they produce representations are those of *hypertextuality*, in the sense used by Genette (1982: 12–14), explained in chapter 1.

As was mentioned in chapter 1, school books are *hypertexts* both of the dominant socio-political *hypotext* and of their respective disciplinary *hypotexts*; they are the transformation or rather the recontextualization (Bernstein, 1996) of these hypotexts to education. Therefore the discourses of textbooks are never identical with their disciplinary discourses.

Methodology and Theoretical Basis of the Study

Geography school books are multimodal texts. They use an array of verbal and visual modes in order to transmit values and meanings. Kress explains that 'since meanings are made as signs in distinct ways in specific modes ... That which is represented in sign or sign complexes realizes the interests, perspectives, values and positions of those who make the sign [...] representation is always 'engaged.' It is never neutral' (Kress, 2003: 37, 44).

This standpoint rejects the idea of arbitrariness, maintaining that,

> The relations between signifier and signified are always motivated, that is, the shape of the signifier, its 'form,' materially or abstractly considered, is chosen because of its aptness for expressing that which is to be signified. (ibid.: 42)

Therefore,

> We have to find ways of understanding and describing the interaction of such meanings across modes into coherent wholes, into texts. (ibid.: 37)

Zionist Ideological Basis of Geography School Books

As was mentioned before, Zionism has 'recognized at the very outset the importance of teaching territorial identity' (Bar-Gal, 1993b: 421). Hence, geography curricula in Israel are meant first and foremost to inculcate, as the national curriculum defines it, 'Love and Knowledge of Our Homeland.' This objective, which marked the curriculum in the first half of the twentieth century, when geography was renamed 'homeland studies,' although most of the Jewish citizens were not born in Israel, continues to stand out in today's much more scientific geography textbooks (Bar-Gal, 2003).

The ideological basis of geography teaching in Israel consists of the Zionist message regarding the redemption and resettlement of the Homeland by the Children of Israel who, possessing exclusive historic rights to the Land, have returned home after 2000 years of exile.

Yiftachel (2006: 61) explains that in Israel 'an exclusive form of territorial ethno-nationalism developed, in order to quickly "indigenize" immigrant Jews, and to conceal, trivialize or marginalize the existence of a Palestinian people on the land prior to the arrival of Zionist Jews.'

The work of ideological solidarity and power is at the base of the two levels of ethnicity in Israel (defined by Yiftachel, 2006: 18): at the level of ethno-nationality the Jewish ethno-nation is consolidated by the blurring of differences between different Jewish ethnicities, while non-Jews as a whole are segregated and marginalized; at the level of ethno-class, members of the Jewish ethno-class are privileged while the non-Jewish ethno-classes are underprivileged.[3]

The social exclusion of Palestinians is not only a historical fact but mostly a geographic one. Byrne notes in his book *Social Exclusion* (2005: 2), that 'exclusion happens in time, in a time of history; it determines the lives of individuals and collectives who are excluded *and* the lives of individuals and collectives who are not.' Israel, as other ethnocratic regimes, 'construct[s] historical narratives about the dominant ethnonation as the rightful owner of the territory. Such narratives degrade all other contenders as historically or culturally unworthy to control the land or achieve political equality' (Yiftachel, 2006: 19).

The geography school books studied here offer very little information about the region or about Arab-Palestinian life, be it agriculture, social settings, rural or urban changes, during the 2000 years of Jewish 'absence,' but they do mention at length Jewish yearning for the lost homeland. For instance in *TMC* (p.54) next to a map of the Mediterranean countries, we find this text:

> If this map had been drawn 100 years ago there would not have been a special colour for the Jews because most Jews lived in

> other countries (the Jews had been in exile for 2000 years). The Land of Israel is the land of the Jews. During the many years the Jews were away from their country [...] they yearned to come back to it and resettle it [...] In their hearts they kept saying 'If I forget thee Oh Jerusalem may my right hand forget its cunning' (Psalms, 137: 5). When the Jewish people came back and the state of Israel was founded, Jerusalem, our capital, became once again the most important Jewish centre of the Jewish people.

In this paragraph 2000 years of civilization are reduced to nine words in brackets, while the story of the yearning for the mythicized homeland takes up more than eight lines of the scientific text.

Geography textbooks, in their endeavor to teach how to 'know and love our homeland,' hail the Zionist achievements in agriculture (taming the desert, diverting rivers and drying swamps), in forestry (restoring the glory of biblical forests while erasing the traces of Arab villages and agriculture) and in construction. Consequently the discourse of geography school books is often made of political, historical and scientific discourses, reinforced by biblical verses, patriotic songs and heroic poetry. Visually this mix includes maps that have very little to do with reality, ideologically drawn graphs and images. These various verbal and visual components are designed to immortalize Jewish dominance through its presentation as legitimate from time immemorial. The legitimation draws its authority mainly from the Bible and the divine promise to grant unto the children of Abraham the entire area 'from the river Prath to the uttermost sea' (Deuteronomy, 11: 24). As political geographer Yiftachel argues, religion serves secular education in Israel in forming a collective narrative that 'helps rupturing the borders and legitimating the teaching about the divine land' (2006: 121).

An edifying example is found in *TMC,* a geography school book for the fifth grade (p.60). In the chapter 'One sea with many names,' one finds, next to the map of 'Israel' which includes the Palestinian occupied territories (Figure 3), not the different names given to the Mediterranean sea by the different nations living along its coasts as could be expected by the title, but only biblical phrases that introduce the various biblical names of the Mediterranean while reiterating the divine promise.

These verses are the answer to the opening question of the chapter:

> 'The Mediterranean sea is already mentioned in the Bible. Is it also called the Mediterranean in the book of books?'

The wind-rose drawn on the land (unlike the wind-rose drawn on the sea) bears the biblical terms for North, South, East and West: Yama-Kedma-Tzafona-Negba, another hint that this country has always been Hebrew. These names, which also constitute the title of the map, are part of the verse: 'And thou shalt spread abroad to the

ים אחד ושמות רבים לו

היס התיכון כבר מוזְכָּר בתנ"ך. האם גם בספר הספרים הוא נקרא הים התיכון? וכך כתוב בתנ"ך:
בספר שמות כג 31:
וְשַׁתִּי אֶת גְּבֻלְךָ מִיַּם סוּף וְעַד יָם פְּלִשְׁתִּים.
בספר דברים יא 24:
...מִן הַמִּדְבָּר וְהַלְּבָנוֹן מִן הַנָּהָר נְהַר פְּרָת וְעַד הַיָּם הָאַחֲרוֹן יִהְיֶה גְּבֻלְכֶם.
בספר יהושע א 4:
...וְעַד הַיָּם הַגָּדוֹל מְבוֹא הַשָּׁמֶשׁ יִהְיֶה גְּבוּלְכֶם.

2. *מהם שמות הַיָּם התיכון בתנ"ך?*
3. *פָּרשו שניים משמותיו של הים, כלומר: מה מקור השמות ועל פי מה נִתְּנו השמות לים?*

בתקופת המקרא (התנ"ך) השתמשו במִלה **יָם** לציון צַד מערב.
בספר בראשית כח 14 נאמר:

וּפָרַצְתָּ יָמָּה וָקֵדְמָה וְצָפֹנָה וָנֶגְבָּה.

(פירוש הפסוק: בעתיד תתרחב ארצך מערבה, מזרחה, צפונה ודרומה.)

4. *עיינו במפה א' 2 והסבירו: מדוע המִלה* **יָם** *מציינת את הכיוון מערב?*
5. *האם גם בְּמִצְרַיִם נכון לְכַנּות את צַד מערב בשם* **יָם**? *בדקו במפה שבאטלס והסבירו.*
6. *באֵילו מדינות נוספות לחופי הים התיכון אפשר לקרוא לצַד מערב בשם* **יָם**?

מפה א' 2: **ימה וקדמה צפונה ונגבה**

11

Figure 3 (*TMC*: 11) One sea with many names
Courtesy of Maalot publishers and the Ministry of Education, Jerusalem.

west, and to the east, and to the north, and to the south' (Genesis, 28: 14). The verse itself features next to the map, in a column of biblical quotes which all include the divine promise in greater detail:

> Exodus 23: 31: 'And I will set thy bounds from the sea of Suf [the Red Sea] even to the sea of the Pelishtim [the southern shores of the Mediterranean], and from the desert to the river.'
>
> Deuteronomy 11: 24: 'Every Place whereon the sole of your foot shall tread shall be yours. [...] From the river, the river Prath [Syria and Iraq] to the uttermost sea shall be your border,'
>
> Joshua 1: 4: 'From the wilderness and this Lebanon as far as the great sea ... towards the going down of the sun, shall be your border.'

However, only the verse regarding the 'spreading' is interpreted, within brackets, into Modern Hebrew:

> (The interpretation of the verse: In future your country will expand to the west, and to the east, to the north and to the south).

The column of biblical verses is the Given of this page, given Hebrew directionality (from right to left) which may suggest chronological relations between the verses and the map: the divine promise was there first, and the map followed. The verses are connected to the map by straight horizontal vectors which signify a strong connection that may be that of a narrative or cause and effect, (Kress and Van Leeuwen, 1996/2007). The map, being on the 'new' (left) side of the page, is thus presented as the realization of the divine promises – the modern fulfillment of the ancient prophesies. The insertion of biblical verses into the scientific text endows the text with the sanctity of the Bible and its divine truth, and gives the bible and the divine promises a scientific real-time validity.

Since genres can be defined by their function (Van Leeuwen, 2005a), one may define this whole page generically as 'legitimation', for it legitimates the occupation of Palestinian lands relying on the highest authority for the Jews – the Bible. The answer to the hypothetical question, 'why doesn't the map show the internationally recognized borders of Israel?' is: 'Because the Bible says so.'

Representation of Palestinians by Racist Verbal and Visual Discourse

Morgan (2003), a social and cultural geographer, notes that since 'images are means of persuasion to hold certain beliefs and values,' the crucial questions in Geography are: 'Who consumes it? What do they make of it?' (p.254–255). These questions relate to Van Leeuwen's questions regarding visual presentations (2000: 92):

1) What are the kinds of people and things depicted in the image and how do we recognize them as such?
2) What ideas and values do we associate with these depicted people, places or things, and what is it that allows us to do so?

These questions, which may be asked about any visual sign, are crucial to teaching since 'much of the message of the multimodal text comes across before a word of text has been read' (Van Leeuwen, 1992: 36). As we shall see, in Israeli geography school books the exclusion of Palestinians and their representation as impersonalized elements, as 'problems' and 'threats,' is obvious before a word of the written text is read.

Palestinians, as was mentioned before, are seldom depicted at all. When depicted it is never as modern, productive, individual human beings but as stereotypes of the 'problems' and 'threats' they constitute for Israelis. Stereotypization, as scholars of racist discourse assure us, leads very easily to Racist discourse (Allport 1958, Essed 1991).

Geography school books use strategies of visual racist representation (detailed in chapter 1), to depict the Palestinian citizens of Israel.

1) Portraying Palestinian citizens as primitive, parasite, and vile.
2) Portraying Palestinian citizens as outlaws by defining their houses illegal construction.

3) Portraying Palestinians as thieves, *Geography of the Land of Israel* p.100:
   'The struggle for water: The Palestinian authority steals water from Israel in Ramala.'
4) Portraying Palestinian citizens as the enemy from within, *Geography of the Land of Israel,* (p.240):
   The purpose of the foundation of Mitzpim* is to preserve the national land and protect it from illegal invasion by the non-Jewish population, to acquire land for development in order to prevent a territorial sequence of non-Jewish settlements, for fear that an Arab sequence would cause the detachment of Galilee from the state of Israel.[4]
   * Mitzpim are Community settlements built on top of mountains in the Galilee, overlooking Arab villages in the Galilee.

This paragraph reiterates the official Israeli stance. As Yiftachel notes (2006: 78), 'Since September 1997, the Israeli government has announced on several occasions the introduction of new strategies to block "Arab invasion" of state lands [...] ensure Jewish control over state land and prevent Arab expansion and illegal building.' The project of Judaization of the Galilee started in the 1970 out of fear of leaving the north of the country in the hands of Arabs'. As Yiftachel (2006: 125) reveals 'policy documents of the time urge the government to continue to settle the frontier for "national" Jewish reasons, as evident from a Jewish Agency 1978 plan which states: "We must continue to bring Jews to Galilee and the Negev. The rapid increase in the numbers of Arabs in these regions and their wide-spread practices of seizing state land illegally, presents us with two main options: let the situation evolve naturally so we lose these regions, or reinvigorate the tradition of Jewish settlement and save them from Arab hands"...'

Dichotomies and Impersonalization

'Racist discourse always deals with dichotomies' (Wodak and Reisigl, 2001).

Israeli school books of geography, as Israeli political, social, and educational discourses, use many sorts of dichotomies in order to distinguish Jews from non-Jews. As mentioned before, one such dichotomy is the clear division of the land and all aspects of life in Israel into Jewish versus non-Jewish. For example in *SIS* (p.55), there is a map titled: 'Rural habitation in Israel: blue: Jewish villages, red: non-Jewish villages.' Verbally, defining people as a non-entity (that is, 'non-Jews') serves to impersonalize, segregate and exclude them. Visually, one may argue that marking Jewish settlements in blue and Non-Jewish settlements in red is also ideological since blue is the colour of the Israeli flag and red is the colour of danger.

This division which may seem irrelevant since it says nothing about agriculture or rural life can only be understood on the ground of the major aim of Zionism – the 'Judaization' of the Land, which implies its 'de-Arabization' (Yiftachel, 2006). From this point of view the map's message is, 'Look how much we have achieved and how much more we still have to achieve.'

As Yiftachel (2006: 42) states, 'Territoriality [in Israel] is expressed by the division of "our" and "their" space and by the dynamics of expansion and contraction. Ethnic settlement has been a major (indeed constitutive) feature of the Israeli ethnocracy.' He further explains (p.127) that the 'Judaization' project has created a pattern of group membership shaped by three intertwined elements: ethnic affiliation, group spatiality (location, local attachment and spatial control) and level of economic development. Ethnic affiliation, openly stated in Israeli discourse and marked on Identity Cards, is intertwined with the two other components, therefore emphasizing the ethnic nature of settlements points also to their economic level and their land rights.

As was mentioned before, the indigenous non-Jews, regardless of their origin and faith, are sometimes called by the generic hyperonym: Arabs.

However, non-Jewish immigrants who are accepted into Israeli citizenry (mostly from the former USSR) and are classified, both by the state's population registry and in geography school books as 'others.' Their privileged status is expressed in *GLI*: 149, where a population-pyramid divides the Israeli population into 'Jews and others' versus 'Arabs.' This differentiation is not only between 'them' and 'us' but rather between 'them' and 'us and all the non-them.' The book does not provide any explanation as to who these 'others' are, but the impression remains that some 'others' deserve to be included in the Jewish group, as long as they are not Arabs.

The 'Arabs' in the diagram are depicted in stereotypical-racist icons (Van Leeuwen, 2000): the mustached Arab man wears a Ghalabia, a kaffiyah and is followed by a camel, the woman wears traditional dress and is crouching on the ground; The Jews-and-others are depicted as a 'normal' – though caricaturistic – Western couple, unmarked by any 'Jewish' or 'other' object-signs (Figure 4).

Tradition vs. Modernity

Following the above mentioned map, of rural life in Israel, *SIS* (pp.59–61), offers a series of case studies of different forms of rural settlement (3 Jewish and 1 Arab) in which Jewish settlements are classified both by their religious tendencies, as 'religious' versus 'secular' and according to their specific way of life (village, moshav, kibbutz etc.). But the village of Yama is defined ethnically only as 'an Arab village,' not as a specimen of the villages of its kind.[5] The title of Yama's case study is 'From Tradition to Modernity,' a dichotomy not applied to the Jewish religious village Bnei-Reem, which is praised for combining modern technology with Jewish tradition, a combination made possible initially thanks to the aforementioned 'Arab family who dwelled in the area [and] served as "Sabbath Goy" (p.63) only to be replaced later by a "Sabbath clock". '

Active versus Passive Participation in One's Life

Van Leeuwen counts 'passivation' as one of the ways whereby racist discourse describes social actors, along with impersonalization, functionalization and genericization.

In the chapter quoted above, the case studies of Jewish settlements offer rich descriptions of their lives, quotes and testimonies from 'the mouth of pioneers' and current inhabitants. The 'case study' of Yama does not quote any human speech, except for an indirect semi-quote from the 'elders' who thank Israel for the 'Modern revolution' it has brought into their lives, and pledge, as a token of their gratitude, to be 'a bridge for peace' (p.59).

פירמידות הגילים: אוכלוסייה יהודית
מול אוכלוסייה ערבית, 2000

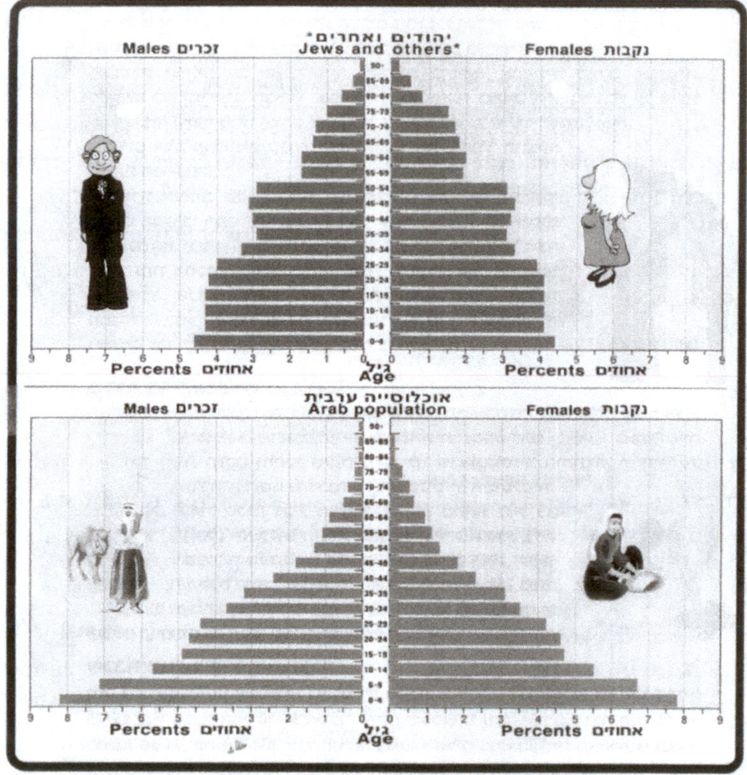

מתוך: שנתון סטטיסטי לישראל, מס' 52, 2001

Figure 4 (*GLI:* 149): Age Pyramid: Jewish population versus Arab population 2000

In the Jewish settlements, 'reforms' and 'innovations,' 'development' and 'cultivation,' are presented in active verbs, which emphasize the active part of the people in these processes (*SIS*: 60, 62). But Yama's 'modernization' processes are packed into non-human nominal clauses which emphasize the passivity or inaction of the villagers in improving their own life, thus concealing Israeli responsibility for their 'backwardness' while presenting Palestinian strife as self-generating processes. For instance in Arab villages 'infrastructures slowly improve' and 'their lands are diminishing' (*SIS*: 58). 'In Yama, like in other [Arab] rural settlements, there are only few services and the bus passes only three times a day.' (p.56). These facts are presented as natural or self-generating phenomena, though they are part of a very clear policy of discrimination and land confiscation.

The Palestinian citizens' objection to Israeli regime of exclusion and segregation is termed as we have seen, reluctance to contribute anything for the general good (*GLI*: 303) and is explained by their being a clannish society.

Double Connotation

An interesting sort of dichotomy is when the same term is used for conveying two opposite notions. One example is the term 'detached garden cottages' Or 'land-ridden houses.' In *SIS* (p.66) we read about Jewish outpost settlements (Mitzpim):

> Many people aspire to live in a community settlement like Rakefet, because its inhabitants are advantaged with a high standard of living expressed in a rustic and serene atmosphere, clean air, detached garden-cottages and a variety of community activities.

However, in *GLI* (p.303) one reads:

> The Arabs refuse to live in high-rise buildings and insist on living in land ridden houses.

These examples show that words do not have meaning in themselves, but are injected with meaning according to context (Kress, 2003) and that 'meaning does not exist outside semiotic and discursive forms and processes' (Hodge and Kress, 1993: 158). While the Arabs are 'unwilling to give anything for the general good' – namely give up their lands – and while all their attempts to build on their own land for their children are termed illegal, the Jews in Rakefet and other such outposts are allowed to 'build for the next generations' on previous public or 'state lands' (confiscated from nearby Palestinian town of Sakhnin) that were 'de-frozen' for that purpose (*SIS*: 64).

Marginalization and Segregation

The only information the reader receives about the 'Arabs' who live 'on the national margins' (*GLI*: 146) is negative. The general tendency to present 'Israel's Arabs' as a backward 'sector' and exclude them from any account of social, cultural or economic life is manifest in *PIS* (p.76), where a graph depicting average marriage age for women as one of the characteristics of development, manages to locate Israel as the last bar in a line of 'Developed Countries' thanks to a minuscule footnote that says, 'The graph refers only to the Jewish population' (Figure 5).

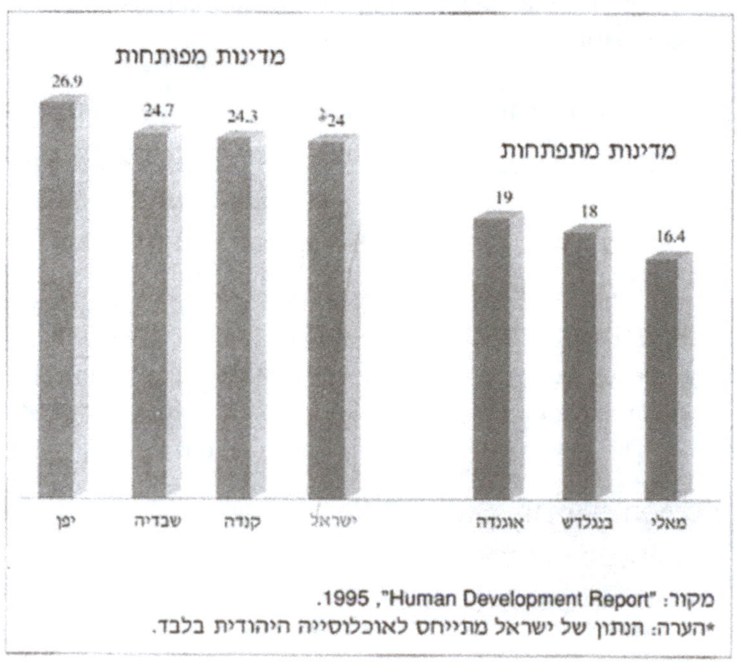

Figure 5 (*PIS*: 76): Average marital age for women in a number of countries 1990

*Note: The Israeli data refer only to the Jewish population.

Courtesy of The Centre for Educational Technology

The Power of Maps

Oxford, Dorling and Harris (2003: 154) mention the main elements that need to be included in a map:

1) A title that explains the major theme being mapped, region and data.
2) A legend with a clear explanation of what each symbol represents, with the text to the right of each symbol.
3) The source of the data: where the data were obtained, when they were collected and by whom.
4) Labels that would indicate features of interest.

The following examples show how Israeli school books manipulate cartography for the purpose of excluding Palestinians, for emphasizing Arab threat and for blurring the international borders of the state while legitimating the occupation of Palestine.

Mental Maps: Centre and Peripheralness

> Mental maps are a critical variable – occasionally the decisive factor – in the making of public policy (Henrikson, 1994: 50).

'Mental maps' are ideological constructs which may have little to do with geographical evidence. They reflect individual or societal perception or reflection of the world. For instance, in European maps Europe is the centre of the world. The drawing of maps is highly influenced by mental maps or by the political ideologies the state is interested in diffusing. The power of mental maps, especially in a small place such as Israel can be fatal for the underprivileged citizens, for as Henrikson explains,

> The sensation of peripheralness itself cannot be altered, of course, by simply shifting or reducing the graphic frame of the map. (1994: 56)

The marginalization of Arabs is emphasized in all geography school books, where Arab cities and villages within Israel are missing from maps and Palestinian life-world is absent from the texts. Many of these Arab villages are legally termed 'unrecognized villages,' and their inhabitants are legally defined as 'present absentees,' namely people who remained in Israel after being expelled from their villages and live on other lands. The 'unrecognized villages' do not receive any municipal or governmental services. That means that about 100,000 citizens are subjected, by law, to a permanent 'state of exception', which ' is precisely this topological zone of indistinction, which had to remain hidden from the eyes of justice' (Agamben 1998: 37). In Israel this state of exception is legalized.[6] That is why a sentence such as 'In the late 1960s the [Arab] village of Yama in the Sharon region [the very heart of Israel] was connected to the central water system and at the end of the 1970s to the national electricity grid.' (*SIS*: 58) can be written in a school book without any further explanation.

Thus, the Arab citizens are pushed in spite of Israel's small frame, to the margins of consciousness and social reality, as it is well expressed in the following statement from *GLI* (2003: 197):

> Factors that inhibit the development of the Arab village:
>
> [...] Arab villages are remote from the centre, the roads to them are difficult and they have remained outside of the process of change and development, they are hardly exposed to modern life and there are difficulties in connecting them to the power and water networks.

None of these 'remote' villages is depicted on any map though they are all situated within the 'narrow waistline of Israel' which at its widest part is 50km wide (30 minutes drive) and at its narrowest part is equal to the distance between Manhattan and JFK airport – 15 km, 9 minutes drive – as emphasized in Israeli maps issued by the Ministry of Foreign Affairs.[7] However, Jewish Mitzpim (outposts)[8] such as Rakefet, built on hilltops overlooking those 'remote' or non-existent villages, and Jewish colonies such as Ariel or Alon Shvut and Bet-El, situated beyond the official borders of Israel, are presented in all school books as examples of a high standard of living, not as remote, marginal, deprived settlements.

Arabs are marginalized in Israeli school books as they are excluded from Israeli cultural discourse and social life (see Yiftachel, 2006, Yona, 2005). For example, in a history book for grades 8 and 9: *From Conservatism to Progress* (p.269), we learn that, 'In the years 1881–1882 thousands of people arrived at Jaffa port: from Russia, from Rumania, from the Balkan and even from far-away Yemen.' Needless to say, Yemen is closer to Jaffa port than Russia, but on the 'mental map' of the book's authors and of the numerous committee members and counselors who authorized it, the centre is still Eastern Europe, the spiritual centre of Zionism and the origin of the dominant social group in Israel. As Henrikson (1994: 55–56) remarks, 'One of the unfortunate consequences of colonialism and the condition it engendered, [...] is a feeling that the centre is elsewhere.'

Regarding the influence of mental maps, Bar-Gal argues,

> Israeli citizens of the present acquired political beliefs in the past from which each has built their 'mental map'; these maps will influence their decisions at the ballot box on the question of the future borders of the state. (1993b: 421)

Shifting the Centre

> It is through the lens of a map [...] that we see, know and even create the larger world (Henrikson 1994: 52).

Maps have both a synoptic quality (show what is happening in an area), and a hypnotic quality – a suggestive effect. 'Cartohypnosis' (a term coined by Boggs 1947) is the subtle persuasiveness of maps which 'causes people to accept unconsciously and uncritically the ideas that are suggested to them by maps' (Henrikson, 1994: 50).

Kress and Van Leeuwen argue that 'the centre is not always identical with the focus of the map. [...] For something to be presented as Centre means that it is presented as the nucleus of the information to which all other elements are subservient' (Van Leeuwen and Kress, 1996: 30, 90). The shift of attention to the non-central focus is made possible by the use of colour, size and perspective.

In *TMC* (p.53) a map titled: 'Expand your knowledge: Jews, Christians and Muslims around the Mediterranean' (Figure 6) has, right above it, two lines of orientation: 'Many nations dwell around the Mediterranean: Jews, Arabs, Italians, Greek, Spanish and others.' The 'others' are the Tunisians, the Moroccans, the Algerians and the Turks, all included in the generic name 'Arabs' represented by two huge, dark-pink 'Muslim' blocks surrounding tiny 'Jewish' Israel. A light-pink unnamed block of 'Christians' is also depicted. But the strong 'Jewish' hue of tiny Israel – dark purple – and the fact that none of the other blocks is named, render Israel the most salient feature of the map and its focus, the first item to attract the eye. Arnheim argues (quoted in Henrikson, 1994: 58) that studying maps can actually makes the viewer feel 'the underlying spatial forces of the map structure as "pushes and pulls" in his own nervous system,' for shape and colour in maps have an animating effect. In reading maps, the first to meet the eye are the expressive qualities of the map carried by stimulus data such as colour.

Monmoniers (1996) notes in his book *How to Lie with Maps* that 'Colour is a cartographic quagmire,' (p.163), and that '[...] simultaneous contrast will make the lighter colour seem lighter and the dark colour seem darker' (p.172).

The legend of the *TMC* map indicates that the colours depict the 'majority' in each block and the editorial text under this map specifies: 'On the map, at the eastern side of the Mediterranean, there is a prominent spot of colour which represents the Jews living in our state – the state of Israel.' However, in the area named Israel, the dark purple covers all the occupied Palestinian territories including the Gaza Strip, thus representing as Jewish majority the combined population of about 5.5 million Jews and 5.5 million Palestinians. In the Muslim blocks there are neither Jews nor Christians, and there are no Jews in the Christian block. But in Cyprus a third of the country is painted Muslim and the Balkans contain some uneven 'Muslim' stripes of various sizes, which are not accounted for in the legend. Neither the stripes nor the third of Cyprus represent majorities but they reinforce the effect of Muslim encroachment. Van Leeuwen (1992: 51) observes that since maps are analytical, the relations they show are

Figure 6 (*TMC*: 53): Jews, Muslims and Christians around the Mediterranean Legend: Majorities: Black: Jews; Dark grey: Muslims; Light grey: Christians.

Courtesy of Maalor publishers and the Ministry of Education, Jerusalem.

not dynamic but static. This map conveys static relations of power or threat in the Middle East, by means of colour.[9]

This map contains additional elements not accounted for in the legend.

The Cartography of Exclusion

> The territory no longer precedes the map, nor survives it. It is the map that precedes the territory [...] that engenders the territory. (Baudrillard, 1983: 2)

Henrikson argues that 'cartography like politics is a 'teleological discourse,' reifying power, reinforcing the status quo, and freezing social interaction within charted lines.' Therefore, 'the map has always been the perfect representation of the state' (ibid.: 58, 59, 60). Maps can naturalize exclusion more than any other device. In Israeli school books the maps make the 'indistinction' of Palestinian citizens and non-citizens real and visible.

Bar-Gal notes, that Israeli curriculum planners have neither resigned to man-made borders, nor have they given up teaching about the Greater, Promised Land of Israel that goes way beyond the state's official borders and is presented in geography school books as *'a whole geographic entity.'* This 'geographic entity' is presented in all municipal, commercial and 'physical maps' adorning school corridors, ministries and banks. It comprises Israel, parts of Lebanon, Palestine, most of Jordan (called the Eastern Land of Israel) and portions of Syria and Egypt and creates the idea of 'natural' boundaries for the newly formed Israeli nation state. Israeli maps present therefore not 'the "State of Israel" which has achieved international legitimation [but] the "Land of Israel" which has divine legitimation' (Bar-Gal 1993b: 430). As Bar-Gal asserts, (1996: 69),

> The educational system continues to present the map as a miniature model of reality, and less often emphasizes that this map is a distorted model, which sometimes can 'lie,' and contain items that are completely different from reality.

None of the books is called *The Geography of the **State** of Israel*. The titles are usually ***Israel*** or *The **Land** of Israel*, which entails the inclusion, in all maps, of territories beyond the state's official borders, including the occupied areas that were seized during the wars but whose legal status does not make them a part of the state.

IMS is the only book of those considered here that declares from the outset it would teach about the State of Israel. However its maps include, as an integral part of the state, the Palestinian territories that are outside Israel's official borders but omit Arab cities inside Israel (such as Nazareth, Acre, or Um El Fahem). On the first map: 'Israel and its neighbors 2002' (p.7, Figure 7), the areas controlled by the Palestinian authorities (areas A) are encircled with a very thin broken line, which usually expresses temporariness. Other Palestinian areas (B, C), which are under military occupation and have never been annexed to Israel, are not marked at all and seem as part of the state. Similarly, on page 23, a map of universities includes the tiniest Jewish university-extensions that were erected in the illegal settlements of Ariel, Alon Shvut, or Elkana but excludes all major Palestinian universities in the same areas, such as Bir Zeit, Al-Quds and Bethlehem university, although the latter are much bigger and better known all over the world.

Two other maps present the Palestinian territories as what Henrikson terms geographic or toponomyc silences that is, as colourless spots within the state of Israel. Geographic silences are created usually by

> The removal or alteration of place names – the renamed locations of conquered people or minority groups – {which} create 'toponomyc silences' namely 'blank spaces,' silences of uniformity, of standardization or deliberate exclusion, willful ignorance or even actual repression. (Henrikson, 1994: 59)

On the map depicting the distribution of 'Arab population in Israel 2002' (*IMS*: 16 Figure 8) Palestinian regions are colourless and defined as 'Areas for which there are no data,' that is to say as areas within the state of Israel where there is no 'population'; on the map depicting the distribution of employment (*IMS*: 33) there is a colourful graph depicting the Israelis who work in the occupied Palestinian territories but no data about Palestinian employees. These are labeled in the verbal text, as we have seen above, 'foreigners' or 'host workers.' Their being

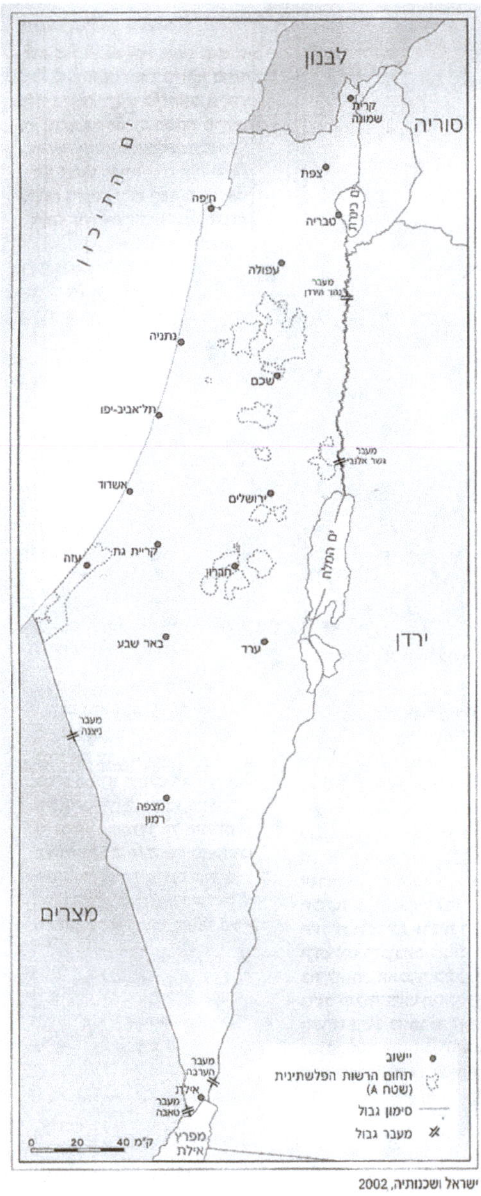

Figure 7 (*IMS:* 7): Israel and its neighbors 2002

Courtesy of the Centre for Educational Technology, Tel Aviv.

9א. תפרוסת האוכלוסייה הערבית במדינת ישראל לפי נפות, בשנת 2000

Figure 8 (*IMS*: 16): The Arab population in Israel 2000

Courtesy of the Centre for Educational Technology, Tel Aviv.

employed in 'unprofessional jobs' is the only information the school books give about the sort of work Palestinians do. Moreover, treating the Palestinians as foreigners points to an odd geographical perception: the Palestinian territories – except for area A – are presented as part of Israel and yet the inhabitants of these same territories are foreigners. However, the readers may not be aware of this peculiarity because the occupied territories are not marked as Palestinian areas. As Henrikson explains,

> Maps are powerful and persuasive sometimes explicitly and nearly always implicitly. Every map is some one's way of getting you to look at the world his own way. They do it by conveying they have no such interest. They are convincing because the interests they serve are masked. (Henrikson, 1994: 58–59)

The 'toponomyc silences' regarding the presentation of Palestinian areas are the visual expression of the Zionist slogan, 'A land without people for a people without land' which has always justified the policy of occupation and colonization. This is most apparent in the map of Jerusalem, 'the historic capital of the Jewish people,' (*IMS*: 174–175) titled 'Jerusalem as capital – government, culture, administration and national sites,' where no Palestinian cultural sites or administrative buildings are depicted in the eastern side of the city, which is inhabited almost exclusively by Palestinians. This map convinces the viewer that Eastern Jerusalem is an empty place where the only important sites are Temple Mount and the Wailing Wall, marked as 'national sites.'

Cartographic Bad-Practice

GLI is the most blatant, both in its verbal and in its visual representations. As demonstrated very vividly on the map 'Israel following the Oslo Accords' (Figure 9), international laws and decisions are presented as inapplicable to Israel in this text book. Across the West Bank one sees white rectangles bearing the inscription that Samaria and Judea (Hebrew names of The West Bank) are 'in a process of dynamic changes' (right rectangle), but the 'Gaza strip will remain under Israeli

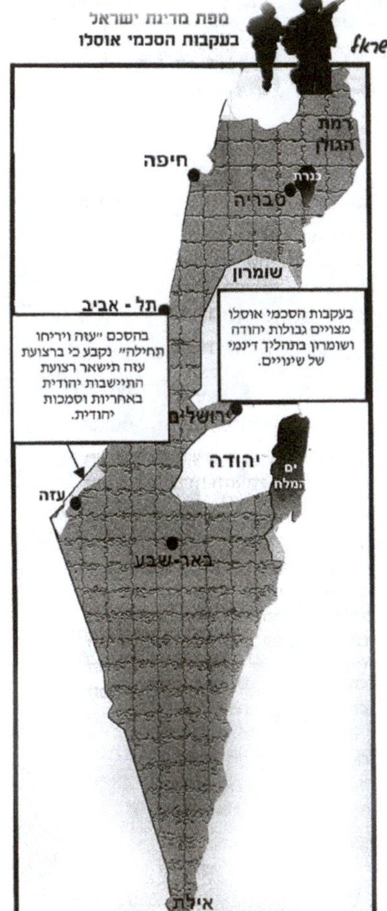

ציוני דרך נוספים בקביעת גבולות מדינת ישראל

מלחמת יום הכיפורים

באוקטובר 1973 פרצה מלחמת יום הכיפורים בין ישראל למצרים בגבול הדרומי, ובין ישראל לסוריה בגבול הצפוני. המלחמה לא שינתה את גבולות הקו הסגול אך בעקבות הפרדת הכוחות עם הסורים בוצעו שינויים קלים בקו הגבול.

חוזה השלום עם מצרים

מוחמד אנואר אל-סאדאת, נשיא מצרים, מנחם בגין, ראש ממשלת ישראל וג'ימי קרטר נשיא ארה"ב חתמו בקמפ דיוויד, ב-17 בספטמבר 1978, על הסכם שלום בין מצרים לישראל. בעקבות הסכם השלום החזירה ישראל למצרים את חצי האי סיני. כך חזרנו לקו הגבול הבינלאומי הנמשך מרפיח ועד לטאבה.

סיפוח רמת הגולן

במלחמת ששת הימים נכבשה רמת הגולן מידי סוריה. בדצמבר 1981 סיפחה ישראל את שטחה של רמת הגולן לתחומה, והחוק הישראלי הוחל על שטח זה עם כל המשתמע מכך.

הסכמי אוסלו

בשנות ה-90 הוחל במגעים דיפלומטיים עם הפלשתינאים והוחלט בהסכמי ביניים על הקמת הרשות הפלשתינאית בשטחים מסוימים ביהודה, שומרון וחבל עזה. שטחי הרשות הפלשתינאית לא סומנו בספר במפת ישראל, היות ואין מדובר עדיין בגבול בין-מדיני.

Figure 9 (GLI: 17): Israel after the Oslo Agreements

control' (left rectangle). The bottom rectangle on the right-hand side of the page explains that 'the areas accorded to the Palestinian authorities were not marked on the maps in this book because they have not yet acquired the status of international borders.' However, Jewish colonies in the West Bank and the Golan Heights, whose annexation has not yet acquired international status either, are marked as part of the state, and the two soldiers erupting from the map's frame with rifles pointed toward Syria and Lebanon, reassure readers that Israel has not come to terms with, and will not abide by, man-made borders. This kind of map is what Oxford, Dorling, and Harris (2003), define as 'cartographic bad practice':

> It is bad practice to clutter the map with unnecessary information or chart-junk, namely, decoration that may draw attention away from the important information. (2003: 154)

The important information in this case should be, as the title promises, the internationally agreed borders and the areas returned to the Palestinian authority in consequence of the Oslo accords, but except for the title – which is also misleading – none of the necessary elements is included in this map. No reference is given as to the source of the data, and the map clearly includes unnecessary elements unlikely to feature in any atlas. The conclusion must be that this map is not meant to teach the students about cartography or international borders but rather to transmit a very clear message regarding the inapplicability of international decisions in Israel. As Bar-Gal explains,

> The borders of Israel as presented on the map represent the right-wing ideological perception which refuses to see the area of the West Bank and Gaza as territory under a different sovereignty. (Bar-Gal, 1993a: 125)

To sum up, in all the maps presented in this chapter 'Persuasion is foregrounded and instruction and exposition backgrounded' (Kress and Van Leeuwen, 1996: 90).

Ideological Images

Photographs

Photographs, even documentary ones, may have symbolic meaning and may be analyzed not only semiotically but also iconographically and iconologically. Such an analysis would seek to find out what the photograph represents within a certain context of culture or situation and to link it with 'themes, concepts or conventional meaning' (Woodrow, 2003), in order to provide the 'why' behind the representations analyzed (Van Leeuwen, 2001: 116). The analysis would then reveal 'the basic attitudes of a nation, a period, a class, a religious and philosophical persuasion – [...] condensed into one work' (Panofsky, cited in Woodrow, 2003).

One representation I would like to analyze in this way is found in *PIS* (p.150) in a sub-chapter called: 'Case study 4: Many refugees in the world are running for their lives.' This chapter is analytically structured: it shows many sub-kinds of what is classified as 'refugees.' A map shows concentrations of refugees in 1992, a million of whom, it states, are in the region of Israel. Altogether there are seven photographs: three 'close-shots' of Jewish refugees from 1945 and 1956, one close-up of Israeli soldier-doctors tending to a Rwandan baby, one 'long-shot' aerial photo of Rwandan refugees, one 'long-shot' aerial photo of Somali refugees, one 'long-shot' of Haitians, and one 'very-long-shot' of an empty shanty town defined as 'Jabalia refugee camp in the Gaza region.'[10]

All the refugees except for the Palestinians are presented as human beings 'running for their lives,' though all of them except for the Jewish ones are shown from a very long distance, as 'phenomena' rather than as individuals. However, their troubles are detailed in the text and their escape routes are depicted on maps that contain all the necessary facts the reader might need in order to understand their circumstances: size of the country, composition of the population etc. The only refugees that are not depicted 'running for their lives' are the million refugees in the Israeli region, whose vicissitudes are neither described in the text nor depicted on any map.[11] The only representation of these refugees is the aerial photograph of the refugee camp of Jabalia. Van Leeuwen (1992: 49) writes about such aerial photographs:

> It is the angle of the omnipotent observer, placed high above the madding crowd or to use an even stronger image: the angle of the pilot who flies too high to be able to see the people on whom he is dropping his bombs [...] it is the kind of knowledge which education is still primarily concerned to reproduce.
>
> The caption of the aerial photograph of Jabalia reads:
>
> 'One of the big refugee camps, whose inhabitants live in over-crowdedness and poverty.' (p.153)

This is the only caption that does not specify who the inhabitants are and how they became refugees. Poverty and over-crowdedness are presented in terms of *existentialization* – as given conditions or rather as timeless circumstances that 'simply exists' (Van Leeuwen, 2008: 67), a situation into which those inhabitants happened to fall or to be born, detached from any cause or human agency. The editorial text above the Jabalia photograph explains:

> The population in the refugee camps is growing fast and the conditions of life are very hard –the rate of unemployment is high, the houses are crowded and poor and the standard of health services, education and hygiene, is low.

This account is given without any specification. 'The population is growing fast,' resembles reports about an epidemic, such as the increase of mosquitoes or rats in places where *the standard of hygiene is low.*

On the back side of the page, as 'counterpart' or 'negative' of the Jabalia photograph, (p.154), is a photograph of 'Jewish refugees on their way to Israel' during the 1950s, showing Kurdish Jews crowded in an airplane. Kress and Van Leeuwen maintain (1995: 34) that 'Connections are realized as vectors [...] on double spread, on two sides of a page or through pages.' The text above the photograph confirms the connection between the two sides of the page:

> Contrary to the Arab refugees, of whom many still live in refugee camps and their problem has not been solved [by the Arab

countries] – the problem of Jewish refugees from Islamic countries has long been solved. [...] The state of Israel has invested a lot of effort in the absorption of these refugees.[12]

Racist Cartoons

In *GLI* Palestinians are represented only by racist icons and cartoons, such as the classical Arab with a moustache, wearing a kaffiyah, riding or followed by a camel (Figure 10).

This image of the Arab, repeated throughout the book in variations (with or without a crouching woman, with or without a pack of children, riding the camel or leading it) whenever 'Arabs' are discussed, is always placed outside the frame. On a map which depicts 'the Geographic distribution of Arab villages and cities in Israel' (p.145, Figure 11), two figures of 'Arabs' are placed outside Israel, on the other side of the river Jordan, clearly separated from their residential areas, as if relocated across the border, in the kingdom of Jordan, where Israel has always tried to transfer them. The natural border – the river, as the

Figure 10 *GLI*: 195: A traditional society

התפרוסת הגיאוגרפית של
היישובים הערבים בישראל

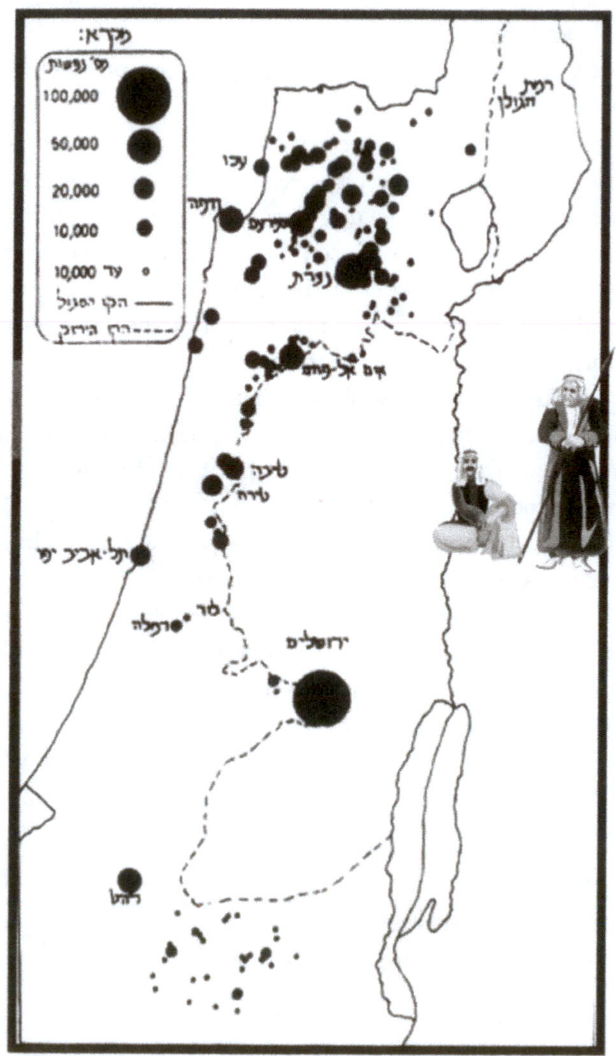

Figure 11 *GLI*: 135. Geographic spread of Arab population in Israel

oval frame in Figure 1, segregates these people and places them in an entirely different domain.

These borders or frames limit symbolically the interaction between the figures and the place; create barriers that 'may be removed only by those who hold the key' (Van Leeuwen, 2005: 16).

Contrary to the Arab population map which excludes the Arabs from the land, a Jewish immigration map shows figurines that are clearly inside the frame (Figure 12). On this map, which is at the New-Ideal spot (top-left) of a page entitled 'Immigration to Israel as an influential demographic factor,' the airplane bringing in the Jewish immigrants obscures parts of Syria, the flag of Israel is draped across the country, covering the whole of Palestine (Gaza Strip and the West Bank), and the Jewish immigrants march directly into the occupied Palestinian territories. At the bottom of the image one sees a contract of citizenship which Jewish newcomers sign upon arrival. These two maps visualize the fact that while the indigenous population is pushed out, Jews from other countries are brought in to replace them and populate their lands.

The icons of the 'Arab' accompany all the maps, the graphs and the verbal texts that discuss 'Arabs' in this textbook. They seem to fulfill the function of 'illustration,' or 'elaboration' (Van Leeuwen, 2005: 230), for they specify visually the characteristics of 'Arabs', showing what 'Arabs' look like. But since no map, graph or 'pyramid' shows Arab doctors or lawyers, businessmen, academics, artists or industrialists, this illustration – connoting all Arabs – restricts the image of the 'Arab' to clown-looking primitive farmers and nomads, who hardly represent any Arab either in Israel or in Palestine today.

The Meta-narrative of 'Development' and the Power of Colour as a Semiotic Resource of Meaning

This section discusses 'classification images' (Van Leeuwen, 1992: 54, Morgan, 2003) which are used to convey development and underdevelopment. Classification is an instrument of ordering the world and of control (Hodge and Kress, 1993: 63). One classification which freezes power relations in Israel is the above mentioned Jews versus

Figure 12 *GLI*: 136. Jewish immigrants arriving at Israel

non-Jews and another classification, related to it, is the categorization of developed versus underdeveloped societies. Such 'Monopolistic, undifferentiated, two-valued and rigid categorizations,' to use Allport's terms (1958: 171), are usually irreversible.

Israeli geography textbooks teach that 'an historical event, the resurrection of the Jewish nation, had an impact on the landscape' (Bar-Gal, 1993a: 60). This 'impact' is often termed 'development' or 'progress,' and is manifested in Zionist achievements such as the taming of the desert, afforestation, massive construction and the diversion of rivers. Although these projects are, as Yiftachel (2006: 38) notes, 'Wrapped in a discourse of development, modernity, and democracy, the very material reality is unmistakable, entailing minority dispossession and exclusion.' Palestinian (and Druze and Bedouin) citizens are included in this meta-narrative of development as underdeveloped, non-Westernized sectors that Israel is 'modernizing' and cultivating just like the landscape (Bar-Gal, 1994: 231).

Israeli school books attribute 'underdevelopment' to the general 'Arab' way of life which is 'traditional' and 'clannish' without mentioning Israeli development projects that exclude and impoverish them.

The sharp distinction between developed and undeveloped societies goes against current thinking of developmental geography which claims that,

> Meta-narratives, such as 'development', are to be mistrusted [and] 'development' should be questioned. The world with its varieties cannot be understood using only a small number of concepts; the people who get to choose which concepts tend to come from wealthy areas and they describe the world according to their own vision of how it should be and call these concepts universal. (Page, 2003: 98)

Page maintains that 'If development is to be regulated it needs to be scrutinized' and suggests to 'analyze discursive tactics employed by the advocates of development ...' stating that 'current geographical work sets out to disturb the simplicity of development propaganda in order to deepen our understanding of different places [...] Development

Geography {has} dispensed with the view that anything can be justified as long as it is labeled "progressive" ' (ibid: 101).

One of the most common representations of underdevelopment is the 'Oxfam image' (Hicks, 1980: 13) of the primitive farmer with his primitive plough, which connotes nothing but 'backwardness' (Van Leeuwen, 1992: 56). *PIS* (p.110) presents a quadrangle of photographs, titled 'From traditional to modern life in the non-Jewish population' (Figure 13). On the right (the 'Given' part of the page reserved for the past, the known and uncontested)[13] we see 'traditional agriculture in the Galilee' and a 'traditional' village. On the left side (reserved for new information) we see their counterparts: 'Modern construction in the suburbs of the Arab town Um El Fahem' and a modern machine-cultivated field (at the New-Ideal spot). The blurred figure of the farmer in the 'traditional' field is seen from a great distance and

Figure 13 (*PIS*: 110): From traditional to modern life in the non-Jewish population

Top right: Traditional agriculture in the Galilee

Bottom right: Traditional construction in the Arab village Dier-Hana in the lower Galilee

Top left: Modern agriculture in Taybe, an Arab village on the coastal plain

Courtesy of Dr. Zvi Ron

Bottom left: Modern construction in the suburbs of the Arab town Um El-Fahem.

in profile, namely 'impersonally as a type rather than as individual' (Van Leeuwen and Selander, 1995: 46). He hasn't any ethnic object signs, such as a kaffiyah or an 'Arab' dress, but a khaki shirt, oversized khaki trousers and a khaki woolen cap, which are the usual Israeli hand-downs to poor neighbors. Disadvantage and dependence upon Jewish good will have become, according to this representation, what Ogbu (1986: 96–97) defined as 'secondary cultural characteristics.' Ogbu explains that 'secondary cultural characteristics are [...] those different cultural features that came into existence after two populations have come into contact, especially in contact involving the subordination of one group to another.' In the Israeli context poverty and backwardness stand for 'Arabness' or rather for 'non-Jewishness.' The farmer goes from left to right, receding away from, and turning his back on the 'modern' machine-made field on his left, which is located at the New-Ideal part (top-left) of the quadrangle, above a caption: 'Modern agriculture in Taybeh, an Arab village in the coastal plain.' Thus, backwardness, which resides in the Arab-populated Galilee, gives way to modernity the closer one gets to the Jewish centre.

The houses of the 'traditional Arab village in Galilee,' located at the bottom-right spot (Real-Given), have flat roofs designed to collect rain water. The colour of their walls is that of the land that surrounds them. The houses are connected to each other and face a common centre. By contrast, the 'modern construction in the suburbs of the Arab town Um El Fahem,' at the New-Real location (bottom left), consists of scattered individual western-looking houses topped with precipitous red tiled roofs – designed for snowy weather – on an uncultivated slope of a rocky hill, with no roads leading from one house to another. Progress therefore means the passage from community life to individual habitation and from mid-Eastern functional construction, shapes and colours to Western ones.

The Power of Colour as a Semiotic Resource of Meaning

> Colour is a semiotic resource like any other: regular, with signs that are motivated in their constitution by the interests of the makers and not at all arbitrary or anarchic. (Kress and Van Leeuwen, 2002: 345)

Colour has three dimensions: hue, value – which refers to the colour's lightness or darkness – and saturation (chroma) which refers to the colour's intensity or brilliance (Monmoniers, 1996: 164). Van Leeuwen and Selander (1995: 506) note that 'greater sharpness and colour saturation makes the represented object more real.'

Aerial photographs are good examples of the manipulative use of distance and colour. Although both Jewish and Arab villages are usually represented from above, aerial photographs of Jewish settlements manage to acquire a postcard look, showing individual houses, fields and landscape that we can almost touch (Van Leeuwen 1992), while Arab settlements are represented from a much longer shot, as blueprints (e.g. *SIS*: 62–65). Israeli settlements, even those located in the Negev desert, such as Bnei-Reem mentioned above, are always depicted in western saturated colours: White-washed houses with precipitous red roofs, lush green vegetation and cultivated flowers. This, according to Zionist-Israeli ideology, connotes the 'impact' of Jewish return, which 'made the wilderness bloom.'

Colours, just like verbal language, may represent ideational, interpersonal and textual meanings. *Ideationally,* 'colour can denote specific people, places and things as well as classes of people, places and things, and more general ideas' (Kress and Van Leeuwen, 2002: 347). In Israeli geography textbooks 'Jewish' colours connote progress, a high standard of living or Western imported culture, whereas 'Arab' natural colours connote mid-Eastern non-development (Bar-Gal, 2000) hence non-Jewishness.

Interpersonally, 'the use of colour acts on people and manipulates them. Colour states a status and a mood' (Kress and Van Leeuwen, 1996: 349). Monmoniers (1996: 170) argues that '[...] because of the embedded emotions or culturally conditioned attitudes some colours carry a subtle added meaning that could affect our interpretation [...] or our feelings towards the elements portrayed on the map.' This observation can also be applied to photographs. The colours of Arab villages – faded yellow, brown, gray and olive green – connote in Israeli consciousness threat and alienation (Bar-Gal, 2000). As Monmoniers remarks, 'a range of greens and blues is generally preferable to a range of yellow and yellowish green' (p.170) in Western eyes.

Textually, or in terms of 'mode,' 'colour and the coordination of colours can create cohesion.' (Kress and Van Leeuwen, 1996: 349). In terms of cohesion, the contrast between the two colour schemes – the 'Arab' natural colours vs. the 'Jewish' manufactured or imported ones, stand in contrast or opposition to one another, and may represent the power relations between the two cultures. Jewish-Western domination over the Eastern-Arab landscape is what Israeli education presents as development. As Bar-Gal maintains (2000: 172), the presentation of places in geography textbooks are made in accordance with the perspectives of their authors.

Conclusion

The view that no sign is created in isolation or in a disinterested fashion and that no sign is 'neutral' or independent of Ideology is shared by geographers and social-semioticians alike. Israeli school books make use of scientific visuals, which are presented as unbiased, for the inculcation of political ideology and discriminatory ideas. The mendacious maps and demeaning images, embedded in the ethnocentric discourse, determine students' perception of their country and of their neighbours.

The books do not present the critical nature of scientific discourse but rather use geography to enhance Israeli ethno-nationalism and 'ethno-regionalism' which 'denotes both a geographic reality and a political process' (Yiftachel, 2006: 166). In this process the presence of Palestinians is erased from the landscape and from the country's life-world, which consists of 'these [...] spheres of sociality [which] provide a repository of shared meanings and understandings [...], the background against which communicative action takes place' (Finlayson, 2005: 52).

Geography school books teach Jewish Israeli students to see themselves as masters of the Land of Israel/Palestine, to control its population, its landscape and its space, and to do whatever necessary to increase Jewish domination and its 'development' which means its expansion.

3

LAYOUT AS CARRIER OF MEANING: EXPLICIT AND IMPLICIT MESSAGES TRANSMITTED THROUGH LAYOUT

Introduction

This section examines the function of layout in the representation of the Arab-Israeli conflict in three history school books. The methodology derives from the works of Kress and Van Leeuwen[1]. The analysis suggests that understanding layout may help answer larger questions, concerning 'the transformation of social practices into discourses about social practices in specific institutional contexts' (Van Leeuwen, 1996: 35).

The chapter elaborates two concepts, 'ideological layout' and 'punctuation of semiosis.' It argues that layout can 'punctuate semiosis' or meaning-making in two different senses: First in the sense of 'bringing (conventional-official) semiosis to a temporary stand still in textual form' (Kress, 2000: 141) and second, in the sense of puncturing or piercing a hole in the conventional or official meaning, and thereby criticizing it. In either case layout creates new complex signs that either support or contradict the verbal and visual texts it presents.

Kress and Van Leeuwen (1995: 33) explain that layout means composition in space or positioning things in space, so that it would feel 'just right.' Our sense of layout derives from our sense of balance and the function of balance can be shown only by pointing out the meaning it helps to make 'visible' (Arnheim, 1974: 27).

Layout places the various meaningful elements into the whole and provides ordering, cohesion and coherence among them. Therefore it plays an indispensable part in getting the message across (Van Leeuwen, 2005: 181).

Today, when most texts and especially textbooks, are multimodal, layout plays a crucial role in transmitting meanings, interpretations and ideologies. As we can see in this chapter and the ones that precede or follow it, layout may transmit meanings that are not always explicit either in the verbal or visual texts.

Reading Paths as Access to Knowledge in the Multimodal Text

Multimodal texts are constructed of verbal and visual discourses and multimodality opens the question of directionality and the question of 'point' (Kress, 2003: 157): What elements are to be read together? As was mentioned in the methodology section of this book, Kress explains that whereas in reading verbal texts (the world as told) there is a distinct and strict 'reading path' one must follow in order to make sense of the writing, this reading path being top to bottom, left to right or right to left in Hebrew and Arabic, multimodal texts (the world as shown) allow readers to design their reading and to follow a to-be-constructed path of reading, which depends on certain qualities of the text, as will be specified below, and on what Fairclough calls Member Resources, namely cultural resources, traditions, preferences and meanings every reader brings with her to the act of reading and meaning-making. Thus, the reader is much more active in constructing the reading path of a multimodal text, which is actually established according to principles of relevance to the reader.

Kress and Van Leeuwen (1995: 35) stress that 'different readers will in all likelihood follow different reading paths, and which paths they will follow will depend on their socio-cultural position, for cultural factors play a significant role in the perception of salience, and different cultural groupings are likely to have different hierarchies of salience'.

Reading images is harder given the pre-established reading path of the written page. Kress makes it clear that in order to read the multimodal text one must know about the constituents of image as we know about the constituents of sentences. The significance of elements depends upon their placement in the layout of the page or double-spread, which is a framed space. Shape, size and colour may determine what will be read first and what will be read second, which may be different for different readers. These principles are utterly different from ordinary reading. As Van Leeuwen explains (2005a: 85) the multimodal text is not always a staged, goal-oriented process. It must be analyzed as a kind of map, a spatial structure allowing a number of trajectories; or as the layout of a building, a spatial structure designed to facilitate a range of specific activities.

The logic of placement encourages us to see margins and centres for instance but doesn't compel us as in writing.

The elements that help us constitute a reading path are salience, colour, texturing, spatial configurations of various kinds, the meaning of specific kinds of elements, either natural or human made, all of which allow one to build a reading path, tracking the path of the narrative through all the different elements, the verbal, the visual etc.

Methodology

The analysis of layout in this and other chapters seeks to find the meanings of both the 'lexicon' of layout, namely the meanings of each part, and its 'syntax' – the meanings created by ordering and the relationships between the parts. The analysis constantly takes into account the intertextual relationships layout as a whole and each of its parts have with past and current social and political texts.

The Structure, Function and Possibilities of Layout

Layout is regarded by Van Leeuwen and Kress (1995) as a text or rather as intertext, namely as one semiotic entity. Being a 'spatial display' of visuals and verbal 'chunks,' layout 'may lend itself with greater facility to the representation of elements and their relation to each other' (Kress, 2000: 146). By assembling different texts and visuals on the same page, double-spread, or even whole chapters and books, layout brings 'the process of semiosis [...] which is always multimodal [...] to a temporary standstill in textual form' (Kress, 2000: 141,152). Structurally, elements in layout can be 'disconnected, marked off from each other, or connected, joined together' (Van Leeuwen and Kress, 1995: 33). What may seem as collage or bricolage is actually a transformation of ideologically motivated signs into new meaningful wholes or new 'complex signs.' This transformation is achieved through the three signifying systems that are involved in layout: information value, framing and salience, 'all serving to structure the text, to bring the various multimodal elements of the multimodal text together into a coherent and meaningful whole' (Van Leeuwen and Kress, 1995: 26).

Information Value

The placement of elements in a layout endows these elements with specific information values that are attached to the various zones of the visual space (Van Leeuwen and Kress, 1995: 26). A given element does not have the same value and meaning when placed on the right or on the left, in the upper or in the lower section of the page, in the centre or in the margins. Each of these zones accords specific values to the element placed within it. When a layout polarizes left and right, placing one kind of element on the left and another, perhaps contrasting, element on the right, the elements on the left are presented as Given (in Hebrew the elements on the right are presented as given, since writing runs from right to left). For something to be 'given' means it is presented as something the reader already knows, as a familiar and agreed upon departure point for the message. For something to be 'New' (right in English, left in Hebrew) means it is presented as something not yet known to the reader, and hence it becomes 'the crucial point of the message, the issue to which the reader must pay special attention. The New is therefore in principle problematic, contestable, the information at issue, while the Given is presented as commonsense and self-evident' (Van Leeuwen and Kress, 1995: 27). Van Leeuwen and Kress explain that 'such structures are ideological in the sense that they may not correspond to what is the case either for the producer or for the consumer of the layout' (ibid.). The information is presented as though it had that status or value for the readers, who have to read it within that structure, even if that valuation may then be rejected by a particular reader.

When a layout polarizes top and bottom, placing different, perhaps contrasting elements in the upper or lower parts of the page, the elements placed on top are presented as the Ideal and those placed at the bottom as the Real. For something to be Ideal means that it is presented as the idealized or generalized essence of the information, and therefore as its ideologically most salient part. The Real is then opposed to this in that it presents more specific information (e.g. details) and/or more 'down to earth information' (e.g. real data) and/or more practical information (e.g. practical consequences, directions for actions etc.) (Van Leeuwen and Kress, 1995: 28).

The opposition between Ideal and Real can also structure text-image relations. 'If the upper part of a page is occupied by text and the lower part by one or more pictures (or maps or charts or diagrams) the text will play the ideological lead role, and the pictures will play the subservient role, which however is important in its own right as specification, exemplification, evidence, practical consequence and so on. If the roles are reversed, so that one or two pictures are at the top section, then the Ideal, the ideologically foregrounded part of the message, is communicated visually, and the text will serve to comment or elaborate' (ibid. p.29). Such ideological foregrounded parts of the message may be posters or maps as we shall see later on.

Visual composition may be structured along the dimension of centre and margins. 'Just how marginal margins are will depend on size, and, more generally, the salience of the centre' (Van Leeuwen and Kress, 1995: 30). In the series of school books *Living Together in Israel*: A *Textbook in Homeland Studies, Society and Civics* for years 2–4, published in 2006 by the Centre for Educational Technologies, Palestinian, Jewish-Ethiopian, Bedouin and Druze children living in Israel are completely excluded from the main texts and visuals of 'Israeli Life' and are confined to strongly framed 'windows' where they are depicted on pages of different colours, as decontextualized and marked specimen of Israeli 'minorities' or 'ethnicities' to be observed, but without any connections to the rest of the population and with no share of the lifeworld represented in the book. On the cover of every booklet, a colourful drawing of people of all ages represents the Israeli population. None of these people is Arab or black or even brown as 'oriental' Israelis, who are the majority, are. In each of the booklets there is a 'gang' of children who act as guides and take the reader on a trip in Israel, to meet the people and become acquainted with the places, and who greet the Jewish newcomers. In this gang, except for one blond child called Sasha – who became one of the group – a hint to the successful absorption of Russian Jews – all of the children are Israeli-born. The Arab, Druze and Ethiopian children mentioned in the framed 'windows' are not part of this gang but are represented as 'other' types of human beings. This way the booklets teach the very young readers, both verbally and visually, that these children, framed hermetically in their special 'windows,' are indeed marginal, excluded or marked types in our society, but never included in 'our' group. A chapter in the booklet for year 2, called 'Sometimes it is hard to be different,' relates a meeting between an Israeli (Jewish, white) boy and a French one, connoting that to feel 'different' means to travel to another country. Immediately after this chapter there is a coloured 'window' titled 'A meeting with ...' and the life story of Sundus, a girl from the Arab village Tuba, in the Hula Valley. The girl, Sundus, speaks of her village and family without mentioning any connections between themselves and the Jewish villages and Kibbutzim around them, as if this village or the family were an island in a decontextualized space. The very same account is given about Muhamad, the Bedouin boy, and Gila, the Ethiopian girl who unlike the Russian girl, was required to change her name into a Hebrew one but is not yet a part of the Israeli society. This way, from the age of seven Israeli Jewish children learn to marginalize Palestinians, Druze, Bedouins and black Jews and see them as excluded from the mainstream life in the state of Israel. When the book presents in its margins the 'minority children' of Israel (Arab-Palestinians, Druze, Bedouins and Ethiopian Jews), it depicts them not only as lesser in numbers but as marginal socially and culturally. The children reading these pages are taught by the books to see their society as composed of central people or central children and marginal ones. However, as this example shows and as we shall see further down, marginal 'windows' can be much more salient than the central text due to their colours and very strong frames.

Regarding the centre of a page or double-spread, Van Leeuwen and Kress emphasize, following Arnheim (*The Power of the Centre*) that 'even when the centre is empty it will continue to exist in absentia, as the invisible (or denied) pivot around which everything else turns' (1995: 30). The centre, as we shall see later on, can separate two parts of the text or it can be a mediator, bridging and linking two extremes.

Salience

'Layout also involves assigning degrees of salience to the elements on the page' (Van Leeuwen and Kress, 1995: 33). Regardless of where they are placed, salience can create a hierarchy of importance among the elements; select some more important, more worthy of (immediate) attention than others. The elements of a layout are made to attract the reader's attention to different degrees, through a wide variety of means: placement in the foreground or background, relative size, contrast in tonal value or colour, difference in sharpness and so on. Hence, the Given may be more salient than the New or the New more salient than the Given, or both may be equally salient.

Salience is judged on the basis of visual cues. Readers are intuitively able to judge the 'weight' of the various elements of the layout, and the greater the weight of an element the greater its salience. Salience is not objectively measurable but results from a complex interaction, a complex trading-off relationship, between a number of factors: size, sharpness of focus or, more generally, amount of detail and texture shown; tonal contrast (borders between black and white have high salience); colour contrast as was explained in chapter 2 (between highly saturated and 'soft' or faded colours, or the contrast between red and blue, or different hues of green), placement in the visual field, perspective (foregrounded elements are more salient than backgrounded elements, and overlapping elements are more salient than the overlapped ones); and also quite specific cultural factors, such as the appearance of a human figure or a potent cultural symbol. Hence, 'Salience does not only have an aesthetic function; it also plays a vital role in structuring the message' (ibid.: 34).

Framing

The semiotic work of all frames is to connect or disconnect to a certain degree (Van Leeuwen, 2005). Verbal texts are framed by punctuation: 'Most cultural and social frames are intangible but in writing punctuation creates concrete, material frames. Punctuation is the result of implicit or explicit structuring and planning. Punctuation indicates how the writer wanted to parcel his piece' (Kress, 2003: 124–125).

Kress (2003: 122–123) explains that 'semiosis is ceaseless; without "fixing" and without framing we would never have anything tangible and graspable [...] Without frames there are no elements and without elements there is no structure and without structure there is no meaning. Framing marks things off but it also decides what will be included.'

Frames can be 'diegetic,' namely part of the represented world – like a mirror frame or a border on a map, or non-diegetic, namely superimposed on the representation (Van Leeuwen, 2005: 11), as the above mentioned 'windows' in school book reports.

Visual framing devices (frame lines or white spaces between elements) can disconnect the elements of a layout from each other, 'signifying they are to be read in some sense as separate and independent, perhaps even contrasting items of information' (ibid.). As we shall see strongly framed 'windows' can transmit a message that contradicts or criticizes the main text.

Frames can segregate, put people or places in entirely different territories, as belonging to two different orders. As we saw in chapter 2, in *The Geography of the Land of Israel* whenever Arabs are depicted in drawings or on maps, they are placed outside the border or outside the frame, and this placement creates symbolic barriers and limits symbolically the interaction between the figures and the place.

Contrast

Pictures on the same page can differ in terms of quality, for instance – as was mentioned before – when Arab and Jewish settlements are presented by aerial photographs, the 'Jewish' photos look like tourist postcards while the Arab ones look like blueprints, with faded colours and blurred shapes.

Register in Layout

Van Leeuwen (2005) explains that we can also speak of register in the context of layout: just as in language, one chooses one's lexicon and syntax according to context (what is said to whom and in what kind of relationships), so it is in layout – one makes semiotic choices in different contexts: what sort of information to include in the layout, in what shape, size and colour, and in what order. In school books these choices are determined by the rules of recontextualization and distribution because they have to convey ideology and educational messages, according to age.

Connective Devices

The connections between the elements of layout are expressed in vectors, or in repetitions of shapes and colours, which convey that the elements thus connected are to be read as belonging together in some sense, as continuous or complementary. The vectors may be oblique, and they may connect elements on one page, on a double-spread or on two sides of the page (Van Leeuwen and Kress, 1995) as we have seen in chapter 2 where the aerial photo of the empty refugee camp of Jabalia was contrasted with the close-up photograph of Jewish refugees on the other side of the page.

Reading Path

Information values, salience and framing, vectors and repetition of shapes and colours, determine the 'reading path' of the page. The reading path is 'the trajectory followed by the reader in scanning or reading the text' (Van Leeuwen and Kress, 1995: 26). Van Leeuwen and Kress explain that 'in densely printed text, reading is linear and strictly coded. Such texts must be read the way they are designed to be read – from left to right (or from right to left) and from top to bottom, line by line. Any other form of reading is cheating and may produce a slight sense of guilt in the reader' (1995: 35). But today, when 'the non-linear texts become more common, [...] linear reading is gradually losing ground in many, perhaps most domains' (ibid.).

Textbooks are not meant to be read linearly or from cover to cover, for they are 'used' and interrogated rather than read for pleasure; many of them include chapters that must be read for matriculation and others that are meant for general instruction. Hence, they can be read in more than one way. Their reading path is less strictly coded and less fully prescribed. Teachers can choose to read the book's chapters and the individual pages in different orders, starting from the questions, from the images or from the main text. In addition, the layout of the pages sets up particular reading paths, particular hierarchies and sequences for the hypothetical readers within and across different elements. Such reading paths begin with the most salient element, then move on to the next most salient element and so on. The pictures are usually noticed before the text, and one can discern the message of the whole page or whole book by reading the images alone (Van Leeuwen, 1992).

Regarding the textbooks studied here, all but the history textbooks *50 Years* and *Face* are multimodal and therefore offer several reading paths. *50 Years* and *Face* are densely printed texts, which lack colour, photographs and maps, and therefore offer a single obliging reading path. This is compatible with the simplistic narratives and the committed single point of view of these books, as we shall see later on, regarding all the major events in Israeli-Jewish history and in the Israeli-Palestinian conflict. In that they resemble what Podeh named the first generation of Israeli textbooks, 1950–60 (Podeh, 2002). One may assume that the regression to an all-text school book which imposes one reading path and one perspective is grounded in the current stance of the Ministry of Education to return to the good old times and the good old teaching, to omit problematic subjects and versions and not to risk different reading paths that would encourage critical reading and distract the students from the single interpretation prescribed by the book. All other books offer multimodal texts in every page.

The new 'meaningful whole' created by layout constitutes 'a kind of intertextual punctuation' (Kress, 2000: 142), realized through the 'weaving' of modes and genres, social ideologies and facts. Each part of this intertext has meaning both in itself and as a part of the new complex sign that the layout creates. Hence, the reading of multimodal texts involves understanding the relationships between the parts of the layout as well as between each part – and the layout as a whole – with other texts. As Kress maintains, intertextuality 'can be seen as a category with strong ideological, social and political effects' (Kress, 2000: 143).

The following examples show that the official Israeli-Zionist narrative is usually conveyed through the editorial text and images, while the critical voice of the historian is inserted through layout.

Example No. 1: Layout as Reproduction of the Official Narrative[2] (*The 20th*: 78–79)

In this double-spread there are two axes. The photographic axis is analytic, for it represents the two main parts of the ideal 'New Jew'

Figure 14 Land of Israel types: Top-right: Land Labourers. Bottom-left: A Jewish guard from the Hashomer group

Courtesy of Illan Rot Archives, Hertzlia, and Mapa Publishers, Tel Aviv, Israel.

perpetuated by Socialist Zionism: a Jewish farmer and a Jewish guard in the Land of Israel; these 'New Jews' had been re-indigenized; they have cast off their diaspora appearance to resemble the natives of the Land: sun-tanned, healthy and well-built, wearing an Arab kaffiyah, mastering an Arab horse and the art of cultivating the Land.[3] The farmers look with anticipation towards the future (or towards the New-Ideal part of the double-spread) while the guard looks indignantly towards the past (or towards the bottom-left or the Real–Given part of the double-spread). These indigenized immigrants are presented in the right-upper caption as 'Land of Israel types' namely, as indigenous natives rather than as the Eastern European newcomers they were at that time (both photographs were taken in 1905).

Ruth Firer, who analyzed the meaning of each photograph by itself, neglecting to take into account the layout as a whole complex sign or as a whole semiotic unit, writes about the 'Land of Israel Types':

> They have open, optimistic faces, are well built and sun-tanned, as is the young guard who rides a noble black horse and is dressed in modern clothes with an Arab Kaffiyah and Aqal on his head. He too is very athletic, sun-tanned, healthy and optimistic. (2004: 74)

Firer ignores in her description the colonialist connotations of these photographs, especially of the sun-tanned 'optimistic European' with the gun, who rides an Arab horse, and wears a Lawrence-like Arab Kaffiyah in addition to his 'modern' European clothes.

The photos are strongly connected to each other by a diagonal vector and form the most salient part of the cross-shaped composition of the double spread, constituting its main message: the conquest (which is termed 'redemption') of the ancient homeland by its returning sons.

The 'Arab' axis of the double-spread, ignored by Firer completely, is composed of two 'windows' containing 'sources' regarding the Arab indigenous population or as it is labeled, 'The Arab question.' This axis is less salient for there are no human beings in the 'windows.' The green window at the Given-Real part (bottom-right), titled 'A missing question,' is a quote from a speech titled 'A missing question,' given in

1907 by Yizhak Epstein, a Zionist leader who was born in Palestine, and who, as a linguist and an educator, studied and knew very well the different tribes that populated the region. Epstein warned the Zionist Congress that, should it go on ignoring the Arab population, whom he called 'the true masters of the Land', Zionism would be short-lived; the other end of this axis is the New-Ideal yellow window – a sheet of data showing the increase in Jewish and Arab population between 1800 and 1931. The caption, at the extreme Ideal and New spot (top-left), is a 'proleptic' account[4] which reminds one of events that would happen more than 40 years after the events specified in this double spread. It states that by 1948 the Land would be 'emptied of most of its Arabs.' The relationship between the two 'windows' can be interpreted as question and answer: The answer to the 'missing question' is that in 40 years this Real-Given 'question' would be 'solved,' for the Land would be almost 'Arab-free.' The inescapable intertextualization of this double spread with the present occupation of Palestinian lands, eviction of Palestinian residents and the constant Israeli efforts to Jewify and 'de-Arabize' the whole of Israel/Palestine, carries the message of this layout far beyond its scope.

Example No. 2: Layout as Reinforcement of the Official Narrative versus Layout as Criticism (Figure 15: *MTII*: 238–9)

This section analyzes two double spreads which depict Jewish and Palestinian refugees. Israel's refusal to reintegrate the Palestinian refugees is presented in all books as a national necessity: The Palestinians or 'Arab refugees' as they are called, could not be returned because Jewish refugees, especially from Arab countries, were brought to Israel destitute and in great masses. History and geography textbooks alike, praise the Israeli government for taking care of its own (Jewish) refugees who were settled in old Palestinian 'abandoned' villages and cities, denouncing the Arab states for not taking care of theirs.

The most salient part of the double spread is its top left, namely the New-Ideal spot that shows people who look directly into the viewer's

Figure 15 The creation of the 'Palestinian problem'

Courtesy of Israeli Government Press Office and Mapa Publishers, Israel.

eyes: a young family of Jewish newcomers, which serves in Zionist iconography as a symbol of the realization both of Zionist ideals and biblical prophesies: the ingathering of the Children of Israel in Zion. The family, whose eyes meet the viewer's in what Kress and Van Leeuwen (1996) named Demand, is seated on improvized suit-cases in the middle of an empty nameless street in 'the abandoned village of Yahud'. In the Israeli reality, their 'demand' is interpreted as a request from those who brought them to Zion to fulfill their promise and provide them with a home and livelihood.

The caption under the photograph emphasizes this promise and uses it as explanation for Israel's refusal to reintegrate the expelled Palestinians:

> In the first years of its existence the state absorbed hundreds of thousands of Olim [Jewish new-comers] who came destitute. Many of them were lodged in the abandoned Arab villages, one

> of which is the abandoned village of Yahud, where this photograph was taken in 1948.

A diagonal vector goes from the family of the newcomers – the Zionist ideal and its 'new' or recent realization – to the Real-Given spot, usually reserved for the past and the uncontested, where one sees a smaller photograph of an empty flooded street with two unrecognizable figures at the distance. The closer figure carries a huge box on its head. Showing these people from such a long distance impersonalizes them and turns them into icons of 'refugees,' symbols of a universal 'problem.'

The flooded empty street may represent any poor neighborhood anywhere in the world, when the rain surprises the authorities and washes out whole families from their miserable homes, reminding them of their 'lot.' But the caption defines what we see as 'the Palestinian problem':

> The 'Palestinian problem' has ripened in the poverty, inactivity and frustration that were the lot of the refugees in their miserable camps.

The metaphoric style of the caption equates people's misfortune caused by other people with some sick natural process and attributes their plight to destiny. The location of the photograph (Real-Given spot) and its caption, and especially the inverted commas framing 'the Palestinian problem' indicate that this 'problem' is known, undisputed and self-evident. Van Leeuwen (1996: 60) counts as one of the features of racist discourse the reference to humans by a noun that does not include the semantic feature '+ human', or the 'representation of social actors by means of a quality assigned to them, for example the quality of being a problem.'

Podeh (2002), who studied Israeli textbooks of history up until the late 1990s, comments on this photograph and praises the writer for 'not attempting to conceal the wretched, poverty-stricken conditions of the Palestinian refugee camps,' and for using 'a realistic photo.' Podeh even suggests that the fact that this photo followed a photograph of Jewish refugees about to be settled in the 'abandoned' Palestinian village Yahud 'may insinuate that there is a parallel between the Palestinians and Jews immigrating to Israel' (2002: 195). Podeh failed to see that the photos do not 'follow' each other but are placed in different corners of the double-spread: The Jewish family at the New-Ideal spot (top left) and the 'Palestinian problem' namely the flooded human-less street, at the Real-Given spot (bottom-right) which, as was explained earlier, is reserved for things past, or for down-to-earth facts. As Kress and Van Leeuwen explain (1996: 58) the diagonal vector suggests a narrative or causal links: The (absent) Palestinians who populated the Land in the past became refugees so that the Jewish refugees could repopulate their 'abandoned' villages.

Moreover, Podeh did not take into account the fact that while the Jewish refugees are represented by a family who looks straight into the viewer's eyes, the Palestinian refugees are represented by an environmental hazard, as an ecological 'problem.' Not taking the whole layout into account as one semiotic unit, prevented Podeh from picking up on the racist tone of the caption which defines human beings as 'a problem' and presents the horrible conditions faced by Palestinian refugees as devoid of human agency and responsibility. In that he obeyed the logic of the caption, according to which the 'Palestinian problem' has 'ripened' by itself, almost like a malignant growth or plague which has no accountable cause. Furthermore, Podeh does not consider the fact that unlike the 'Jewish' photo, no name, date or location is assigned to the flooded street, which could have been any flooded street in any poor neighborhood in Tel Aviv or New Orleans, thus equating a human-caused catastrophe with an ecological disaster situated nowhere or rather anywhere.

Podeh's observation about the placement of the two photographs which 'may insinuate that there is a parallel between the Palestinians and Jews immigrating to Israel' is better applied to another layout offered in the banned book, *A World of Changes* in a chapter called 'Israel – a new state' (Figure 16). This layout is an instance of what Van Leeuwen and Kress (1995: 38) define as 'Connectedness,' where 'an element is visually joined to another element through similarities of colour and shape.' The two photographs – one of the same Jewish

Figure 16 Israel – a new state *A World of Changes*
Left caption: New Olim (Jewish newcomers); Right caption: construction works in the abandoned village of Ein H'ud whose name was changed to Ein-Hod, 1949

Courtesy of Israeli Government Press Office and Maalot Publishers, Israel.

family of refugees we met in the previous example and one of an empty ruined Palestinian village being reconstructed by Jewish masons – are of identical size, identical quality and identical old black and white colours, and both occupy the centre of their respective pages. This composition suggests much more openly a parallel between the two fates, the parallel Podeh hypothesized could have been in the mind of the authors of the above double-spread.

Between the two bound pages of history presented in *A World of Changes* there is a divide. Arnheim (1988: 137) explains that centres can divide and create a bridge at the same time. The bridge also creates symmetry, in which the Given and the New support and condition one another. The dividing-bridging centre can be a mediator or a situation that distances the two margins, or it can lead from one to another, as in this example: one group is absent because the other one is present.

The non-representation of the Palestinians in their ruined village creates a 'blind spot' (Barthes, 1980: 855), from which these people are excluded but in which their existence is nevertheless assumed and 'proven' by the village's former name, mentioned in the caption. The blind spot reminds one of Lacan's example of the book which is absent from the shelf but its non-occupied slot among the other books proves its existence as a missing book.

The similarity created between the two groups of refugees in this layout is historically accountable. Both groups – the present Jews and the absent Palestinians – were victims of the same sort. Both were driven out of their original homes that were seized and appropriated by those who drove them out, in the same political circumstances – Zionism and the establishment of the state of Israel. Therefore one may see the photographs not only as 'connected' but as two parts of a 'covert taxonomy':

> A taxonomy in which the superordinate is only indicated [...] or inferred from such similarities as the viewer may perceive to exist between the subordinates [...] The proposed equivalence between the subordinates is visually realized by a symmetrical composition. The subordinates are placed at equal distance from each other, given the same size and the same orientation towards the horizontal and vertical axes [...]. For participants to be put together in a syntagm which establishes a classification means that they were judged to be members of the same class and are to be read as such. As in language, naturalization is not natural. (Van Leeuwen and Kress, 1995: 81)

The carrier in this covert taxonomy is 'an absence, a carrier that is not there but that is implied' (ibid.). This carrier may be the social exclusion of both groups of refugees, who would indeed be socially excluded for generations to come.

The two photographs constitute therefore two halves of a whole, a historic whole and a tragic whole. Like the two halves of an Alexandrine verse in classical French tragedies (Barthes, 1969), each of the halves is a partial statement on its own and does not convey the whole meaning of the tragedy or the whole story, until it receives its completion from the other half. Here, the presence of one group determines and is determined by the absence of the other.

This double tragedy is referred to in the editorial text surrounding the photograph of the Jewish 'newcomers' as they are called:

> In its first years Israel had to cope with the absorption of a big wave of new comers unprecedented in its scope in comparison with other immigration countries. [...] The problem of dwelling was solved in two major ways: 1.) The government rejected the demand to return the families of Palestinian refugees to their homes and decided to appropriate all the abandoned houses in their villages and cities and to settle there many of the Jewish newcomers from east Europe and the Arab Countries. 2.) The government also initiated the foundation of temporary tent and tin shacks camps. (p.177)

The taxonomic relations between the two photographs are reinforced by the caption at the right side of the ruined village, which makes the invisible carrier – social exclusion – quite evident:

> Construction work in the abandoned Palestinian village Ein H'ud whose name was changed to Ein Hod, 1949.

Although the notion of Palestinian desertion of the land is expressed in the terms 'abandoned village' and 'abandoned houses,' it is problematized by the photograph that shows ruined houses being reconstructed. People who abandon their homes and flee in terror do not raze their village to the ground before they leave.

This caption also reveals – through intertextualization with the Israeli historical and social texts, that are only hinted at, which of the alternatives mentioned in the main text, regarding both groups of refugees, was finally chosen: The Palestinian lands of Ein H'ud were confiscated and the remaining villagers live to this day on a small part of their previous land as 'present absentees' deprived of all rights and services, in what is legally called an 'unrecognized village.'[5]

Regarding the Jewish refugees, it is well known in Israel that the Jewish village of Ein Hod which was rebuilt on most of Ein H'ud's lands is an exclusive colony of well-known artists and a tourist site, being a hosting village for art exhibitions. Its reconstruction was never meant as a solution for destitute Jewish newcomers from Arab countries like those shown in the photograph. These participants of the so-called mass-immigration of the 1950s were lodged for years in 'temporary' refugee camps (called Maabarot) of tin shacks or tents, and as we find more explicitly in another history school book studied here (*The 20th:* 214–216):

> [...] The new comers did not choose where to live, and nobody asked for their opinion on the matter, and in many cases their allocation was done through deceit and against their will. More than once whole families refused to step down from the trucks when they had found out where they were brought to.

Thus, both groups were twice excluded – first from their home-lands and then in the new state of Israel where they finally ended up. To sum, this layout is the arresting of a process of an alternative, non-official meaning making, which equates the two groups of refugees, Jewish and Palestinian,[6] thus producing – through the creation of a covert taxonomy as well as through various levels of intertextualization – a whole new sign, semiotically as well as socially.

This layout is different from the previous one, which was the 'congealing' of the official semiosis and presented one group of refugees as 'demanding' (and deserving) human beings, at the New and Ideal spot, and the other as an impersonalized poisonous, dehumanized 'problem.'

Example No. 3: Problematizing Symbolic Meaning

This section analyzes layout as a process of problematization, where the title is problematized by the photograph and the established symbolic or iconological meaning of a photograph is problematized by it caption.

The photograph features in a chapter titled: 'The Palestinians – from refugees to a nation,' which reproduces the Israeli version of the way the Palestinians became a nation (quoted in chapter 1). The first lines of the chapter explain that, by declaring themselves a nation, the Palestinians transformed the refugee problem into an international problem (*The 20th:* 244).

In other words, the 'Palestinian problem' may have changed labels, but not its essence. However labeled, whether 'refugees' or 'nation,' the Palestinians remain a problem for Israel. The introduction to this chapter states:

> This chapter explores the development of the Palestinian problem, which stands since the beginning of the Zionist enterprise in the heart of the Middle Eastern conflict, and the attitudes within the Israeli public regarding the problem and the character of its solution. (*The 20th*: 244)

Facing this text, at the top centre of page 245, above a section titled 'The Palestinians wage a terrorist war against Israel,' is a photograph of an Israeli soldier carrying a wounded crying girl, titled: 'Galil Maimon rescuing his wounded sister' (Figure 17).

Since it was taken in 1974, this photograph has become an icon in the Israeli discourse against Palestinian terror. Its iconic value may stem from its classic universal image of 'rescue': a soldier rescuing a wounded young girl. The soldier runs from an invisible danger, which may allow several interpretations. For instance, non-Israeli audience usually interprets it as Palestinians running away from an Israeli attack, which seems compatible with the title. But Israelis never

32

הפלסטינים, מפליטים ללאום

פרק זה סוקר את התפתחות הבעיה הפלסטינית, הניצבת מאז תחילת המפעל הציוני בלב הסכסוך המזרח־תיכוני, ואת הגישות בציבור הישראלי כלפי הבעיה ואופי פתרונה.

2. הפלסטינים מנהלים מלחמת טרור נגד ישראל

Figure 17 The Palestinians: from refugees to a nation

Courtesy of Israel Sun and Mapa Publishers

interpret it as anything save as 'the real image or face of Palestinians,' which is the face of terror, whether they are a nation or not, namely as Israelis running from a Palestinian terrorist attack.

The photograph occupies the upper centre of the New-Ideal side of the double-spread, it is big, foregrounded, and therefore the most salient element and the first item to be read, namely the item that affects the reading of both the title and the editorial text.

Both the photograph and the opening paragraph send a very strong anti-Palestinian message. The fact that no Palestinians are shown in this chapter that is supposed to relate their history, only the consequences of their criminal actions, already colours their route 'from refugees to a nation' with the blood of innocent children.

Ruth Firer (2004: 80) notes that it is 'the only photograph in all the textbooks that shows blood.' However, 'in spite of the pain and the shock the photograph deals with a brother who rescues his sister, which is a positive angle of the story' (2004: 81). Firer ignores the anti-Palestinian message this photograph conveys, being concerned about the Jewish-Israeli students being exposed to such a horrifying photograph so close to their conscription.

But the anti-Palestinian message, transmitted by the photograph and the editorial text, is seriously problematized by the caption on the left side (the extreme New and Ideal) of the photograph:

> On the 16th of May 1974, 90 school-pupils were taken hostage in the course of a Palestinian terrorist attack. Following a concept that there should not be any negotiations with terrorists, an IDF force attacked the terrorists. In the course of the attack 16 children were killed. In the photograph: Galil Maimon is rescuing his wounded sister.

The caption not only relates the event depicted in the photograph but also shatters its iconological meaning by ascribing a whole different aspect to it. The term 'concept' is not only meant to blur human agency and responsibility but also to resurrect an old recurrent debate: Whether or not to negotiate with terrorists. The official Israeli policy – never negotiate with terrorists, which has always been presented in Israeli public discourse as an irrevocable principle, is presented here as 'a concept,' one of myriad possible concepts, suggesting that it may not be the only possible one or even the correct one. This caption suggests that the blame for the casualties in this attack lies with this concept that sends Israeli soldiers to kill children and harm their own sisters who might have been saved by negotiation. In view of this caption, although the photograph retains its value as an image of rescue and bravery, it has now acquired a different meaning: the soldier who may have killed some of the children in an avoidable attack, nourished by a debatable policy, this emissary of a stubborn and maybe false principle, managed to rescue his own sister, whom he may have wounded himself.[7] Galil Maimon is transformed by the caption from an emblem of Israeli heroism into a symbol of the Israeli popular leftist slogan: 'Shoot and cry,' a soldier who may have shot his own sister and then cried, trying to save her.

It seems there is a semiotic chain here, first the photograph problematizes the title, then the caption, presented as the Newest (perspective) and most Ideal (way to write history), problematizes the photograph and thereby the whole text.

The motivation for choosing this photograph may have been be just that: take a symbol, an iconic photograph, and show it in a light that may have escaped the viewers. Had the writer wanted to deliver the simplified canonical narrative, he would have chosen a much more recent and clear-cut photograph of a terrorist attack: a bombed bus, bodies scattered in the street or soldiers being killed while looking for pieces of their comrades' flesh, which are abundant in the Israeli press as well as in educational publications. Instead he (or the editor) chose to present the official message alongside this iconic photograph, which seems to complement it, and then problematize the message through the caption.

This problematization, which questions the conventional semiosis, is the essence of the new complex sign created by the layout.

Rephrasing Barthes' question regarding historical discourse (1967), one should ask then: What does this double-spread say with what it says? For as Jenkins comments,

> The histories we assign to things and people are composed, created, constituted, constructed and always situated literatures ... they

> carry within them their author's philosophy or 'take' on the world present, past and future. (1991: 86)

The answer could be: it says that being an historian means being the one who chooses to problematize the simplified story, the established collective memory. Moreover, bearing in mind Kress' comment, that the representation of a state of affairs is affected both by the interests of the producer of the sign and his interest *vis-à-vis* his assumed audience (1993: 180), a more precise version of the above Barthian question may be: what does this layout say to its special audience, high school students about to enlist in the Israeli army?

This layout may suggest that things are not what they seem: heroism is questionable, terrorism is questionable, nationalism is questionable, unquestionable official government policy is nothing more than 'a concept,' so the text you are reading may not be what it seems either.

What Barthes (1980: 818) says about individual photographs may be apposite to this layout as well: 'It is subversive not because it frightens or revolts but because it makes one think.'

Since Israel's policy towards the Palestinians has not changed, this new sign may serve the students as a 'thinking device' (Wertsch, 1991) about the present political situation and their near- future part in it.

Example No. 4. Disrupting Chronology: The Relations between Given and New as Argument and Criticism: Israel and the Neighboring Arab Countries

Van Leeuwen and Kress argue (1995: 27) that the polarization of Given and New is ideological and may not always reflect what is Given and New chronologically. Pages 234–235 in *The 20th* present, in a sub-chapter titled: 'The Arabs determine Israel's status in the world,' an account of the relationships between Israel and the Third World. At the top-centre, a photograph shows two tall young black men, in khaki uniforms and large Safari hats, looking attentively at a shorter white woman, who faces the reader, holding an orange-tree branch and apparently showing it to the men (Figure 18). In Van Leeuwen's terms (2000) the black men are the patients of the action and the woman is

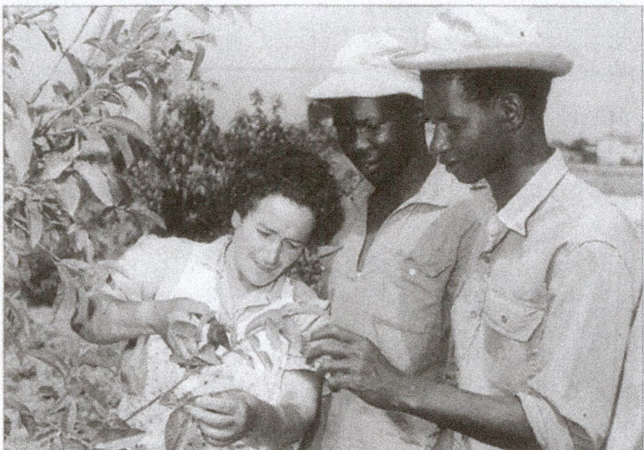

סטודנטים אפריקאים רבים הגיעו לישראל להתמחות במיגזרים שבהם היה לישראל ידע ייחודי בלעדי: השקיה, פיתוח המידבר, תיכנון קהילתי ואזורי. הסטודנטים הנראים כאן לומדים שיעור בטיפול בעצי פרי.

אשנב

"חוק ירושלים", אוגוסט 1980

לעיתים דואגת ישראל לערער בעצמה את מעמדה הבינלאומי על־ידי מעשים בלתי־שקולים. דוגמה מובהקת לכך היא "חוק ירושלים", שעבר בכנסת באוגוסט 1980 ביוזמתה של גאולה כהן מתנועת ה"תחייה". חוק יסוד זה בא לקבוע שהעיר המאוחדת תישאר לנצח בירתה של מדינת ישראל. רוב המשקיפים ראו בכך "שער עצמי". לא זו בלבד שהחוק היה מיותר, שכן ירושלים המזרחית סופחה ממילא באורח רשמי מיד אחרי מלחמת ששת הימים; אלא שהוא העלה את ירושלים על סדר היום הבינלאומי, נתפס כהתגרות בערבים ובדעת הקהל העולמית, וסופו שהשיג את ההיפך ממה שביקש להשיג: הוא החליש את מעמד ישראל בעיר הבירה שלה. למרות זאת, החוק עבר ברוב עצום, שכן מפלגת העבודה שישבה אז באופוזיציה לא העזה להצביע נגדו, מחשש שתיחשד בחוסר מחויבות מספקת לעניין ירושלים.

התוצאות היו צפויות מראש: הגוש הערבי־מוסלמי יצא בשצף־קצף נגד החוק וישראל הוקעה בכל פורום בינלאומי אפשרי, לרבות מועצת הביטחון של האו"ם. גרוע מזאת, 12 מדינות לטינו־אמריקניות וכן הולנד, שהמשיכו, על אף כל הלחצים, להחזיק את שגרירויותיהם בירושלים, נטשו בזו אחר זו את הבירה.

פתחו את שגרירויותיהן בירושלים, אך לא תמיד הן תמכו בה בזירה הבינלאומית. הסיבה היתה המלחמה המתמשכת במזרח התיכון.

4 את מעמד ישראל בעולם קובעים יחסיה עם הערבים

דווקא הניצחון הגדול במלחמת ששת הימים סימן את תחילת תהליך ההידרדרות של תדמית ישראל בעולם. מצד אחד היו הכל משוכנעים כי לישראל הצבא, המודיעין והטייסים הטובים בעולם. מצד שני, המצוינות הזאת שמה קץ לתחושות האשם שחוללה השואה. הישראלים נתפסו עתה כחזקים, והפלסטינים – כחלשים. האיבה לישראל ולציונות הפכה לאופנה בקרב האינטליגנציה של השמאל.

תופעה זו צברה תאוצה והתרחבה בעקבות מלחמת יום הכיפורים. מדינות ערב גילו את עוצמת נשק הנפט, ואירופה גילתה עד כמה פגיעה כלכלתה. מדינות אירופה הגיבו בבהלה. בעוד הקרבות מתחוללים בחזית הקפיאו האנגלים את מכירות הנשק לישראל; הגרמנים, האיטלקים והספרדים סירבו לאפשר למטוסי התובלה האמריקנים, בדרכם לישראל, להשתמש בשדות התעופה שלהם; צרפת מכרה מטוסי מיראז' ללוב, אימנה טייסים מצרים ותמכה בגלוי במתקפה הערבית. משבר הנפט הפך את הסכסוך הישראלי־ערבי לבעיה אירופית כאובה: ישראל הצטיירה כגורם המאיים על שגשוגה הכלכלי של היבשת.

המתקפה הדיפלומטית הערבית הצליחה

234

Figure 18 The Arabs determine Israel's relationships with the world

Courtesy of the Lavon Institute and Mapa Publishers, Israel.

the agent. The whole scene is situated in an orchard. The explanation is given in the caption, on the right side of the photograph:

> [In the 1950s] African students arrived at Israel in order to specialize in domains in which Israel had a unique and exclusive knowledge: irrigation, the development of the desert, community and regional planning. The students shown here are having a lesson about the maintenance of fruit trees.

With this image in mind the reader should turn to the editorial text right under the photograph:

> The diplomatic Arab attack succeeded beyond expectations in the Third World, and especially in Africa, who suffered more than anybody from the head-spinning rise of petrol prices. Already following the Six Days War Guinea had cut off her relationships with Israel [...] It seemed that Nasser's dream to drive Israel out of Africa was about to come true [...] Almost all the African states broke up one by one their relationships with Israel.

The message conveyed by the title of the chapter, the editorial text and the photograph hovering above it is the well-known Israeli political message at the time: We helped them grow oranges and they betrayed us (20 years later) because of Arab conniving and the price of oil. However, even before turning to the editorial text the reader is drawn to another, more salient, text. In a strongly famed green 'window' presented as the 'given' and 'real,' usually reserved for the past and the known, we are confronted with a 'proleptic' account[8] of an event that happened more than 10 years after the events reported in the main text and about 30 years after the event depicted in the photograph: The 'Jerusalem Law' August 1980.

> Sometimes Israel herself takes care to undermine her own international status with her indiscretion. A perfect example of such indiscretion is 'The Jerusalem Law' that was passed in the Knesset in 1980. [...] All [international] observers saw in this

> law an 'own goal.' Not only was the law unnecessary [...] but it was perceived as an open provocation against the Arabs and the whole world. [...] The results were expected: the Arab block reacted with foaming rage and Israel was denounced in every possible international forum. [...] 12 Latin-American states and Holland [...] abandoned the Capital [Jerusalem] one by one.

The framed green window creates an immediate clash with the photograph and contradicts the editorial text, which is bound to be read after it, being less salient and presented as New in relation to the green 'window.' The strong framing, achieved through disconnection and colour, emphasizes the discontinuity between the elements and at the same time indicates that though they seem separate, they may affect one another (Van Leeuwen and Kress, 1995: 34). As Arnheim emphasizes (1988: 55), 'The frame defines the picture as [...] a centre that exerts its dynamic effects upon its surroundings.'

The unconventional Given-New relationships of the different chunks of history on the page raise the question of implication or of what Grice calls Implicature (1989), for it is a diversion from the expected 'orderly manner' of the chronological representation in history textbooks. As Grice explains, every transgression from convention has implicature, or as Kress puts it, is motivated by interest. Hence, placing the account of future events as first on the page, in the Given-Real part and in such a strong frame, is bound to be motivated by interest, for it becomes the ground on which the editorial text is understood. The editorial text, discussing the 1970s, is read in the light of Israeli indiscretions posterior to it (1980), which entailed international denouncements and the loss of friendly allies. Therefore, reading the editorial text after reading the green 'window,' one may reason that perhaps it was not Nasser's conniving that made the African countries break up their friendship with Israel but some (unmentioned) Israeli indiscretion such as would have been committed 'sometime' in the future, and which made Israel hateful in the eyes of the world.

This unusual order may also imply that history repeats itself, and therefore the ordering of historic events on the page is inconsequential. The past is not different from the present or the future, and the given or known is neither given nor known, just as the new is anything but new.

It may further imply that Israel learns nothing from past experience, as is suggested at the end of the double-spread, which gives another proleptic account, this time of the Oslo agreements between Israel and the Palestinian authorities in 1994:

> Never has Israel's position been as bright and glamorous as after the Oslo Accords [...]. Will the window of opportunities remain open, or will it be closed again? The answer is first and foremost in the hands of Israel itself. (p.289)

The historian's interpretation of the past, expressed in the layout, is explicitly intertextualized with the present and with the future.

Conclusion

This chapter showed that layout is a powerful means not only for perpetuating official narratives but also for creating alternative interpretations and weaving the writers' own perceptions into the official educational discourse. Layout allows 'punctuating' or puncturing conventional semiosis, breaking taboos and conveying some daring messages, which – it must be emphasized – may be revealed only by a multimodal analysis. Layout enables new meanings to be inscribed over old conventional ones without erasing them altogether, thus turning them into one layer in a sort of Palimpsest (Genette, 1982). This Palimpsest is the new complex sign created by layout, which 'provides new elements and new resources for the further process of ongoing semiosis' (Kress, 2000: 152).

4

PROCESSES OF LEGITIMATION IN REPORTS ABOUT MASSACRES

On the Desire To Be Precise

Nathan Zach

And then there was a major exaggeration in the body count
There were some who counted about a hundred and some
counted several hundreds
And this one said I counted thirty six burnt women
And his friend said you are wrong, it was only eleven
And the error is deliberate and political, not accidental
And since I am started I will also say
That only ten women were slaughtered because two were shot
And there is one that is questionable and it is not clear
If she were slaughtered, raped or merely slashed in the belly
And also in the matter of the children the last word has not yet
been said
Everyone admits that six were crucified and one was tortured
Before his head was crushed but who will assure us
That all those who had disappeared with nobody knowing
their whereabouts
Were indeed thrown – all of them or some of them – into the sea
Because if that is so – how can we account for the blood stains?

With things like these one should not lend oneself to
exaggerations
And one should recognize and beware: this is a matter of life
and death
And one might – God forbid – err in the reports
For such has, my learned friend, happened before.
And all that day great disputation was in that place
And if it had not been for the terrible stench that rose there
They would have come to complete precision – or to blows
Since the desire to be precise is no less human
Than the desire to kill, to rape, to crush, and to exterminate
Your enemy, your opponent, your next door neighbour,
the suspicious stranger,
Or just
Every man, woman or child in the world.[1]

Introduction

During the 1948 war, called the 'War of Independence' by Israelis, and '*Nakba*' by Palestinians, nearly 800,000 Palestinians were uprooted from their land, 530 villages leveled to the ground and 11 urban neighborhoods vacated of their inhabitants (Pappé, 2006).

After the establishment of the state of Israel, the Israeli army committed massacres both of Israeli-Palestinian citizens and of Palestinian refugees in their Jordanian villages and refugee camps.

Although, as Rabinowitz (2001: 74) notes, 'The Palestinian tragedy, with 750,000 refugees and displaced persons, colossal loss of homes, land, means of livelihood and honour, remains consistently silenced in Israeli historiography,' these facts are not entirely absent from current Israeli history textbooks. Along with the persistent claim that most Palestinians fled on urgings by their leaders to leave their homes, most books mention that some of them were indeed expelled or massacred. Some textbooks (especially the most recent ones published in 2004, 2006 and 2009) tend to present the massacres as routine battles or military operations; other books view the massacres as transgression from official plans but legitimate them by the positive outcome they have brought about – the establishment and maintenance of a coherent and secure Jewish state with a Jewish majority.

A 'massacre' is defined as:

1) The act or an instance of killing a number of usually helpless or unresisting human beings under circumstances of atrocity or cruelty.
2) A cruel or wanton murder.[2]

This chapter examines reports about massacres in seven Israeli secondary school history books and one civic studies school book, all published between 1998 and 2009. It aims to show that massacres are legitimated by their outcome, through a complex rhetoric that involves both verbal and visual means.

The study uses theories and analytical tools of Critical Discourse Analysis, Social Semiotics and Multimodal Analysis to examine the linguistic, discursive, generic and multimodal strategies of legitimation employed in these school books. The analysis is based primarily on the works of Van Dijk (1997), Martin Rojo and Van Dijk (1997), Van Leeuwen (2000, 2007, 2008), Van Leeuwen and Wodak (1999), Hodge and Kress (1993) and Coffin (1997, 2006). The argument I wish to put forward in this chapter is that Israeli mainstream school books often implicitly legitimate the killing of Palestinians as an effective tool to preserve a secure Jewish state with a Jewish majority.

Three events that involved intentional or wanton killing of helpless Palestinians are reported in some Israeli mainstream school history books:

1) The Dier Yassin massacre in 1948
2) The Qibya massacre in 1953
3) The Kaffer Kassem massacre in 1956

In addition, one event of intentional killing of Jews is also mentioned: the Altalena affair of 1948. Following are details of the massacres as they appear in history books written for the general public, not designed for primary or secondary instruction.

1) The Dier Yassin massacre, 9 April 1948: on this date, Dier Yassin, a village west of Jerusalem that had reached a non-aggression agreement with the Hagana (the official pre-state armed forces), was attacked by troops from the 'dissident' underground groups Etzel and Lehi. The perpetrators massacred most of the inhabitants of the village. The number of victims – still debated today – was estimated at between 110 and 245. Pappé (2006: 91) explains the debate: 'Recent research has brought down the accepted number of people massacred at Dier Yassin from 170 to 93 [but] at the time of the massacre the Jewish leadership proudly announced a high number of victims so as to make Dier Yassin the epicentre of the catastrophe – a warning to all Palestinians that a similar fate awaited them if they refused to abandon their homes and take flight.' The number 245 was endorsed at the time by Jewish, international and Palestinian authorities. The Etzel radio declared on the April 14, five days after the massacre, that most of the other villages were evacuated thanks to their action in Dier Yassin: 'In one stroke we have changed the strategic situation of the capital,' it declared proudly (Morris, 2002: 159). The massacre was marked as 'a crucial accelerator' of the evacuation of Arab cities and villages up to June 1948, especially in central and south Palestine (ibid. p.160).

The village was populated the following summer by Jewish newcomers, despite objection from scholars such as Martin Buber and Ernst Simon, who believed this massacre was 'a black stain on the honour of the Hebrew nation' and therefore the village should be left empty as 'a horrible tragic symbol of the war, a sign of warning to our people, that no military or practical needs should justify murders of that sort.'[3]

Dier Yassin has not yet become 'history' in Israeli consciousness. It is still 'a living event, an event whose meanings are still negotiated, whose reference invokes strong emotions and whose discourse is loaded with speech acts of threat, blame and justification' (Dayan and Katz, 1992, quoted in Blum-Kulka, 2000).[4] One example of this discourse is a TV report from April 1997, analyzed by Blum-Kulka. The report shows a demonstration of Palestinians who wished to commemorate the day of the massacre in the Orthodox Jewish neighbourhood of Har Nof that was built of the razed village of Dier Yassin. The television reporter took a rather subversive stance on the matter by presenting the different perspectives 'in a blunder': the accusatory one and the justificatory one, and let the viewer decide how to interpret this report. Regarding the number of casualties and the identity of the guilty parties, the report presented the unresolved controversy by stating:

> More than 125 inhabitants were murdered in the course of its conquest by the forces of the Hagana, the Irgun and the Lehi. Our reporter Yotam Binur says that years afterwards the prime minister Ben Gurion apologised for the murder but military officials say the massacre caused a massive escape of Arabs from their villages in Israel and enabled the establishment of a Jewish majority.

Then the camera turns to the Palestinian-Arab MP Hashim Mahmid who claims:

> Tens and hundreds of people were murdered here and everybody should know that. One mustn't forget that such cases had happened. My people also have memory. They also have the right to remember just like the Jewish people has.

By naming the Hagana as one of the murdering forces the reporter is clearly taking side in the ongoing discussion about the Hagana's reponsibility for the massacre; the apology made by Ben Gurion to King Abdallah of Jordan means that he acknowledged the crime. The militaries believe it was a 'founding crime' for it had positive effects for Israel, and the Palestinian perspective voiced by MP Mahmid is that this massacre was part of the Palestinian Shoa.

2) The Qibya massacre (based on Morris, 2000: 176–178): On the night between 12 and 13 October 1953, Palestinian infiltrators from Jordan killed a woman and her two children at their home in Yahud (a former Palestinian village cleansed in 1948 and repopulated by Jewish immigrants). Prior to this killing, IDF Unit 101 had raided the Burij refugee camp in the Gaza strip, killing 20 people. The Yahud infiltrators escaped to the village of Rantis, 5 km north of Qibya. The Prime Minister, chief of staff and other generals decided, without consulting the cabinet, to retaliate. The massacre, called reprisal or retaliation in the public discourse, was committed by Unit 101 which was founded for that purpose, headed by Major Ariel Sharon. The official version claims Sharon was ordered to clear the village and demolish some houses. However, Morris found out the order was 'to commit destruction and maximum killing in order to drive all the inhabitants out of their homes,' that were to be demolished. 69 people were killed and 45 houses demolished. As news of the massacre emerged, the Israeli government, especially Prime Minister David Ben Gurion, denied it, stating that all soldiers were at their bases that night and that the massacre was committed by farmers enraged by robberies: These farmers, the announcement said, were holocaust survivors and newcomers from Arab countries where revenge is common. Later Ben Gurion said the soldiers did not know there were people in the houses that night and that most of the victims were persons who were buried under their demolished homes. Later still he justified the reprisals saying they restored security both to border-settlements and to central Tel Aviv (*Haaretz* 15 December 1955. Quoted in *50 Years of Wars and Hopes*, 2004: 245)

The only one who publicly denounced the massacre on moral grounds was Professor Yeshayahu Leibovitch (1903–94), one of Israel's most prominent scientists and scholars, a devout Jew and a major militant for peace and social justice. Right after the massacre, Leibovitch published an article called 'After Qibya', in which he concluded that since Zionism has applied the value of sanctity to mundane matters such as the state, the land and the weapon, it endowed them with absolute moral legitimacy: 'If the people and their security, if the homeland and its peace, are the holy of holies and if the sword is Israel's rock – then Qibya is possible and permissible as well [...] this is the horrible punishment for the grave sin of taking God's name in vain.'

3) The Kaffer Kassem massacre (based on Rosenthal, 2000, Segev, 2006, Karpel, 2008[5]): Following upon the establishment of the state of Israel in 1948, the Arab-Palestinian citizens were placed under military government, requiring permits to go in and out of their homes. Curfews were laid every night from 19:00 to 6:00 in the morning. In the lead-up to the 1956 war with Egypt, the government and the army devised a plan (Plan Mole), to divert attention from their true intentions and to 'encourage' Palestinians living near the border to flee to Jordan, and subsequently block their way back. On the first day of the war, the army decided to advance the daily curfew on Palestinian towns and villages from 19:00 to 17:00 but the village Mukhtars were only advised of the change half-an-hour before its onset, so they could not notify the farmers working in the fields or outside the villages. Nevertheless, the order given by Army Colonel Shadmi was to shoot and kill anyone who would be out after 17:00.

Although most junior officers decided not to obey the order, Lieutenant Gavriel Dahan, the commander at the western entrance to Kaffer Kassem, stopped the carts, bicycles and trucks that brought workers back from the fields, ordered the people and their families to stand in line and instructed his soldiers to 'cut them down.' Within an hour, 47 people – among them 11 children and 17 women – were killed at the northern and western entrances and in the village itself. The bodies were hurriedly buried during the night in the neighboring village of Jaljoulia by villagers forced to do the task.

After six weeks during which the Israeli government denied the event and censored its publication, there was no alternative but to charge the soldiers with murder.[6] The defendants claimed they had obeyed the orders of their superiors but the judge ruled they should have disobeyed a manifestly unlawful order and sentenced them to jail terms varying between 7 and 17 years. The commanding officer was charged with a fine of 2 pounds. They were all released by December 1959 by presidential amnesty and their ranks were restored to them. Gavriel Dahan himself has been appointed delegate of the Jewish Agency in Paris. In 1994, the mayor of Kaffer Kassem, Sheikh Darwish Nimer, wrote a letter to Prime Minister Yitzhak Rabin requesting state recognition of the massacre but received no answer.[7]

The Kaffer Kassem massacre is remembered in Jewish-Israeli consciousness mainly for being the source for the court's unprecedented ruling against compliance with 'manifestly unlawful orders.' In Kaffer Kassem itself it is commemorated every year, but Israeli officials rarely attend the ceremony. In 1999, Education minister Yossi Sarid decided the massacre should be commemorated in Israeli schools, a requirement renewed by minister Tamir in February 2009, right after the raids on Gaza. Tamir demanded that schools commemorate this massacre for it was 'a milestone of Israeli society that has inculcated in generations of commanders and soldiers the moral boundaries within which they have to operate' *(Haaretz*, 16 February 2009). Professor Tamir, like most of the school books studied here,[8] failed to mention that the verdict was not carried out to its term and said nothing about the suffering of the villagers.

As Uri Avneri wrote in *Maariv* (1996):

> The personal stories of the survivors of Kaffer Kassem sound like the stories of the Jews from the Valley of Death; stories that every Arab child knows by heart and no Jewish child in Israel has ever heard of. (quoted in Rosenthal 2006: 79).

The Nature of Legitimation: Theoretical Background

The theoretical basis of the following analysis, regarding the nature of legitimation and its various types, is founded primarily on works from the fields of social semiotics and critical discourse analysis (Martin Rojo and Van Dijk, 1997; Van Dijk, 1997; Van Leeuwen and Wodak, 1999; Van Leeuwen, 2007, 2008).

Martin Rojo and Van Dijk (1997: 560–561) define legitimation as the act of 'attributing acceptability to social actors, actions and social relations within the normative order,' in contexts of 'controversial actions, accusations, doubts, critique or conflict over groups relations, domination and leadership.' Legitimation is related to the speech act of defending oneself which 'requires as one of its appropriateness conditions that the speaker is providing good reason, grounds or acceptable motivations for past or present action that has been or could be criticized by others [...]. Institutions justify their actions when they fear disagreement or condemnation, challenge or attack' (Van Dijk, 1997: 256).

In the case of massacres, legitimation is top-down: the state legitimates its actions downward 'using norms and values that are ostensible in the specific culture' (Van Dijk, 1997: 255). When the actions of the rulers are compatible with cultural and traditional norms and values, and can be accounted for, they are not legitimated. For instance, Israeli cleansing actions that involved massacre but were not controversial, do not undergo a process of legitimation in school books. They are legitimated a priori and are usually termed 'operations.' Such are the cleansing operations of the Palestinian cities Lydda and Ramla in 1948, or of villages near Dier Yassin such as Kastal and Hulda, which as the books inform us, were effected 'according to the official plan Dalet' (*AHH*: 314; Naveh et al. 2009), and with the tacit consent of Prime Minister Ben Gurion (*The 20th*). Nevertheless, details that would make the students question the orders from above, such as the fact that 426 men, women and children were indeed murdered in Lydda and Ramla, 176 of them inside the mosque, and that 50,000 people were driven out in the night, 'stripped of their belongings' (Pappé, 2006: 167), are omitted from the reports.

The Ideological Basis of the Legitimation of Massacres in Israeli School Books

The inclusion of massacres in school books may have the semblance of a very courageous educational act. However, the analysis shows that although the books may denounce the actual manner of killing, all the reports use semiotic devices to build up legitimating claims that justify the outcome. Most of these claims stem from the Zionist-Israeli ideology which '[...] propelled by the myth of a pure nation state inherently harbors the possibility of ethnic cleansing in situations of mixed geography' (Yiftachel, 2006: 60).

The goal of achieving an Arab-free land is never spelled out explicitly in Israeli school books, but the crucial importance of a Jewish majority is, as in the following closing paragraph of the chapter that includes the report on Dier Yassin massacre (*The 20th*: 195):

> In the eyes of the Israelis the flight of the Arabs [enhanced by the Dier Yassin massacre] solved a horrifying demographic problem and even a moderate person such as [the first president] Weitzman spoke about it as 'a miracle.'

Ideology has two contradictory components, solidarity and power, which nevertheless 'mingle with complex promiscuity [...]. While 'solidarity blurs differences, power exacerbates differences' (Hodge and Kress, 1993: 157). Hodge and Kress add that the ideological complex of solidarity and power provides the means of legitimation for rulers and institutions, especially where practices of discrimination are concerned.

Zionist-Israeli ideology, professing Jewish historical rights on the land of Israel/Palestine, Arab threat and the need to keep the regime of segregation for Jewish security, legitimates the ethnic inequality and Jewish dominance in Israel, which is at the base of the legitimation of expulsion and massacres.

Legitimating Norms and Laws

> The sign of legitimacy is the people's consensus. (Lyotard, 1984: 30)
>
> The norm is what turns the prescription into a law. (Lyotard, 1988: 142)

In legitimating controversial actions, the writer has to convince readers that the shared norms were appropriate in each particular situation and that the event was one of the actions specified by the norms as permissible or required (Finlayson, 2005: 36–37). Legitimation, says Van Leeuwen, is 'founded on the principle of right and wrong [...] justified according to culturally specific values and norms' (Van Leeuwen, 2007: 101). That is why a decontextualized analysis of legitimation is impossible. Each group has its own norms and values that organize the actions of the group and legitimate them (Van-Dijk, 1997: 257).

Lyotard (1985: 31) argues that the grand narratives of emancipation (such as Zionism, NPE) allow people to pass judgment on foreigners or on those within the society who don't share its ideals on the basis of laws which others may not recognize. Lyotard gives as examples the conquests of the crusaders, who executed all those who did not believe in their missions, the persecution of communists in the USA, and one should add: the way Israeli law treats non-Jewish foreigners such as host workers, non-Jewish minorities within the state of Israel and above all – the Palestinians in the occupied territories 'whose lives are dispensable with impunity.'[9]

Yiftachel explains that both segregation and justification are needed to maintain the system of disproportionate Jewish control and to marginalize rival civil agendas (Yiftachel, 2006: 105). This need – accepted and justified by the majority of Israeli Jews[10] – is constantly translated to laws, policies, discourses and practices (ibid.: 115). However, many times the practices precede the law that legalizes them. Van Leeuwen (2007: 97) notes that 'contemporary law makers increasingly believe that, if most people are doing it, it cannot be wrong, and should be legalized.' In Israel, although Palestinians – both citizens and non-citizens in the occupied territories – are discriminated by law, many times the discriminatory practices and harsh measures precede the laws that legalize them, overriding court ruling.[11] However, most oppressive practices against Palestinians are justified by laws or by norms that the Supreme Court finds very hard to fight.[12] Such are the law of citizenship or the norm of collective 'punishments' and extrajudicial assassinations of Palestinians[13]; this conduct is inconceivable in relation to Jewish citizens, or even to Jewish terrorists, nor would it match norms of appropriate behaviour or justice in other democratic institutions.[14] Hence, when one says an action is aligned with norms we must ask: whose norms?

Legitimation is often accomplished by persuasive (or manipulative) discourse, which describes actions as beneficial for the group or for society as a whole, reinterpreting these actions as being acceptable, or at least justified as morally or politically defensible in the 'present circumstances', namely during crisis or in the face of external threat (Martin Rojo and Van Dijk, 1997).

The claims that legitimate the killing of Palestinians in school books often present the massacres as 'norm-conformative actions' according to norms that are both Israeli-specific and generally Western, such as the 'war on terror' or the protection of citizens. For example, 'Infiltrators penetrated Israel to commit terror acts, and the state was forced to protect its citizens' (*AHH*: 331, Qibya massacre), or 'The operations [one of which was the Qibya massacre] were also intended to strengthen the feeling of security and the morale of the citizens of Israel, who suffered from a constant threat on their lives – at home, in the fields, on the road and on excursions' (Domka et al. 2009: 160).

The Israeli-specific norms often rely on the authority of the Bible. Thus, the justification of the Qibya massacre as an 'appropriate response' to the murder of a Jewish mother and her two children, is compatible with 'biblical' norms such as 'kill whosoever sets out to kill you,' with its modern interpretations of deterrence, and the 'eye-for-eye' norm of revenge.[15] This norm, based on a skewed interpretation to the biblical eye-for-eye principle, still serves as rationale for Israeli actions against Palestinians today.[16] This traditional interpretation proves Bourdieu's remark, (quoted in Van Leeuwen 2005: 55), that 'tradition is learned ignorance,' for this phrase does not encourage revenge but rather making amends: Its meaning is that the injured party should get financial compensation equivalent to the damage.[17] However, the literal interpretation of eye for eye as retaliation is completely admissible in Israeli culture and politics though it may not necessarily conform to universal norms. As Van Leeuwen maintains, 'legitimation is always the legitimation of the practices of specific institutional orders, by means of particular norms, values and "facts"' (2007: 92).

Here are two examples regarding the Qibya massacre and other such legitimated 'reprisals':

Domka et al. (p.159) who specify that 'between 2,700 and 5,000 Palestinian infiltrators, most of them unarmed, were killed during the years 1949–1956 by the forces of the IDF [and] PM Moshe Sharet criticized the behaviour of the IDF towards these infiltrators,' nevertheless end the chapter about the killing of these mostly unarmed infitrators with the coda (p.161): 'These actions contributed to the strengthening of the feeling of security among Israeli citizens.'

One of the questions following this chapter presents a newspaper from 1956 whose main headline is:

> 50 Egyptians were killed, 40 were taken prisoners – the greatest operation since the War of Independence.

And the questions are:

1) In what way can such a headline influence the morale of Israeli citizens?
2) Why did Israel choose to carry out 'reprisals,' though they often involved the killing of innocent people?

The obvious answers, according to Israeli norms, would be: retaliation and deterrence, which contributed to the morale of Israeli citizens according to this book.

In the same line, though less bluntly, Naveh et al. (2009: 205) pose a question regarding these 'reprisals':

> Do you think the reprisals were enough to deter the Arabs from acting against Israel?

Types of Legitimation

Van Leeuwen (2007) distinguishes four key categories of legitimation:

1) *Mythopoesis*: Legitimation conveyed through narratives whose outcome rewards legitimate actions and punishes non-legitimate actions.
2) *Rationalization*: Legitimation 'by reference to the goals, the uses and the effects of institutionalized social action' (2007: 91).

3) *Moral evaluation*: Legitimation by reference to discourses of value or value systems, which are not made explicit and debatable but are only hinted at, by appraisals that 'trigger a moral concept' (2007: 97).
4) *Authorization*: Legitimation by reference to the authority of tradition, custom and law, and of persons in whom institutional authority of some kind is vested.

Following are examples of legitimation according to these categories:

1) *Mythopoesis*

In the following reports, the telling of the event (its suzjet) is governed by 'mythological logic,' which is 'a logical model capable of overcoming a contradiction' (Noth, 1995: 376). The story of the massacre unfolds in such a way that the negative act is counterbalanced or even rewarded by positive consequences such as victory or rescue, and the conflict between evil and good results in the victory of good, namely in positive consequences for Israel, as per the following:

Dier Yassin massacre: the slaughter of friendly Palestinians brought about the flight of other Palestinians which enabled the establishment of a coherent Jewish state (all books).

Qibya massacre: the slaughter of Palestinians in their homes brought about some confidence to Jews in their homes (*AHH*) and restored morale and dignity to the IDF (*50 Years*, 2004; *Face* 2006; Naveh et al. 2009).[18]

Kaffer Kassem massacre: 1) A Barbaric crime brought about an enlightened verdict (*AHH*; Domka et al. 2009; Naveh et al. 2009).

2) The slaughter – enabled by the military government and its permanent situation of curfew – was the starting point of a process that ended (many years later) with the abolition of this same military government (*The 20th,* 1998).

Effect-Oriented Legitimation

Coffin (1997) explains that in history textbooks events are appraised in their capacity to bring about good and bad, big or small, changes, hence they can be legitimated by their effects. In effect-oriented legitimation 'purposefulness is looked at from the other end, as something that turned out to exist in hindsight, rather than as something that was, or could have been, planned beforehand' (Van Leeuwen, 2007: 103).

Effect-oriented legitimation is part of instrumental rationalization, itself part of rationalization legitimation. Instrumental rationality legitimates actions 'because they correspond to the criterion of utility, namely 'in reference to purpose or function they serve, needs they fill' (Van Leeuwen, 2007: 105). Instrumental rationalization is more common in legitimating massacres than theoretical rationality which legitimates practices by reference to a natural order of things and is grounded in whether or not the action is founded on some kind of truth, on 'the way things are,' e.g. 'the only thing the Arabs understand is force' (*MTII*, 1999: 273, Qibya massacre).

Since most books do not present the massacres as purposeful actions, the reasons for the killing are usually concealed and the effects foregrounded, serving as justification. For instance, 'In the months after that [the Dier Yassin massacre] the Jewish community was privileged with many military successes' (*JIP*: 284). The word 'privileged' is the same as 'rewarded' in Hebrew and according to Jewish and other traditions that believe in rewards for good deeds, one is rewarded for his good actions. Hence effect-oriented legitimation is compatible with the 'mythological logic' mentioned before. Likewise Bar-Navi (1998) writes in *The 20th* that the massacre did not 'inaugurate' the flight of the Arabs but 'accelerated it greatly.' By using such festive verbs to describe the consequences of the massacre the books implicitly evaluates it as a positive thing according to Israeli norms and values.

In the same line, the massacre of Qibya 'restored the feeling of security and the morale of the citizens of Israel.' (Domka et al. 2009: 160).

Only *50 Years* and *Face*, with their right-wing military orientation, mention the restoration of the sense of security as a reason for the 'reprisals' and as their cause thus emphasizing the success of these operations. *50 Years* presents a 'sun' of factors that encouraged the government to authorize the 'reprisals' and points to the 'strengthening of the morale' as one of them (p. 243). It ends the chapter by enumerating the successes of these operations saying:

'The 101 unit restored the morale and dignity to the army and helped it become a deterring vigorous army whose long arm can reach the enemy deep in its own territory,' (*50 Years:* 244).

Face counts 'restoring the security of the Israeli population, both morally and practically' as a major reason for these actions, and as one of their achievements as well (pp.294, 297).

The legitimating effects are never the direct results of the massacres but what they brought about, often without the knowledge of their perpetrators and without there being a 'law-like connection' between the actions and their consequences. (Ricoeur, 1983: 136–137). Ricoeur explains, quoting Von Wright, that there is a difference between doing something and bringing something about, in which case the action is not the direct cause of its results. 'Bringing about concerns actions by means of which we do something so that something else happens [...] including the things that we bring about through other people' (p.138). In reports of massacres the latter applies.

In effect-oriented legitimation 'those involved might be able to predict the outcome, they cannot fully bring it about through their own actions. There is no identity between the agent of the action whose purpose is to be constructed, and the agent of the action that constitutes the purpose itself' (Van Leeuwen, 2007: 103).

Within rationalization legitimation we can also find use-oriented legitimation and means-oriented legitimation, realized in clauses with 'facilitating' processes such as 'allow,' 'promote,' 'help,' 'teach,' 'build,' 'facilitate' (Van Leeuwen, 2007: 103). For example:

> The escape of the Arabs solved a horrifying demographic problem. (*The 20th*: 195)

Palestinians' panicked escape that solved the 'horrifying demographic problem' was brought about by the impact of the massacre of Dier Yassin, or by the rumours that followed it, an outcome which was not entirely foreseen though it was very welcome by its perpetrators. Menahem Begin, the Etzel commander, wishing to legitimate the Dier

Yassin massacre, wrote in his book *The Revolt* (1951: 164): 'The massive flight [enhanced by the Dier Yassin massacre] soon developed into a maddened, uncontrolled stampede. Of the almost 800,000 who lived on the present territory of the state of Israel, only some 165,000 are still there. The political and economic significance of this development can hardly be overestimated.'

Legitimation through Moral Evaluation

In most of the reports studied here, morality and political utility are bound together. Some reports speak of 'moral and political implications' of the massacres or about their being a 'moral and political burden' (*The 20th*, *MTII*) etc. As Van Leeuwen (2007: 105) argues, 'in contemporary discourse, moralization and rationalization keep each other at arm's length [...]. In the case of rationalization, morality remains oblique and submerged, even though no rationalization can function as legitimation without it.'

The reports that legitimate the massacres on moral grounds resort to legitimation through conformity to norms and the authority of tradition, by calling the slaughter 'a punitive action' (*AHH*) and by emphasising the massacre was an appropriate response to terror.

A specific form of moral evaluation used in these reports is naturalization, which in fact 'denies morality and replaces moral and cultural orders with the 'natural order' when 'natural actually means justified or true' (Van Leeuwen, 2007: 99). In such cases, 'morality and nature become entangled' (ibid.). *The 20th* (p.184), for instance, brings as a legitimating claim the words of Nathan Yellin Mor, the commander of the Dier Yassin killers from Lehi underground organization, who apparently did not know the slaughter was going to take place and was very surprised by the news:

> I know that in the heat of battle things like that happen, and I know that people do not preplan it in advance. They kill because their friends have been killed and they want an instant revenge. I know that many nations and armies do such things.

Naturalization is close to what Van Leeuwen terms the authority of conformity, which 'relies on normality and is based on the knowledge that everybody does that.' In such cases, 'the answer to the "why" question is [...] "because that's what everybody else does," or "because that's what most people do"; and if "everybody else (or most people) is doing it, so should (or can) you." No further argument' (2007: 101). In the example above, equating the murderers with 'everyman' or 'every nation' everywhere, Yellin Mor naturalizes the act of slaughter and distances it from the initial analogy he himself made with the crimes of the Nazis ('When I remember how my mother and my sister were led to slaughter I cannot accept this massacre' ibid.); if everyone does that, it is 'natural' and therefore legitimate in these special circumstances.

Moral legitimation is achieved by means of generalization, abstraction and evaluation or appraisal (Van Leeuwen, 2007: 99).

Abstraction is a 'way of expressing moral evaluations by referring to practices (or to one or more of their component actions or reactions) in abstract ways that "moralize" them by distilling from them a quality that links them to discourses of moral values.' Thus, the massacre of Qibya is moralized by being defined as 'punitive action' (*AHH*) or as an 'Israeli reaction to Arab hostility' (*MTII*).

Appraisal

The system of appraisal enables writers 'to write in a way that their position is buried from view' and 'render the historian as relatively impartial, neutral arbiter of truth' (Coffin, 2006: 140). Coffin states that appraisals can be found in any lexico-grammatical component and is typical of genre. In the present reports, appraisals express mainly judgment and appreciation. Judgment is the 'institutionalization of feeling,' for 'it serves to appraise human behaviour by reference to a set of institutionalized norms (an ethical framework) about how people should and should not behave' (Martin and White, 2005: 44).

Judgment has two sub-categories: 1.) Social esteem by which 'normality' (is the person's behavior unusual or special?), capacity (is the person competent?) and tenacity (is the person dependable, committed, daring? etc.) are valued. The reports studied here use social esteem in order to evaluate the personalities of the killers.

2.) Social sanction, by which veracity (is the person honest?) and propriety (is the person ethical, beyond reproach?) are valued (Coffin, 2006: 139–45).

The reports studied here use social sanction in cases of de-legitimation, i.e. the killers of Dier Yassin were 'dissidents' (*The 20th*), and the order in Kaffer Kassem was 'unlawful' (*BCI*).

From the category of appreciation, the reports mostly use social valuation, which may express admiration or criticism, and is sensitive to the specific institutional setting (Martin and White, 2005). Both social esteem and social valuation are used in order to depict the perpetrators of the massacres as competent and morally upright members of Israeli society, i.e. the soldiers of Unit 101 who committed the Qibya massacre 'excelled in their audacity' (*The 20th*) and 'were all volunteers' (*AHH*) or 'superb warriors' (*50 Years*); they were 'endowed with extraordinary courage, improvization, perseverance in the hardest conditions, tenacity and loyalty to wounded friends' (Naveh et al. 2009: 204). Usually, the appraisal of the perpetrators of massacres is categorical; whether they are appraised as 'superb warriors' or 'dissidents,' the judgment is very clear and unequivocal.

It is clear from these examples that massacres as moralized actions exemplify Habermas' argument that 'morality here is in no way connected to explicit norms of moral conduct. It has emptied itself of all definite normative content and sublimated to a process of argumentation and application of possible normative contents' (Habermas, 1992: 568 in Van Leeuwen and Wodak, 199: 108).

Legitimation through Personal Authority

Van Leeuwen (2007: 94) explains that 'one of the forms and contents of legitimation, is "because I say so," where the "I" is someone in whom some kind of authority is vested.' When Yellin Mor states: 'I know that many nations and armies do that,' without offering any example, he relies on his personal authority as a commander and as an expert. When President Weitzman is quoted saying that the flight of 'Israel's

Arabs' was a miracle, his authority is used to legitimate the consequences of the massacre.

Personal authority legitimation also includes commendation through role models, achieved in the reports studied here mainly through glorifying photographs and captions, which describe the actors as outstanding heroes.

Multimodal Legitimation

Moral values can be connoted visually or represented by visual symbols (Van Leeuwen, 2007: 107). The images in the report studied here suggest that in addition to the perpetuation of the Israeli myth of beautiful death (Zertal, 2004), Israeli education perpetuates the myth of 'beautiful killers', using visual means to show the combatants – who are the most 'significant others' of Israeli youth – engaged in heroic activities. Not all the killers are represented visually. Those who are not thought of as role models – like the killers of Kaffer Kassem who were border guards, considered lesser or marginal soldiers, or the killers of the Altalena affair, which is considered a blot on Zionism and Jewish solidarity – are never shown. The 'dissident' killers of Dier Yassin are not shown either but in their stead we see, next to the report about the massacre of Dier Yassin in *AHH* the Hagana legitimate cleansers of the Palestinian village Al-Kastal, about 3 km from Dier Yassin. The Kastal operation does not need legitimation for it was a pre-planned part of the official Plan D.

The photos depict the soldiers in 'manly' poses, with the object-signs that connote excellence and heroism in Israel: red military berets of paratroopers, dark khaki combat garb, parachutist wings and parachutist red boots. One such photograph (Figure 19) accompanies two of the reports about the Qibya massacre, depicting the 101 soldiers – headed by Ariel Sharon – with chief of staff Moshe Dayan who came to congratulate them. The photograph in this case is not only an elaboration of the verbal text – it does not just reveal who the 101 soldiers were – but a legitimatory device, for it shows the men who set the high standards of the Israeli army and later rose to the highest political positions. Such heroes could not have done unjustified wrong.

מחוץ לגבולותיה של ישראל שמטרתן הייתה להעביר את המסר כי אם לא יהיה שקט בצד הישראלי, לא יהיה שקט גם בצד הערבי. פעולה צבאית גדולה נערכה בכפר **קִבְיָה** בירדן (אוקטובר 1953). פעולה זו באה בתגובה על רצח אישה ושני ילדיה ביישוב **יהוד**. בפעולה פוצצו בתים בכפר ונהרגו 69 אזרחים ובהם נשים, זקנים וילדים. האו״ם גינה את ישראל על הפעולה. נוסף לפעולות הענישה נגד כפרים ערביים, שמהם יצאו מסתננים, ביצעה ישראל גם פעולות יזומות נגד מתקנים צבאיים במדינות ערב.

אולם בעיות הביטחון של המדינה החריפו בהתמדה. חוליות מסתננים חדרו ממדינות ערב לשטחי ישראל וביצעו פעולות טרור קשות שזעזעו את המדינה: **במעלה עקרבים** הותקף אוטובוס בדרכו מאילת לתל אביב, ו-11 מנוסעיו נרצחו (17.3.1954); חוליית מחבלים הגיעה למושב **שפריר** בקרבת רמלה, חדרה לבית הכנסת ופתחה באש על המתפללים (11.4.1956). בחדירת מסתננים לקיבוץ **נחל עוז**, בגבול מצרים, נרצח אחראי הביטחון של הקיבוץ ומעשי התעללות קשים נעשו בגופתו (29.4.1956); חייל ירדני ירה על משתתפים בכינוס ארכיאולוגי **ברמת רחל** והרג 10 בני אדם (26.9.1956).

פעולות אלה גררו פעולות-נגד של צה״ל. ב-10 באוקטובר 1956, בעקבות רצח של שני פועלים יהודים בפרדס בקרבת הגבול, יצא צה״ל להתקפה על **משטרת קלקיליה**. פעולות התגמול אמנם חיזקו במידת מה את תחושת הביטחון בקרב האזרחים, אבל גררו בעקבותיהם גינויים מצד האו״ם ומצד מדינות המערב.

הרמטכ״ל משה דיין (עומד, רביעי מימין) בחברת לוחמי יחידה 101 והצנחנים.
בין הלוחמים: מאיר הר ציון ואריאל שרון (עומדים, ראשון ושני משמאל); רפאל איתן (יושב, ראשון מימין).

מן הספרות

הסלע האדום

חיים חפר

״הסלע האדום״ הוא שיבוש של הכינוי ״סלע אָדוֹם״, המיוחס לאתר הנַבָּטי הנמצא בפֶּטְרָה, שבירדן. בשנות החמישים הייתה פטרה מוקד להלומותיהם של צעירים ישראלים הרפתקנים, ורבים מהם שילמו בחייהם על המסע הזה. בהשפעתם של מסעות מסוכנים אלה נכתב והולחן שיר, ״הסלע האדום״, שתיאר מסע אחד כזה. כאשר חזרו ונִשְׁנו מקרי המוות של צעירים שניסו להגיע למקום, נאסר להשמיע את השיר מעל גלי האתר מחשש שהוא מדרבן צעירים לנסות להגיע אל היעד הנכסף.

מעבר להרים ולמדבר,
אומרות האגדות, ישנו מקום,
שאיש ממנו חי עוד לא חזר,
והוא נקרא הסלע האדום.

הו, הסלע האדם – האדם.

ראשון הלך גשש, מרים פניו,
מביט בכוכבים שבמרום,
אך המראה אשר ראו עיניו –
היה מראה הסלע האדם.

הו, הסלע האדם – האדם.

גלגל השמש על ראשם הלם
והם נושמים אבק מדבר וחם
ולפתע – כמו קפא בהם דמם –
ראו הם את הסלע האדם.

הו, הסלע האדם – האדם.

שלשה יצאו לדרך עם שקיעה,
מנגד להטו הרי אדום,
חלום ישן, כפה ומימיה,
לקחו הם אל הסלע האדם.

הו, הסלע האדם – האדם.

בואדי, עת חנו בין אבנים,
אמר אחד, כמו מכה חלום:
רואה אני – פניה לבנים.
ענו רעיו: הסלע האדם.

הו, הסלע האדם – האדם.

משח היריות היה קצר.
גנח אחד: נפצעתי – וידם.
ענו רעיו כפה סלא עפר:
הגענו אל הסלע האדם.

הו, הסלע האדם – האדם.

332

Figure 19 'Chief of staff Dayan with the warriors of the 101 unit. Among the warriors: Ariel Sharon, Raphael Eitan and Meir Har-Zion' (AHH)

Courtesy of IDF archives and the Centre of the Technology of Education, Tel Aviv.

Van Leeuwen adds that 'the mere fact that these role models adopt a certain kind of behaviour, or believe certain things, is enough to legitimize [their actions] and the actions of their followers' (2007: 103). Naveh et al. (2009: 204) explain that these soldiers who were endowed with 'extraordinary courage, improvisation, perseverance in the hardest conditions, tenacity and loyalty to wounded friends, became the myth of the combatant soldier in the IDF.' In all the reports, the heroic photographs are 'ideologically the most potent part of the communication since [they have] the status of not-in-dispute knowledge which unites participants in the communication act' (Hodge and Kress, 1993: 165).

Legitimating Layout

One of the means of legitimation is the arrangement of elements, which can create a legitimating reading path or story. Thus, the heroic photographs are usually grafted on or connected by vectors to glorifying songs or slogans. As a rule, 'Song and poems stabilize collective memories' (Wertsch, 2002: 52), and turn narratives to myths (Barthes, 1957). In *AHH* the Dier Yassin report, is situated between the heroic cleansers of Al-Kastal and the song *Comradeship* written by Hayim Guri, the 'poet laureate of the war of independence' as the book defines him. The song glorifies 'our' beautiful brave soldiers whose comradeship is sealed with blood; the above photograph of Unit 101 (*AHH*) is grafted onto *The Red Rock* – a ditty immortalizing the 'daring' young Israeli 'dreamers' of the 1950s who crossed the border illegally into Jordan in order 'to see the Red City of Petra and die.' The soldiers in the photographs are held up as the embodiment of the songs.[19] In *MTII*, the heroic photograph of the 101 is strongly connected by a diagonal vector to an election poster of the (then) governing labor party, showing a lurking Arab aiming at planes and boats bringing Jewish immigrants to the shores of Israel, with the slogan: 'Growth against Siege!' The soldiers are the concrete response to the Arab threat that hovers above them, or us. In both *JIP* and *AHH*, the Dier Yassin massacre is situated in layouts that depict respectively the hardships inflicted by Arab villagers on the Jews in besieged Jerusalem and the achievement brought about by the cleansing of these Arab villages – the opening of the road to Jerusalem.

Layouts may include glorifying captions that differ from the main text. In one report about Qibya (*MTII:* 273), although the main text states very clearly that most of the Palestinian infiltrations were 'attempts by Arab villagers to return to their homes' and that 'only few of them were armed Palestinians sent to carry out intelligence and terrorist activities,' the caption under the heroic photograph of the Qibya killers claims Qibya was 'a departure base for terrorists,' thus legitimating the massacre.

Legitimating Context

Verbal rearrangement serves to create legitimating contexts. In *50 Years,* the Dier Yassin report, though without visuals, uses contextual or rather co-textual legitimation. The chapter starts – in the tradition of textbooks of the 1950s – with the 'dreadful, cruel and bloodthirsty massacres by Arabs of [Jewish] scholars, doctors and nurses, in order to counterbalance the negative impression created by the Dier Yassin episode.' (Podeh, 2002: 106). It ends with '1200 Jews lost their lives in the first four months of the war, half of whom were civilians' (p.181), ignoring completely the Palestinian casualties. In this context, the Dier Yassin 'affair' or 'episode,' as it is called, is made to seem absolutely justified according to Israeli norms of deterrence and revenge.

Means of De-Legitimation

> To justify does not mean to ratify. It does not mean 'this is what I would have done,' but weighing the action in terms of the agent's goals, his beliefs (even if they were erroneous) and the circumstances he was aware of. (Dray, 1957: 124)

This important distinction may explain the fact that despite the difficulty – especially for young readers – to draw the distinction between not condoning the massacre while endorsing its consequences, the very act of massacre is not always legitimated and sometimes is explicitly de-legitimated on moral grounds, whereas its consequences are legitimated on the ground of utility and effect.

In that the school books follow the general Israeli stance (see Blum-Kulka, 2000).

De-legitimation is realized by the following categories (following Van Dijk, 1997: 259–261):

1) De-legitimation of membership – the killers of Dier Yassin were 'dissidents' (*The 20th*).
2) De-legitimation of action and propriety; for example, in Kaffer Kassem, the soldiers killed helpless, honest, hard-working farmers and their children unscrupulously. Here are two examples (my notes in brackets):

Examples:

1) *The 20th:* 211

[...] On this same day 43 inhabitants of the village of Kaffer Kassem who had not heard of the curfew returned to their homes after a long working day in the fields (*positive appraisal of hard working land labourers*). They were massacred by a patrol unit of the Israeli army without any previous warning. (*Negative appraisal of killers*)

Note: By calling the murderers 'army soldiers' this report does not differentiate between the army and the border guards who are a police-force, as others reports do. This may be considered as implicit criticism of the government that wished to keep the army untainted by the slaughter and presented the massacre as the initiative of the border guards.

2) AHH: 335

On the day the Sinai Campaign started [...] the curfew was brought forward to an earlier hour, 5:00 p.m. That evening, workers from Kaffer Kassem returned to their homes after curfew without knowing it had been changed. The border-guard soldiers who met them at the entrance to the village ordered them to stop, recognised them as the inhabitants of the village and then shot them dead.

3) The *20th*: 184

In this report about Dier Yassin, the killers lacked veracity and ethics: they did not respect the signed agreement with the village and they 'bragged' about the slaughter.

Explicit de-legitimation is usually extravocalised using personal and impersonal authority to make its claims; the most explicit de-legitimation of the Dier Yassin killers is quoted from their own commander; a UN observer denounces the shelling of the ship Altalena, and a judge incriminates the Kaffer Kassem murderers. Negative judgment is usually attributed to political, religious and moral authorities as in 'The massacre shocked the Yishuv. The Hagana, the Jewish Agency and the rabbinical authorities condemned it vigorously. The board of Directors of the Jewish Agency expressed its feelings of abhorrence and nausea regarding the barbaric way in which this operation was carried out' (*The 20th*: 184). This attribution of judgment authenticates the evaluation but also distances the writer from the speech act of de-legitimation and diminishes his/her commitment to it.

De-legitimation is achieved through the following discursive means:

Analogy, usually with the Nazis: The analogy may be quite explicit as in Yellin Mor's speech quoted above, but it can also be inferred from titles such as 'a manifestly unlawful order' or from a sentence such as 'They argued they had followed orders.' Both phrases intertextualize the act and the defendants' argument with the Nazi criminals during the Nuremberg trials.

Comparison: 'Comparisons in discourse almost always have a legitimatory or de-legitimatory function' (Van Leeuwen, 2007: 96). As in the examples above, in some reports about Dier Yassin and Kaffer Kassem (i.e. *The 20th; AHH*), loyalty, integrity, tenacity, human decency and veracity characterize the victims but are lacking in the murderers. The fluctuation between the descriptions of the criminal acts and the positive evaluations of the victims emphasizes the de-legitimation of the killers. However, in all the reports, the de-legitimation of the act or of the actors is a rhetoric phase on the way to the legitimation of the outcome of the massacre.

From De-Legitimation to Legitimation

Even when the act itself is not justified, its consequences and sometimes its actors are. In Domka et al. (2009: 164), a question regarding the Kaffer Kassem massacre creates a condoning reading position towards the killers:

> How were the feelings of threat and suspicion towards the Arabs that were prevalent in Israel in the 1950s, expressed in the actions of the soldiers in Kaffer Kassem?

Naveh et al. (2009: 213) ask a slightly more subtle question regarding this massacre. However, following an account that de-legitimates the killers, the act and the order from above the question opens a crack for legitimation:

'Questions for thought: How can one explain the case in which a unit of border guards shoots and kills Arabs, who were undoubtedly innocent and without any mean intention? (Think in different directions).'

By naming the victims 'Arabs' instead of farmers, families, land-laborers, both questions reframe the victims through 'genericization' as 'the enemy,' ignoring or backgrounding the existence of 17 women and 11 children aged 8–15 who were slaughtered. The suggestion to 'think in different directions' presupposes the possibility of the existence of a reason to kill innocent children and their hard-working parents.

Some texts provide, following the de-legitimation of the manner of killing, a turning point where the text shifts to the legitimation of the outcome. In *The 20th*, Yellin Mor shifts his soldiers' blame from killing to 'bragging' about it. Learning that the murderers made the victims march in the streets of Jerusalem prior to their killing, Yellin Mor said 'I know that many nations and armies do such things but who asked them to brag about it?' (*The 20th*: 184).

Another turning point is offered at the end of the same chapter: (*The 20th*: 184, my comments in brackets)

> The Dier Yassin massacre remained a blot on the struggle of the Hebrew Yishuv for survival and independence. In the political arena, the massacre served as a central charge in Arab propaganda against Israel. But (*turning point*) its most crucial effect was in the short run: Although it did not inaugurate the panic-stricken flight of Israel's Arabs, which had commenced previously, it nevertheless accelerated it greatly *(effect-oriented legitimation)*.

The chapter ends with the quote from president Weitzman who called this effect a miracle.

This paragraph de-legitimates the massacre not because it was cruel and immoral but because it was harmful to the Zionist struggle and to Israel. However, the positive outcome of the massacre overcomes the harm, and is given the last word.

The Discourse and Genres of Legitimation

'Justifying accounts of controversial past actions involve all levels of discourse that may positively influence the opinions of the recipients.' (Antaki, 1994, quoted in Martin Rojo and Van Dijk, 1997: 549).

Van Leeuwen defines the linguistic and discursive means whereby social meanings are conveyed as socio-semantic means, for although these means are part of a linguistic system, 'meanings are cultural and not linguistic' (2008: 24). Regarding legitimation, he specifies that 'we need to consider [...] especially the intricate interconnections between social practices and the discourses that legitimize them' (2007: 111).

Legitimation is achieved through various speech acts such as assertions and questions, various types of interrelated and sometimes contradictory discourses, and various genres, all of which transform reality into a version of this reality (Van Leeuwen, 2007: 110). As was demonstrated in the previous chapters, Israeli history and geography school books use a mix of scientific, Zionist and biblical discourses, songs and poems in order to legitimate Jewish domination over the land of Israel/Palestine.

Legitimation is realized in the reports studied here through the following discursive means.

Exclusion of Elements

No representation of any social practice can include all there is to be represented. The question is what will be included and what deleted. Deletion includes both omission and the suppression of social actors (Van Leeuwen, 2008).

Selection of facts is one of the constraints of every narrative and especially of 'ideologized' narratives. Lyotard (1992: 90) explains that in grand narratives of emancipation (such as Zionism) '[...] many events go into the dustbin of history or spirit. An event will be retrieved only if it illustrates the master's views.' The reports on massacres studied here omit the reasons for the killing, exclude both the immediate and the long-run consequences for the victims and any verbal or visual proof of their suffering, as well as details that may raise unnecessary questions regarding the legitimacy of Israel's actions and goals. They mention social actors either by function or by turning their actions into independent participants. No names are mentioned.

An edifying example is the following report of the Kaffer Kassem massacre from *AHH* (p.335):

> **A Manifestly unlawful order**
> On the day the Sinai Campaign started the curfew was brought forward to an earlier hour, 17:00. That day, workers from Kaffer Kassem returned to their homes after curfew without knowing it had been changed. The border-guard soldiers who met them at the entrance to the village ordered them to stop, recognized them as the inhabitants of the village and then shot them dead. They argued they had followed orders, to shoot and

> kill indiscriminately anyone found outside their homes after curfew. 49 citizens of the village, including women and children, were murdered. The prime minister denounced the murder. The Knesset stood a whole minute to commemorate the murdered [...]. The defendants were sentenced to prison terms of 7–17 years. The judge ruled that a manifestly unlawful order should be clear to every man who is a man. It is a moral test. 'If the eye is not blind and the heart is not corrupt.'

In this report the soldiers are de-legitimated through analogy with Nazis. They recognized the people as honest innocent farmers and (nevertheless) shot them to death. The connective 'nevertheless' is implicit in the text, assumed by the sequence and by the conjunction 'and'; the victims, though appraised for innocence, are of no interest and receive very little paper time. The important consequences of the murder are the trial and the enlightened sentence, appraised in this and all the other reports as unprecedented.

The report succeeds through a careful process of selection and omission of facts in de-legitimating the act, socially excluding the killers, while legitimating the Israeli government and army and hailing the Israeli court. It foregrounds Israeli (judges') courage and moral integrity. For that purpose the text conceals important facts such as the prime minister's order to deny the event for 6 weeks, or his refusal 'to put the army on trial' thereby laying all the blame, as the text does, on the border guards and exonerating their military commanders. The report praises the Prime Minister and the Knesset for commemorating the murdered for a whole minute but avoids mentioning the murderers' release after a short while. It doesn't mention Colonel Shadmi's 'penalty' of 2 pounds fine, or the fact that all the killers regained their positions in the army and governmental offices with the explicit help of the prime minister; it does not mention the overwhelming support of Shadmi by senior officers of the army during the trial and the worry expressed by one of them after hearing the verdict, 'I came here to see whether in the future we will have to go into battle with a lawyer' (Rosenthal, 2000: 45), a concern that was repeated after the raid on Gaza in 2009. Such information would have hindered what seems to be the aim of the report, to fully legitimate the government, the court and the army while de-legitimating the killers as marginal members of society who do not represent Israel in any way, and who supposedly acted independently of the organization that had sent them to do the task. This impression is also achieved by providing the conditions while omitting the reasons for the massacre, so it would not seem pre-planned in the high windows. The orders given to the soldiers are presented as the murderers' argument and not as fact.

Given the missing facts, we would have had the following teleological explanation:

1) Israel wanted to conceal the fact that it was going to attack Egypt and encourage an auto-transfer of its Palestinian citizens to Jordan.
2) Israel considered that attacking Palestinian villages and killing some would divert attention away from the real war and 'encourage' the rest of the Palestinians to flee to Jordan.
3) Therefore, the curfew was changed without the villagers' knowledge and army colonel Shadmi ordered the border guards through their direct commander Major Melinki[20], to kill anyone who would be outside after 17:00.[21]

This report, given in regular history books (e.g. Rosenthal, 2000), has not yet found its way into textbooks, for it could shake the reputation of the IDF as a moral army, that Israeli education is so keen to propagate.

Addition of Elements

The addition of thoughts, intentions or situations that legitimate or at least exonerate the killers is frequently used in reports about massacres. For instance, 'The loud-speaker encouraging the inhabitants of Dier Yassin to leave the village did not work [...] the inhabitants did not leave the village and that is the reason why the number of casualties among them was so great' (Naveh et al. 2009: 113); or 'The soldiers did not know the people were hiding in their homes.' (*50 Years*: 244, Qibya report), an argument made by the Prime Minister at the time, used with much less commitment in Domka et al. (2009: 162): 'The Israeli claim was that the soldiers did not know the inhabitants were hiding in their homes and thought they were bombing empty houses.' Though this argument seems hardly valid in view of the fact that the attack took place at night, it is used especially in the most recent books.

Change of Information

Although *Modern Times II* (1999) and *Building a State* (2009) were co-written by the same author (Professor Eyal Naveh), in the former, Dier Yassin is described as 'a friendly village whose inhabitants made of their own initiative a non-aggression agreement with the Hagana and kept it meticulously despite the pressure from the [Arab] 'gangs,' while in the latter it is described as 'one of the bases of the Arab forces that kept attacking the road to Jerusalem.' This change of information contributes to the legitimation of the massacre and points to a new direction in Israeli education, manifested in *50 Years* (2004) and *Face* (2006) as well, to present this massacre as a justified battle that had gotten out of hand due to 'a series of mishaps' [that] 'turned [the battle] into a massive killing of innocent Arabs' (Naveh et al. 2009: 112–13).

Abstraction and Generalization

These devices are very typical of the questions given at the end of some reports. In *AHH,* the question, 'What were the achievements of the Nahshon operation?' comes right after the report about Dier Yassin, either ignoring the massacre or including it in the achievements of the large-scale official cleansing operation. Following the massacre in Qibya, *MTII* presents the students with two questions:

1) What was the expression of Arab hostility towards Israel?
2) Do you think Israel's reactions to these hostile actions were effective and justified? Give reasons.

These questions express the educational message of the reports: Look beyond the individual (unfortunate) incident of killing at the big picture and at the long-term (positive) outcome for us. The reader is thus made to value the military and social achievements brought by the massacre and remember its advantages, rather than the 'mishaps.'

Modality

Modality has an important role in representation for it is through modality that writers increase and decrease the force of their assertions (Martin and White, 2005: 13–14). As Van Leeuwen reminds us, 'Whoever controls modality controls which version of reality will be selected' (2007: 160).

Different strategies of legitimation use different expressions of modality (Van Leeuwen, 2007: 94). As we have seen, personal authority legitimation contains forms of high obligation modality ('I know'); conformity legitimation may contain implicit or explicit frequency modality such as 'usually,' 'every' (or 'many armies do that,' every nation ... etc.).

The following 'question for thought' regarding the Dier Yassin massacre (*MTII*: 228) exemplifies the strength of modality:

> What political and moral consequences might the affair of Dier Yassin have had, in your opinion?

In this question, 'Modal resources serve to introduce explicit negotiability into the proposition and hence, unlike positive declarative, do not assume or simulate solidarity between writer and reader' (Coffin, 2006: 145). Hodge and Kress (1993: 138) observe that 'all modals contain an element of negation in them, which is the key to their meaning [...]. The underlying pre-modalized form either has its source in the speaker or comes from outside and is regarded by the speaker as an "alien" meaning.' The assumption underlying the above question, or its 'pre-modalized meaning' – that massacres must have moral and political consequences – is negated by the modal form that suggests that a massacre may not necessarily have either moral or political consequences, and that these consequences are interrelated and negotiable.

Fairclough (2003: 219) remarks in the same line that explicitly modalized statements (may, might) can be seen as intermediate between categorical assertion and denial and that they register varying degrees of commitment to truth. In the present question, the modal *might* pushes the assumption underlying the question closer to denial, suggesting that this massacre (renamed affair) escaped both political and moral consequences.

Modality differentiates between legitimation and de-legitimation. When the killers are being either incriminated or wholly justified in their action, their acts are represented in high deontic modality and in active assertions; but when the responsibility of the killers is mitigated, the reports use low modality or the modality of possibility and the passive mode, as in the following extract from *50 Years* (p.244, emphasis added).

'A mixed force of Unit 101 and paratroopers *assaulted* the village of Qibya that *was known* as the departure point of terrorists, and *demolished* 45 houses. [...] 70 men, women and children *were killed*.'

Passive with a deleted actor (were killed) creates the impression of objectivity (Hodge and Kress, 1993: 134) and diminishes the responsibility of social actors; the village 'was known to be a terrorist base' but the text does not specify by whom, as if it was general, universal, accepted knowledge. The switch from active to passive reflects the book's stance that the soldiers were not entirely responsible for the people's deaths, since they did not know that there were people in the houses they demolished that night. However, though the actors are excluded, they are assumed because 'their exclusion leaves a trace' (Van Leeuwen, 1996: 39) which is then evaluated as an independent phenomenon.

The suppression or backgrounding of social actors can also be realized through grammatical metaphors, which turn events and processes into independent participants such as 'In the course of *the takeover* of the houses the people were killed' (*50 Years*); '*the attack caused* the *panic-stricken flight*' (*AHH*); or '*The border* with Jordan, which had been delineated arbitrarily and separated Arab villagers from their lands, *became a real line of fire*' (*MTII*: 273 emphasis added). The border is presented here as having been 'delineated arbitrarily' by no-one in particular (who delineates borders anyway? The students may ask), and became – all by itself – a line of fire. This sentence means in common-sense language that someone (the UN, the state, the government, the army) delineated the border without considering either family relations, property, or livelihood and has thereby created a terrible human misery, separating people from their families, farmers from their lands and crops etc. This unbearable situation was the reason for constant clashes between people who tried to go back home or to their fields and the soldiers who had to guard this 'arbitrary' border. Presenting sad and cruel stories by grammatical metaphors and the passive mode, namely by turning actions and processes to independent protagonists that act by themselves, without human agency, takes the human features out of the drama and exonerates the responsible people from blame.

Low Modality Concerning the Other

All the reports manifest very low commitment to facts concerning the Palestinian victims or Palestinian versions. As we have seen earlier, the number of Palestinian casualties may vary from one report to another and sometimes within the same report. When Palestinian versions regarding the massacres are presented it is always as probability existing only in their 'eyes,' in their 'sector' or in their 'consciousness,' e.g. '*in the Arab sector* the Kaffer Kassem massacre *became* the symbol of the evils of oppression' (*The 20th*: 121) or '*It was argued* that [in Dier Yassin] many of the people were killed not during the battle and that the Jews committed a massacre of the villagers' (Domka et al. 2009: 87); or 'Dier Yassin *became a myth in the Palestinian narrative* [...] and created a horrifying negative image of the Jewish conqueror *in the eyes of Israel's Arabs*' (Naveh et al. 2009: 112–13, emphasis added). To the question (Van Leeuwen, 2005: 160), 'As how true are the truths of each of these different voices represented?' One can surely answer that the Palestinian-Arab voice is represented as less true.

In all these examples, the cruel actions and their effects are presented as an argument made by the victims and not as fact. It must be remembered that both the phrases 'in the Arab sector' or 'in the Palestinian narrative' and the repeated verb 'became' reflect the decision of the writer who, as Hodge and Kress would have it, 'effaces himself from the utterance but leaves a trace of judgment' (1993: 136).

The Genres of Legitimation

From a social semiotic point of view, the question of writers is, 'what is it that we want to mean, and what modes and genres are best for realizing this meaning?' (Kress, 2003: 88). Hence, in text analysis, one should look not only at what is done with words or pictures but who does it, for whom, where and when, and what people do to each other by means of text (Van Leeuwen, 2005).

Coffin (2006: 10) suggests 'viewing historical discourse – within secondary schooling – as comprising a repertoire of different types of text or 'genres,' each of which enables different ways of thinking about the past.' According to Coffin's study, 'The discursive practice central to history is the interpretation and construction of social experience using textual forms and linguistic resources of narrative, explanation or argument as means of positioning and persuading the reader to accept interpretation as fact or "truth"' (2006: 44).

The narrative or recording genres, recount and account, are best fit for the construal of simple stories that lead the reader to accept a single perspective. Judgment in these genres is mostly 'woven into the structure and the lexico-grammar' (Coffin, 2006: 139); therefore they are more apt for legitimation than the arguing genres which are more open for debate and where judgment is 'laid bare.' As Habermas (1975: 71) notes, 'The procurement of legitimation is self-defeating as soon as the mode of procurement is seen through.'

Recount

The recount is designed to inform or to chronicle past events which are regarded by the historian as significant. Coffin notes that 'in traditional textbooks, the historical recount has generally been used for presenting mainstream versions of the past' (2006: 56). Israeli school books are still very 'traditional' in this sense. In a recount, 'events are selected, edited and linearized' (ibid.), which means they obey certain rules of recontextualization, distribution, and evaluation. The historical recount has three stages:

1) Background – summarizing previous historical events or conditions.
2) Record of events – sequencing events as they unfold over time
3) Deduction (optional) – drawing out the historical significance of the events recorded. Coffin notes that 'often a deduction explicitly interprets the historical meaning of events' (ibid.: 56). In the present analysis the deduction may contain the writer's legitimating claim regarding the massacre.

In terms of context, the field of the historical recount (Coffin, 2006: 57) concerns 'contact between different peoples, conflict and war.' The emphasis, says Coffin, is on groups of people, realized through generic participants, as in the texts studied here, where the 'dissidents,' 'soldiers,' the 'Jewish authorities' or the 'Yishuv' (Jewish community in pre-Israel Palestine) act as protagonists in the massacre drama. Although individuals may be referred to in a historical recount, their purpose is often to exemplify and possibly glorify collective activities. Both individuals and groups are defined in terms of their 'institutional' roles rather than their domestic or personal relationships – the judge, the commanding officer etc. The recount also includes non-human participants which are often realized by means of dense, nominal groups such as 'the attack' 'the takeover of the houses,' 'the panicked flight' or 'the crushing victory,' etc.

The 'voice' in recounts is that of the 'recorder.' Coffin warns however, that 'the label of recorder voice refers to reduced authorial intrusion rather than being an indicator of objectivity in any absolute sense [...] objectivity is to some extent a rhetorical illusion. [...] Recorder's voice, although seemingly neutral and objective is not value free. Rather the recorder voice captures the way in which writers create their interpersonal position or particular interpretation of events in a relatively indirect way – through the selection (or omission) and arrangement of [...] tokens of judgment. [...] This style may result in a text having a factual, neutral 'feel.' In other words 'objectivity ' and 'factuality' can be construed through the absence of direct, explicit forms of evaluation and the exclusion of competing, alternative interpretations' (Coffin, 2006: 151).

The recorder voice 'assumes or simulates reader alignment with the writer's world view, thus minimizing the amount of explicit interpersonal work to be done, in terms of negotiating with diverse audience positionings' (Coffin, 2006: 151–152). Therefore in recounts 'there is an absence of negotiation and argumentation, and the writer does not invite the reader to challenge the view of events presented' (p.58). Though in the deduction stage of recounts 'a judgment is made concerning the historical significance of the events recorded, typically, such judgments emerge "naturally" out of the record of events stage' (p.57). Appraisal in recount is 'buried' in 'an array of linguistic techniques that communicate values, create bias and persuade the reader of the truth of whatever message is transmitted' (p.140).

Because of this seemingly unintrusive style, the recount seems to bear a greater resemblance to a chronicle than a historical narrative, although its author writes as a historian and this makes a great difference, for as Ricoeur explains, 'The chronicler has no knowledge of the future and the historian does,' and therefore the narrative sentences 'describe past events in light of subsequent ones unknown to the actors themselves' (1983: 144). In the case of massacres, the recount can report the event in light of its consequences that were frequently unforeseen by the perpetrators themselves but oftentimes are used to legitimate their action retrospectively.

Time is the main organizing principle of the recount, with temporal expressions typically functioning as a point of departure of each paragraph. The temporal or additive connectors may assume the function of causal links. For instance, 'In the months after that [the massacre of Dier Yassin] the Yishuv was privileged with military successes.'

Kress (2003: 1) explains regarding such causality, that 'the simple yet profound fact of temporal sequence and its effects are to orient us towards a world of causality [...] and the narrative is the genre that is the culturally most potent formal expression of this.'

Wertsch (2002) believes that such school book narrative texts, 'instead of serving as containers of precise unchanging information seem to play a role in memory by serving as indicators of 'the sort of things' an individual or a group would say. In the massacre reports studied here we find 'the sort of thing' Israeli society would say about the massacres of Palestinians.

Following are two examples of recount:

1) Dier Yassin massacre (*50 Years*: 180, headings added):
    1) **Record of events:** on the night of 9 April, Dier Yassin, an Arab village west of Jerusalem, was attacked by a joint force of the Etzel and Lehi.
    2) **Ground**: the goal was to capture the village and eject its inhabitants.
    3) **Record of events cont.**: In the course of the battle that developed on the ground, between 100 and 250 persons were killed, including women and children.
    4) **Consequences**: The affair sparked a public debate about the norms of warfare and the ways to treat the indigenous population.

Martin Rojo and Van Dijk (1997: 532) argue that socially legitimation presupposes accusations or doubts, 'whether the social or cultural norms, values or the moral order itself are breached by the action.' This report does not seem to presuppose accusation but it does presuppose doubts, which it answers by inserting a legitimate goal (the ejection of the Arab population) at the point where doubts as to the purpose of the massacre may arise, right after mentioning the attack that was seemingly launched for no apparent reason. The ejection of the population needs no legitimation for it was the most legitimate cause at the time; elaborating and justifying it explicitly would be to 'over communicate' (Van Leeuwen, 1996: 41), for its legitimacy has long been established in Israel and inculcated to all Jewish students, who learn about Palestinians being a demographic threat to the Jewish majority (the popular term used is often 'demographic demon'). Renaming the massacre 'battle' and 'affair' is an act of judgment and an expression of opinion in the ongoing debate regarding this massacre,[22] but typically of the recount the act of judgment is not explicit. The report omits the consequences that affected the victims and their families and mentions only the moral debate it 'sparked' among the Jews, thus legitimating the Israeli public while insinuating that some people may have thought this was the right way 'to treat the indigenous population.'

2) Dier Yassin massacre, Domka et al. (2009: 87, headings added):
   1) **Record of events**: Parallel to the Hagana's breaking of the siege over the road to Jerusalem during the Nachshon operation, the Etzel, with the co-operation of Lehi people from Jerusalem, executed an action against the village Dier Yassin, located at the Western entrance of Jerusalem.
   2) **Ground**: The village was thought to be neutral and even signed a non-aggression agreement with the neighbouring Jewish settlement Givat Shaul. However, its take-over was included in the plan of the Nachshon operation and the headquarter of the Hagana approved the action and helped the attackers logistically.
   3) **Record of events cont.**: In the course of the battle, in which a few Etzel combatants were killed, many of the villagers were killed and the survivors were led to Eastern Jerusalem.
   4) **Consequence 1**: The great number of civilian casualties, including women and children, who died during the battle, had huge repercussions in Jewish and Western public opinion. It was argued that many of them were not killed in battle and that the Jews committed a massacre in Dier Yassin. The Jewish leadership in Israel denounced the action of Etzel and the Palestinian leadership spread news and rumours about the events in Dier Yassin that aroused great fear and rage in Israel and in the Arab countries.
   5) **Consequence 2**: The affair served, it seemed, to accelerate the flight of Palestinians from villages and towns in the areas conquered by the Jewish forces.
   6) **Consequence 3**: Similarly, the affair created pressure from Arabs around the world on their respective states to interfere on behalf of Israel's Arabs and against the Yishuv.

This recount mentions the causal links between the events but does not explain them; it confirms the tight connection between the massacre and the bigger cleansing operation Nachshon, which in other books remains quite opaque, and the cooperation between the 'dissidents' and the official Hagana. By mentioning the non-violence agreement between the village and the Hagana it implicitly blames the authorities who nevertheless included the cleansing of this friendly village in their cleansing operation. It renames the massacre 'battle' and presents the fact that there was a slaughter as someone's argument ('it was argued that') without specifying whose opinion it was. It neither denounces nor praises the soldiers and gives balanced information about the reactions in the world and in Israel/Palestine which allows the reader to make her own judgment.

Account

The social purpose of the historical account is twofold – to record and to explain, or account for, why events happened in a particular sequence. Coffin explains that 'the account makes causal links between events [...] rather than one event merely following on from another; events may take on an agentive role and produce or cause subsequent events' (2006: 58).

For instance, 'The attack *caused* a shock among Israel's Arabs and *accelerated* their panicked flight' (*The 20th:* emphasis added).

In accounts the writer is more intrusive in terms of judging and valuating the past. His/her stance is generally more 'in view.' The voice of the account is the 'appraiser voice' in which writers favor different selections of resources in order to 'manage' the positioning of their readers. 'The selection and construction of events function to position a (compliant) reader to share the writer's view of past events. The reader is positioned to appraise positively or negatively the protagonists, just as the writer does' (Coffin, 2006: 152). Since the writer assumes compliance, clauses tend to use assertions, as in the example above.

Coffin notes that appraisal in account is both explicit and implicit, as in the following example from the report about the Altalena affair, when the IDF shelled a ship bringing Jewish refugees and ammunition for the 'dissident' military organization, the Etzel, also known as the Irgun (*MTII:* 233) (emphasis added)[23]:

> Before the *unbelieving eyes* of the UN observers, the Israeli army bombed a ship that carried ammunition *Israel needed like air*, and killed *Jewish volunteers* who had come *to help Israel* fend off the *Arab onslaught.*

The writer's judgment is made quite obvious by the choice of evaluative nouns, adjectives and similes.

Mode: Coffin notes that in addition to time, cause becomes a text-organizing device in account, often being used as point of departure both at the level of paragraph and at the level of clause. The account makes increased use of nominalization and grammatical metaphor, which makes the discourse more dense and allows the construal of an argument that covers long periods. Also, it makes the text more technical and hence more 'scientific' and 'objective,' almost devoid of human agency. For example:

Most of the *raids were aimed* at *civilian targets*, and included *stake-outs* and *incursions* deep behind the border lines. (*50 Years*, 2004: 244 Qibya massacre).

Civilian targets, stake-outs and incursions are technical terms for Israeli soldiers killing Palestinian civilians. Similar to terms such as immigration, population-explosion or refugee problem, they objectify the human actions and turn them into technical objects for observation and analysis. The technical language allows condensing many events into one category, such as 'stake-outs' or 'incursions' that cover long periods and turn them into elements in a logical argument. Also, by distancing them from every day expressions and values, the technical language detaches the actions of killing from any human characteristic, reaction or empathy.

Account stages are quite similar to those of the recount: background, sequence which accounts for events as they unfold over time, and an optional deduction. As we have seen in the Recount before, the stages do not always follow this order, and the ground can feature as cause and be inserted in the middle of the report, when the most important question of legitimation, 'Why?' arises.

Example: Kaffer Kassem massacre, Naveh et al. (2009: 213, headings added).

1) **Record of events**: On the first day of the Sinai War a horrible event happened [...] Due to the starting of the war the curfew was set earlier than usual [...] without notifying the people who worked outside the village.
2) **Ground**: The villagers were used to curfew during the night, therefore they returned from work after the curfew had started.

3) **Record of events cont.**: In Kaffer Kassem an officer obeyed the orders he was given: to shoot and kill anyone who broke the curfew. His soldiers shot the people who came from the fields at the checkpoint. It is important to emphasize that in the other villages, where farmers arrived home after the curfew hour, the commanders acted compassionately and understandingly, and did not comply with the order to shoot. The killing [...] was revealed to the public much later because of the censorship and the 'military government' which blocked the information [...] The defendants received long terms in jail but all of them were released upon presidential amnesty after a year, due to different sorts of pressure.
4) **Deduction**: The massacre of Kaffer Kassem serves as a warning light to the rule of law in Israel; it was this massacre that engendered the term 'a manifestly unlawful order' [...].

This report creates or rather hints at causal links between the war against Egypt and the curfew, although it leaves them as opaque as possible. However, the writers' view regarding the order, the act, the actors and the consequences are expressed explicitly. The causal links present the conditions without revealing the reasons for the different actions. The text does not explain why the curfew on Arab villages in the centre of Israel should be forwarded due to the opening of a war in Sinai? Why weren't the people notified? Why did the censorship and the military government block the information? What sorts of 'pressure' brought about the criminals' early release?

One reason for this opacity may be that the account could not be more revealing without contaminating the reputation of the army and the government, which could entail the de-authorization of the book by the ministry of education. However it seems revealing enough to make the reader think, look for answers and reach her own judgment.

Explanation

Coffin (1997: 202–203) sees explanation in history school books as a category which forms a linguistic bridge between narrative and argument and is used to justify the interpretation the text advocates.

Dray (1957: 124) argues that to explain is 'to justify with a nuance of appraisal attached to the term.' In explanation, he writes, 'Historians [...] recruit details to the justification of their thesis. [They are] searching warrants, weighing and evaluating causes, testing candidates for the role of causes and all these are activities of judgment.'

As we have seen above, the books never mention the reasons for the massacres so as not to present them as purposeful actions, but they may include reasons or intentions for the purpose of legitimation that usually justify the massacre as part of larger justified and purposeful operations. For instance:

> These actions [one of which was the Qibya massacre] were meant to transmit a message to the host countries (especially to Jordan and Egypt) that they must prevent the infiltration from their lands. Otherwise they would be hurt. The actions were also intended to strengthen the feeling of security and the morale of the citizens of Israel. (Domka et al. 2009: 160)

Or:

> The [101] unit acted for months and performed reprisals beyond Israel's borders, whose aim was to transmit the message that if the Israeli side did not enjoy peace and quiet, there would be no peace and quiet on the Arab side either. (*AHH*: 331)

50 Years (p.244) also gives as explanation the excuse Prime Minister Ben Gurion used at the time, namely that 'the unit did not know that many of the villagers had hidden in the houses' that night. But the real reasons, which may be found in regular history books, usually remain concealed.

Legitimating Purpose: Regarding purpose, Van Leeuwen writes, 'In order to serve as legitimation, purpose constructions must contain an element of moralization' (2007: 101). In both reports quoted above, the purpose was to protect (Jewish) citizens against acts of terror and to punish those who didn't act in the same way. Although the 'intentions' and 'aims' do not constitute sufficient reasons for the massacre in question, they do constitute some kind of moral explanation according to Israeli norms of eye for eye, retaliation and deterrence. This justification is necessary first because the same arguments legitimate present-day actions against Palestinians in Gaza and in the West Bank, and second because the students know that the perpetrators of the Qibya massacre have never been punished, on the contrary – some of them like Ariel Sharon and Raphael Eitan rose to the highest ranks of Israel's army and government. People who rose to such high positions cannot be presented as criminals who have done unjustified wrong or as 'dissidents.'

Legitimating Conditions: As we have seen, beside effects, the reports may state the conditions that allowed the massacre to happen and that may legitimate it (i.e. 'in the heat of the battle,' 'the border was laid arbitrarily,' 'the Israelis were afraid in their homes, on the roads, in excursions,' 'the villagers were not notified' etc.). These conditions are usually the 'ground' for the events that brought about the massacre rather than its direct causes. Coffin distinguishes between sufficient conditions or 'enabling causes' and 'determining conditions.' She explains that enabling relations answer the question 'how' (e.g. they lived by hunting), a question that the legitimation of massacres may wish to avoid. A determining relationship is expressed through conjunctions and prepositions of consequence (e.g. as a result of, in order that, for the purpose of) that link a condition with an outcome and answers the question 'why' (Coffin, 2006: 122), which is the question legitimation is trying to answer (Van Leeuwen, 2007). In history textbooks, Coffin found that 'the overall trend is for causation to be of the determining type within each of the genres and for enabling relations to be relatively rare' (2006: 122). This finding reinforces the assumption that history textbooks are primarily meant to legitimate the actions of the state, or function as a sort of 'supreme historical court' whose task is to transmit 'the "true" collective memories which are appropriate for inclusion in the canonical national historical narrative' (Podeh, 2002: 3). Thus the massacres can become the 'founding crimes' of the nation.

Regarding the massacre of Qibya, for example, *The 20th* and *Modern Times II* legitimate neither the act nor the policy that engendered it;

they do not provide any reasonable cause or positive consequences as later books do (restoring the morale, invigorating the army etc.) and do not justify the massacre through its effects. However, they present the determining conditions for the action which answer the question why? In that they suggest the possibility of viewing these conditions as sufficient explanation for the massacre but leave it to the reader's judgment.

20th (p.219) and *Modern Times II* (p.273): Conditions: 'The border with Jordan, which had been delineated arbitrarily and separated Arab villagers from their lands, became a real line of fire. [The infiltrations were] attempts by villagers to return to their homes [...] only few of them were Fadayun – armed Palestinians – sent to carry out intelligence and terrorist activities [...] But Israel refused to acknowledge the difference and her reprisals were harsh.'

The chapter ends with a reflection that reiterates the conditions and adds theoretical rationalization to the legitimation: 'the only thing the Arabs understand is force':

> Was there an alternative policy to the Israeli one? It is hard to know, for no alternative policy had ever been considered seriously. Within the national leadership, persons like Abba Even and Sharet questioned the efficacy of the reprisals, but the PM [...] and the heads of the security establishment, as well as some politicians, accepted the position [...] that the only thing the Arabs understand is force and saw in the IDF the main instrument for tackling the problems in the region.

Naveh et al. (2009) present the conditions that enabled the Qibya massacre by juxtaposing the two perceptions of the Israeli government: the political one which advocated a solution to the infiltrations by political means and the 'security' one, that advocated harsh reprisals. The text explains that 'in the conditions of the Arab-Israeli conflict, as it had developed in the mid-1950s, the political perception represented by Moshe Sharet had only few supporters and the "security" perception of Ben Gurion and Moshe Dayan prevailed' (p.204).

By foregrounding the conditions and concealing the reasons for the massacre the answer to the question 'why?' is always partial. For example, why were the farmers of Kaffer Kassem or Qibya, or Dier Yassin murdered with their families? The conditions given for the Kaffer Kassem massacre are that, being in the fields all day, they did not hear about the changed onset of the curfew. The way the books present it, these conditions seem to have been sufficient cause for the soldiers to slaughter the workers and their children but evidently insufficient for the court. The conditions for killing whole families in Qibya (the above-mentioned attitude of the government and the murder of a woman and two children in Yahud) were sufficient for Ariel Sharon and his soldiers but seemed preposterous in the eyes of the international community.

Consequential Explanation

Consequential explanation is the best explaining genre for effect-oriented legitimation, which is the most frequent in the reports studied here. Since the massacres themselves can never be presented in school books as purposeful actions, in most of the reports studied here their reasons and conditions are less foregrounded than their effects, which usually take *a posteriori* the place of cause, as in: 'The massive escape of the Arabs [caused by the Dier Yassin massacre] solved a horrifying demographic problem.' The horrifying demographic problem is not presented as the reason for the massacre but becomes its legitimating cause *a posteriori*. This kind of explanation does not authorize prediction but retrodiction (Dray, 1957: 134). Beginning from the fact that the massacre had happened and that we see its effects, we infer backwards through time the antecedent necessary conditions that must have enabled, facilitated or allowed it, and turn those conditions a *posteriori* into cause. As in everyday conversations, 'reasons' or factors leading to unfortunate consequences are reconstructed retrospectively and usually in the form of hypotheses after the fact (e.g. he fell because they had not fixed the road), so that textually they are placed at the end, as 'new' information after the event has been described. As Van Leeuwen specifies (2007: 97), 'The why of the action is never intrinsic to the practice but has to be construed in discourse.'

For example in the Dier-Yassin report of *The 20th*, Nathan Yellin-Mor – the commander of the Lehi participants in the massacre, who apparently had not known about this 'operation' but sought to condone the conduct of his comrades or subordinates, hypothesizes their reasons retrospectively after having denounced the slaughter: 'I know that people do not pre-plan these things, I know they do it because their friends have been killed.' To be sure, in none of the reports about this massacre had this argument been pronounced as its reason. But as Dray says (1957: 122 quoted in Ricoeur, 1983: 129), 'We look for an explanation precisely when we do not see the relationships between what was done and what we think we know about the agents involved. [...] When such a logical equilibrium is lacking we seek to reconstitute it.' And the consequential explanation is the most apt genre for this task.

In the consequential explanation the protagonists are usually abstractions. Hence, 'There is a movement from concrete language to abstract-conceptual presentation and metaphors' (Coffin, 1997: 209). The metaphors which are mostly grammatical, condense processes into nouns, and this shift 'allows the writer to construct experience as an abstract thing that can then be brought into relationship with other abstract things and in this way serve as a basis for further analysis and elaboration of the consequence being focused on' (Coffin, 1997: 217). The following example – part of which was mentioned earlier – is taken from *The 20th*'s report on the massacre at Kaffer Kassem:

> The 1956 war was a good turning point for Israel's Arabs although it began with the tragedy of Kaffer Kassem. But in the long run, the crushing victory, the self confidence of the Jewish citizens and the relative peace at the borders made the military government an intolerable moral and political burden and ten years later it was abolished.

This consequential explanation integrates 'long-term, structural causes with short term precipitating events, [...] and recreate[s] them as a system of causes to an effect, achieving thereby a logical structure where there was none, and a process by which incongruent forms of cause can be made congruent by the use of 'led to,' 'resulted in,' or 'turned x into y' (Coffin 2006:70–72).

The consequential explanation inserts the massacre (renamed tragedy) as the starting point of a positive process. Consequences from two different wars, nine years apart, one of which (1967) had nothing to do with Kaffer Kassem, are all condensed into one causal sequence reconstrued by the writer through a series of processes – turned into 'things' – that brought about a positive change for the victims. Although the relator between the different causes and the positive change is the conjunction 'and,' it has 'a pragmatic effect of continuation' (Chiffrin, 1988: 130) and seems to take the place of 'therefore,' 'hence' or 'so.' The causal connection achieved by the use of the additive conjunction 'and' that precedes the 'ten years later,' creates the link between the abstract causes and the actual abrogation of the military government.

The abstract protagonists in this report – the crushing victory, the relative peace, the self-confidence of the Jewish population, the intolerable moral and political burden – are presented retrospectively as the causes for the 1956 war being a good turning point for the Palestinian citizens. The abrogation of the military government that had oppressed Israeli Palestinian citizens since 1948 serves as cause for the claim that 1956 was a good turning point because this long process (10–12 years) commenced in 1956.[24]

Note that the text is very careful not to create the impression that the massacre or empathy with the victims was the direct cause or had any direct connection with the abolition of the military government, emphasizing it was the outcome of states of mind and circumstances of those who had imposed it in the first place, following their 'crushing victories' over other 'Arabs.' This stance is compatible with the general attitude in Israel at the time. As noted by Boymel (2002: 135),[25] criticism of the military government within Israeli society, 'rather than address the immense difficulty of Arab citizens in living under the regulations of the military government or the need to stop the harsh institutional discrimination against these citizens, was focused on the need of the Jews to decontaminate their young state of the negative image of an undemocratic militaristic state that had adhered to it.'

As was mentioned before in terms of the relationship between writer and reader, the voice of explanation is the 'appraiser voice' and more specifically the 'interpreter voice,' which entails a lack of explicit judgment but a high frequency of inscribed valuation, especially social valuation, appreciation and judgment (Coffin, 2006: 150). Therefore, in the consequential explanation, as in the recording genres, although reasons and consequences are selected and often evaluated by the writer, 'they are presented as categorical, objective 'facts' rather than a set of propositions that have to be argued for. Solidarity between writer and reader is therefore assumed and the process of interpretation is not made explicit, with evaluation often being buried within nominal groups,' i.e. *crushing* victory, *relative* peace, *intolerable* political and moral *burden*, (Coffin, 2006: 150).

Argument

> Historical argumentation is very much about establishing a particular interpretation of past events, and supporting it with proof. (Coffin, 2006: 66)

Although argument as a genre is rare in the reports, the arguments that legitimate the massacre are present – more or less explicit – as their 'high point,' namely as 'what it all adds up to, or rather the thesis of the narrative' (White, 1973: 11).

The main logical parts of any argument (Fairclough, 2003: 81) are Ground, Warrant, optional Backings and Claim. However, these parts 'are mostly implicit, taken for granted or assumed' (Fairclough, 2003: 81). Fairclough adds that 'when this is so one might consider the ideological work the text is doing' (2003: 82).

The *ground* is the premises of the argument. It may be a historical background or a moral ground or both. For instance, the ground for the Dier Yassin massacre in *JIP* (1999) is: 'In the heat of the Nahshon operation, a grave event occurred that would have significance in days to come.' This ground sets the massacre historically within the context of the official cleansing operation and constitutes the moral ground for its legitimation through naturalization (it is quite common that grave events occur in the heat of the battle). Also, this ground states rather explicitly that the significance of the massacre lies in what it would bring about in the future, meaning that it should be judged in terms of effect and utility.

Warrants justify the inference from ground to claim. For instance, 'The prime minister wanted to have a deterring act: there is one government in Israel and it would not bear competition.' (*The 20th*, the Altalena affair)

Backings are optional reinforcements or support to warrants, e.g. 'The Altalena affair was the ticket of Israel into the organized states club' (ibid.).

Claim is the thesis of the argument. In the reports studied here, the implicit legitimating or de-legitimating claim can be implied from titles such as 'A manifestly unlawful order' and 'Israel acts against terror,' or it may appear in the deduction. For instance, 'This blatant tactic isolated Israel in the international arena and shattered the national consensus within Israel, but it seemed worthwhile [...]' (*The 20th*: 250).

Though the ideology which constructs and gives value to historical arguments should normally be a complex one that takes into account both sides and weighs things up (Jenkins, 1991: 38), 'bring difference into existence [...] and hence openness' (Kress, 1989: 12), in school history books arguments may often be 'a site of closure' (Coffin, 2006: 199). As a result, the reader is persuaded to accept one perspective as having greater explanatory power or 'truth' than any other. This is especially true of the two arguing sub-genres challenge and exposition, which introduce competing interpretations in order to overshadow or contradict them. The reports studied here often recur to these sub-genres but not to the sub-genre 'discussion' which 'presents a more balanced range of perspectives on the past, with the purpose of reaching an interpretation based on a careful consideration of all available evidence' (Coffin, 2006: 80).

Challenge is 'an analytical text which argues against commonly held interpretations,' while drawing attention to the fact that the event can be interpreted in different ways (Coffin, 2006: 80).

The stages of the challenge are:

1) Position challenged.
2) Rebuttal of arguments.

3) Marshal opposing evidence and argument.
4) Deduction which summarizes the argument in an antithesis. This antithesis, or alternative interpretation, is then read as the logical conclusion and as a new idea.

50 Years uses challenge at the end of the Qibya report (my comments in brackets):

> Some maintain the reprisals [...] increased Fadayun infiltrations instead of stopping them as was hoped (*position challenged*). However, after the 1956 war the infiltrations stopped and the feeling of personal security among Israeli citizens grew (*rebuttal and antithesis*)

The positive opinion regarding the effective consequences of the Qibya massacre and other such 'reprisals' is presented as fact and is meant to refute or discredit the negative one which is presented as supposition and therefore as a weaker assumption.

Exposition: As we have seen earlier, with regard to the creation of what is labeled 'the refugee problem' some books use exposition to present alternative interpretations without explicitly discussing or refuting them and thus create an impression of balance and debate, though the text leads the reader to a single point of view. At the end of the chapter that includes the Dier Yassin massacre in Naveh et al. (2009: 142), we find this exposition regarding the 'flight' of the Palestinians accelerated by the Dier Yassin and other massacres.

> For Israel, this phenomenon enabled the deployment of Jewish dominion and solved many problems such as security, housing and lack of lands, determining thereby the Jewish character of the state of Israel. By contrast, many Palestinians lost their homes, their land and the Palestinian state they could have received following UN decisions.

This exposition presents the consequences of the war as a tragic dilemma, and the text does not determine the weight of each of its parts. However, according to Israeli-Zionist narrative the two parts of the exposition – or of the dilemma – cannot exist side by side and each one of them must annihilate the other in order to survive. Since the 'redemption' of the Land namely its 'Judaization' or Jewish 'character' is the ultimate goal of the Zionist project, and since a Palestinian state is the most feared threat according to this ideology, this exposition leads to the legitimation of the cleansing of Palestine through its outcome – the acceleration of Palestinian flight which enabled the establishment of a Jewish state while removing the threat of a Palestinian one.

As was discussed in chapter 1 *Face* (p.323) uses the structure of exposition as a rhetorical gimmick, presenting, structurally, two points of view, the 'Jewish' one and the 'Arab' one, regarding Plan D cleansing operations.

While this sort of mock exposition is acceptable and approved of, a 'real' exposition that was not meant for closure but for debate was one of the reasons the book by Domka et al. (2009) was 'collected off the shelves' as soon as it was published. The book presented the Palestinian version regarding the ethnic cleansing in 1948 alongside the Israeli one, using both Israeli and Palestinian sources (such as Walid Khalidi's books). The change requested by the ministry of education was first of all to remove the Palestinian sources from the Palestinian version and to substitute it either with Palestinian texts that are 'more faithful to reality' or with Israeli sources. The reason given was that the writers had not considered the power of the Palestinian texts and the effect they might have on the students.[26] One argument was that 'presenting Arab propaganda as equal in value to the Israeli version is like presenting the Nazi version as equal to that of the Jews regarding the Holocaust.'[27] In order to have the book republished, the authors replaced the Palestinian sources with Israeli ones in the section called The Palestinian Version and gave it less weight without changing the structure; in other words, they reproduced a 'mock-exposition' as in *Face*. This incident manifests the social importance of genre.

As was said above, the genre of argument invites debate and discussion, and this may account for its rarity in Israeli school books. The only book that does present a discussion regarding a massacre is the civics book *Being Citizens in Israel* (2001), which is being thoroughly revised now by the order of the head of the pedagogical council of the ministry of education precisely because it promotes 'criticism against the state.'[28] This book offers a much more detailed account of the Kaffer Kassem massacre and does not conceal the existence of the order to kill everyone who broke the curfew. It then discusses the nature of 'manifestly unlawful orders' – a term coined in the Nuremberg Trials and used in Israel since the massacre of Kaffer Kassem, and the capacity of soldiers to identify such orders. Below are extracts from the report of Kaffer Kassem massacre as it is reproduced in this book and the discussion that follows it (headings and comments added).

Chapter title: The Limits of Obedience to the Law in a Democratic Regime.

Sub-chapter: The duty of disobedience to the law.

Claim: It is important to note that not every disobedience to the law, to an order or to a decree is considered a felony. There are cases – especially in the military system – in which the soldier is obliged to disobey an order or a decree which are manifestly unlawful.

Explanation: A manifestly unlawful order is a rare case of a law or a decree that contradicts in its content the fundamental values of a well-formed society and is totally immoral. The individual is obliged then to disobey the unlawful order and those who obey it should be brought to trial.

Following this explanation is an account:

Input: The example of a manifestly unlawful order was given in Kaffer Kassem, a large Israeli-Arab village east of Rosh ha Ayin, close to the Jordanian border.

Record of events: On 29 October 1956, with the onset of the Kadesh campaign, a curfew was imposed *(by whom?)* on Arab villages between 17:00 and 6:00 the following morning. All inhabitants of the Arab villages between Petah-Tikvah and Natanya had to be at home throughout the duration of the curfew. The order *(given by whom?)* was very stern: There would be no arrests, and curfew breakers were to be shot dead. The order was published the same afternoon, and the Arab villagers who had gone to the fields outside the village early in the morning knew nothing about it. When their working day was done, they returned home as usual, after 17:00. They were shot dead by a border guard unit stationed in the village. Forty-seven people including 15 women and eleven children aged 8–15 were shot dead by the soldiers, upon the order of their commanding officer (*repetition as emphasis*; *mentioning of social actor by function*). It is important to note that Arab villagers from the villages neighboring Kaffer Kassem who returned home after 17:00 were arrested for violating the curfew but were not shot. The border guards understood they were not supposed to execute the villagers who had known nothing about the curfew imposed in their area (*further de-legitimation and marginalization of killers*) [...].

Discussion: The court definition of a manifestly unlawful order is problematic because it does not define clearly and accurately what it is. The definition determines the unlawfulness very ambiguously: 'unlawfulness that pierces the eye and revolts the heart.' The result of this ambiguity often puts many soldiers in a severe dilemma. The difficulty lies in that military law distinguishes between an illegal order which the soldiers must obey and an unlawful order they must disobey; for instance, when a commander orders his soldiers to search a house without a warrant [...] although the order is illegal the soldier must obey. Because of the importance of military discipline, military law obliges the soldiers to obey illegal orders. A soldier who refuses to obey an illegal order will stand trial. However, when the order is manifestly unlawful the soldier must disobey for if he obeys he will stand trial. The soldiers, who are required to make a moral deliberation, face a huge dilemma: should they obey an order that seems illegal to them because the military law obliges them to obey illegal orders or should they refuse to comply because the order is manifestly unlawful and they are bound by the military law not to obey such an order?

The soldier, who is often under stress and pressure, doesn't always know how to act. A soldier who has a sensitive conscience may risk disobedience to an order that revolts his conscience and is actually legal or illegal but not manifestly unlawful. By contrast, a soldier may find himself obeying a manifestly unlawful order that did not revolt his conscience, at least not at the time of the action.[29]

Conclusion: Semiotic Means of Legitimation in Reports about Massacres

The legitimation of massacres in the school books studied here is mostly based on effect and utility. Some books present the act of slaughter as a justified battle, a necessary evil, or as transgression from the official Israeli norm. Other books specify it was committed by the order of army officers. In all the reports the massacre is a departure point for positive changes for the killers' in-group.

Therefore, the main types of legitimation used in the reports are *mythopoesis* with its mythological logic, and *effect-oriented legitimation*, supported by *conformity* to universal norms and *naturalization*. The victims are presented as 'objects whose pain is neutralized,' and who have to be dealt with 'in a rational utilitarian calculus' (Žižek, 1989). Thus, the implicit argument of the reports seems to be that the massacres, regrettable as they may be, were beneficial for Israel, and other nations and armies would have done the same under similar circumstances.

Moral considerations, which play a marginal role in these reports, are usually linked with political ones. The reports advocate the view that under the circumstances, the massacres can be legitimated for their consequences and that they are compatible with Zionist goals and Jewish convictions. Some of them are explicitly approved or condoned by distinguished public figures. The representation of the perpetrators of the massacres as role-models supports the legitimatory claims.

In order to construe a narrative governed by mythological logic and present the massacre as a departure point for positive changes, the reports use the narrative genres *recount* and *account* which create a rhetorical effect of objectivity and lead the reader to accept a single perspective as fact.

The reports template includes the following stages:

1) Legitimating or de-legitimating ground.
2) The act of murder (legitimated or de-legitimated by positive/negative evaluation of killers and victims).
3) Legitimating consequences.

4) (optional) Deduction that includes a legitimating claim in the name of the big picture and the long-term consequences.

This structure serves the books' tone which is mostly authoritative and invites limited debate. That is why genres that are meant for debate such as argument or discussion are hardly used in these reports. Of the arguing genres the reports use the sub-genres *challenge* and *exposition* which are both aimed at introducing competing interpretations in order to overshadow or discard them. As in *recount* and *account*, these genres often include 'deductions' that reinforce a single interpretation and create closure. Reports for the older students use the genre of questions in order to establish a legitimating reading position mainly through abstraction, generalization and modality.

Socio-Semantic Means Used in the Reports

As was mentioned before, Van Leeuwen defines the linguistic and discursive means whereby social meanings are conveyed as socio-semantic means, for although these means are part of a linguistic system, 'meanings are cultural and not linguistic' (2008: 24). One of the most important means is modality, which differentiates between legitimation and de-legitimation and is used to present the Palestinian versions – when they are presented – as less true than the Israeli ones; it is also used to lessen Israeli responsibility for the killing and suggest that massacres should not always have negative moral or political consequences.

The passive mode helps suppress or background social actors and turn human action into independent, objective, 'natural' or autonomous phenomena. Grammatical metaphor is used for the construction of pseudo-logical legitimating arguments, covering long periods by condensing processes and events into human-less nouns or nominal groups.

From the system of appraisal, explicit negative social valuation and social sanction are used to de-legitimate the killers or the act of slaughter and are usually realized through extra-vocalized judgment by personal and impersonal authorities such as military, religious or political leaders and institutions. Positive social esteem and social valuation serve to praise the killers and present them as role-models who could not have done unjustified wrong.

Multimodal means are used to present the perpetrators as role models and create the myth of the beautiful killers.

In summary, the reports herein explored reproduce what Ricoeur termed 'ideologized narratives' which are configured by 'eliminating, shifting emphasis, recasting the protagonists of the action in a different light along with the outlines of the action' (2004: 448).

Implications

The reports about massacres prove Wretsch's contention that school history books prefer the creation of a 'usable past' over accuracy (Wertsch, 2002: 45) and that they usually command the students to forget what Ricoeur (2004) calls 'the other drama' – that of the victims and their circumstances – and look ahead of massacres to the favorable consequences for the Jewish-Israeli nation. Most reports 'simplify the social experience like a controlled scientific experiment' (Coffin, 1997: 220) and position the readers to accept the values and judgments of the dominant discourse. This way, they teach the students the discourse of power, of politicians and generals, and put at stake 'the disciplinary politics of truth' (Coffin, 1997: 201).

Massacres are inserted into the Israeli-Zionist collective memory as the 'founding crimes' of the nation, in a digestible way that exonerates the state of Israel from blame regarding the Palestinian ongoing *Nakba*.

The overall claim of all the reports about massacres is: positive outcome (for us) may condone or overlook evil (done to them) or as Žižek would put it (1989): so much pain (inflicted on them) is tolerable if it prevents a much greater pain (for us).

The determination of the books to justify the wrong by creating legitimating narratives can also explain why in none of the reports do we find what La Capra (2001: 125) calls empathic unsettlement. In the Israeli context such unsettlement may be interpreted as insecurity and empathy towards Palestinians and is therefore inadmissible.[30]

Israeli students embark upon their military service with the conviction that empathy is race or religion-related and has no place in the relationships between themselves and their neighbors who are given to their mercy, and that utility is the only criterion that should guide them in their conduct. This credo was manifest in the words of Yossi Bailin, one of the leaders of the Zionist left, who in pleading for the government to stop the carnage in Gaza in 2009, said: 'It is inhuman, it is un-Jewish, but above all it is ineffective.'[31]

CONCLUSIONS

Gellner (1983: 34) writes, paraphrasing Max Weber, that at the base of the modern state there is the professor, not the executioner, for the monopoly of legitimate education is more important than the monopoly of legitimate violence.

This book elaborated one aspect of the Israeli national narrative as it is taught in Israeli schools – the representation of Palestinians – in Israeli textbooks of geography, history and civic studies. The book's main issues were: 1.) Verbal and visual representation of Palestinians and their life in Israeli school books and 2.) Discursive and visual means that legitimate the exclusion, the discrimination and even the killing of Palestinian citizens and non-citizens.

The analysis of the texts was multimodal, and the mode of inquiry was grounded in social semiotic theory which states that representation is never neutral but always 'engaged' (Kress, 2003) namely ideological.

This last chapter summarizes the findings of the study and discusses their Pedagogical implications.

Israeli School Books Between History and Collective Memory

The study has shown that the main features of collective memory, listed by Wertsch (2002), as prevailing in Soviet school books, can also be seen in the Israeli school books examined here:

1) The books have a 'commemorative voice' which relates unchallenged narratives, especially tragic and heroic ones.

2) They tend to present events 'from a single committed perspective; [are] impatient with ambiguities and reduce events to mythic archetypes' (Novick, 1999: 3–4).
3) They simplify history and focus on stable unchanging group essence (Wertsch, 2002: 47).
4) They are committed to the construal of coherent individual and group identity.
5) They command forgetting, by being based on a very strict selection of facts.
6) They prefer the creation of a usable past over accuracy and often harness the past and manipulate it for the justification of the present. As Nora describes it, 'we take shards of the past and try to glue them together in the hope that the history we reconstruct might seem more like the history we experience' (Nora, 1996: 13).

The books studied here harness the past to the benefit of the present and the future of Israeli policy of expansion, whether they were published during leftist or right-wing ministries.

The present book has shown that Israeli school books of various subjects are governed by the regime of truth or as Tyack, who studies American education (2000: 3) calls it, the Truth Police that controls the books and makes sure they inculcate collective memory grounded in state approved civic truth. Jenkins explains that the truth of power 'acts as censor – it draws the line,' arguing that 'we know that such truths are really useful fictions that are in discourse in virtue of power (somebody has to put and keep them there) and power uses the term "truth" to exercise control: regimes of truth.' (Jenkins, 1991: 39). Jenkins contends that the aim of such regime of truth is to prevent disorder 'and it is the fear of disorder (of the disorderly) [...] the fear of freedom (for the unfree) that connects it functionally to material interests' (ibid.).

The narrative reproduced in the textbooks studied here has another typical trait: It has no sense of the passage of time. It is what Halbwachs (1997) calls a picture of resemblances, unlike history which is a picture of changes.

In the composition of this picture of resemblances Israeli school books express eternal 'truths' about the Jews – usually tragic ones, such as persecution and victimhood, and eternal 'truths' about the non–Jews, who are in this case the 'Arabs.' Israeli school books – in defiance of factual evidence – still present the Palestinians as the 'thugs' and the Israelis as the victims and as the protectors of the land. The centuries-old Jewish saying repeated every Passover: 'Every generation they rise to exterminate us' – reminding one of the constant persecution of the Jews, is still presented in current Israeli school books , as in the political discourse, as an actual fact of the present, ignoring the significant changes in this reality, such as the fact that Israel is a strong state, with unequal military force, that dominates 4.5 million Palestinian Arabs, most of whom are refugees, children or grandchildren of refugees, who have no military force and no civil or human rights.

Historian Confino (2007a) explains the raison d'être of this narrative:

> The collective memory of victimhood has become central in the explanation the Israeli society gives itself regarding its actions in the [occupied] territories. [...] The memory of the Holocaust has become more central as the occupation has become more cruel [...].
>
> Since the 1970s, in Israel, as in the world in general, there has been a change in the memory of the Shoa; [...] it emphasizes victimhood much more than heroism. At the same time the occupation has become harsher and less heroic [for] there is nothing heroic in breaking into a home at night when the babies cry, in detaining a pregnant woman at the checkpoint or in forcing a whole population under curfew so that the children of Israel can celebrate their holiday of freedom (Passover).

Another immutable truth reproduced in the textbooks studied here is the colonialist message about Israeli Jews being the emissaries of progress and enlightenment in an environment where primitive Arabs must be civilized or rather cultivated like the 'neglected' landscape (Piterberg, 2001). Although the Palestinian citizens of Israel pursue modern professions and modern life, their modern ways are never represented either verbally or visually; instead Israeli students learn that their Palestinian co-citizens are slowly 'developing' thanks to the proximity of Jewish cities, villages and kibbutzim.

All these traits make the school books the propagators of collective popular memory more than the product of historical or geographical inquiry. The school books studied here, which are all mainstream textbooks, don't engage students in the historical or geographical disciplinary modes of inquiry but rather induce them to 'master' the master narrative. The tone of the textbooks is mostly authoritative and does not invite debate, even when structurally the text may look like it does. Events are reported from a military-Zionist perspective, which is intolerant to ambiguities and contradicting versions, while the Palestinian versions are usually silenced or 'under told' (cf. Rouhana and Korper, 1997 in Rabinowitz, 2001). The case of Domka et al. (2009) where the Palestinian versions had to be deleted from the book in order for it to be authorized, is an edifying example. The Israeli-Zionist narrative, as it is reproduced in the school books analyzed within this book, reflects the opinion that the Palestinians cannot be viewed but as an obstacle or a threat to be overcome or eliminated. Therefore their stories, their suffering, their truth or their human faces cannot be included in the narrative.

Israeli school books receive authorization only when they reproduce the state-sponsored narrative; therefore despite archives attesting to the systematic master plan of expansion and expulsion (Yiftachel, 2006, Morris, 2002, Pappé, 2006), to the systematic razing of Palestinian villages and to the massacres, and despite documents that attest to the retro-active transfer after the 1948 war, most school books still promulgate the story that the Palestinians fled out of unfounded panic, and present expulsion and massacres as esoteric transgressions or rare cases of necessary evil.[1]

The exclusion of Palestinians in Israeli textbooks can be summarized under the four categories offered by Thompson (1987):

1) **Legitimation**: Representations designed to immortalize dominance through its presentation as legitimate. Such representations are maps of the greater Israel accompanied by biblical phrases reiterating the divine promise to Abraham; the presentation of

land-confiscation, discrimination, marginalization, segregation, expulsion and annihilation of Palestinian Arabs as legitimate practices, justified by security claims and hailed as the realization of biblical prophesies and the Zionist ideal of the redemption of the land.

2) **Dissimulation**: Presentation of events from a single point of view. In the case of the textbooks studied here it is the military-Zionist perspective. Other versions or points of view regarding social and geographical facts (such as settlement, land rights, water disputes, culture and social stratification) are hardly ever considered.
3) **Fragmentation**: Separating people from places, describing the land while ignoring or concealing the existence of its indigenous population. In the books studied here this is done through geographic silence, by changing the names of places and concealing major Palestinian cities, universities, historic and cultural sites from the maps. Fragmentation is also apparent in the description of life in Israel and Palestine without ever mentioning the existence of other cultures, languages or nationalities except for the Israeli-Jewish one and by presenting the Palestinians as foreign workers.
4) **Reification**: 'Representing transitory, historical states of affairs as if they were permanent, natural, outside of time. Re-establish the dimension of society without "history" at the very heart of historical society' (Thompson, 1987: 521). As was mentioned before the picture painted in the school books today is of an immutable reality where Jews are persecuted and have to defend themselves against non-Jewish aggression. Another 'transitory state of affairs presented as natural and outside of time' is Palestinian Arabs' segregated life and their dire conditions, which are depicted as part of their immutable natural lot. This representation is achieved through various multimodal means – racist icons of backward nomads and farmers, and expressions that objectify the people and present their discrimination and segregation as an unchanged phenomenon to be studied, not as processes caused by human agents and socio-political circumstances. These representations reinforce the image Israeli children already have of the Palestinians as violent, primitive and irrational peasants, which, as Rabinowitz

> puts it, 'nourishes an amalgam of right-wing anti-Arab reasoning,' and conceals an image of Palestinians which Israelis can identify as PLU (Person Like Us): 'Rational and educated, possessing the positive characteristics Israeli students tend to associate with their own collectives, a rational, well spoken, responsible Arab – a civilized, stereotype-busting native, with a jacket, a degree and an understanding smile' (Rabinowitz, 2001: 76)

Contrary to Podeh's hopes for 'the appearance of a new narrative in history textbooks [...] that may, in the long run, facilitate the reconciliation process between Israelis and Arabs,' (2000: 29), some of the most recent school books (2003–09) regress to the 'first generation' accounts – when archival information was less accessible – and are, like them 'replete with bias, prejudice, errors, [and] misrepresentations' (Podeh, ibid.). As the study presented here has shown, the differences between the books or between 'generations' of books are very small on the ideological level because none of the books, including the more progressive ones of the 1990s, neglects the job of creating 'a usable past' for the Israeli collective memory; none of them questions the Israeli-Zionist ideological basis or contests its basic assumptions regarding Jewish historical rights to the Land, or the need for a Jewish majority which engenders the need to marginalize, segregate and control the Arab citizens and non-citizens. As Yiftachel notes, the deep chasm often portrayed between rightist and leftist Jewish camps concerns only the extent and brutality of Judaization and not the taken-for-granted existence and necessity of this strategy (2006: 133).

In conclusion, despite researchers' arguments about critical tendencies during the 1990s, and some attempts at showing the multiple facets of the intricate relationships between Israelis and Palestinians, Israeli current mainstream textbooks, explored in this study, present a simplistic and therefore incomplete picture, viewed from a single committed perspective and conveying an unambiguous message: the Land of Israel has always belonged to the Jews, even during the 2000 years of their collective absence and must therefore remain Jewish, in spite of international decisions and laws and in spite of the fact that half the population under Israeli rule is Arab-Muslim.

As Yiftachel explains, this is quite typical of new nation states and especially ethnocracies. However, in the Israeli context this narrative, which is usually the only one Israeli students come to know, may explain – albeit partially – Israeli soldiers' behavior towards their subjugated Palestinian neighbors and towards their discriminated fellow-citizens. This behavior shows that indeed, as Allport maintained, the single-perspective narrative is especially eloquent in times of aggression, when the nation is unified against its 'enemies.' In Israel neither the general social discourse nor the educational one express any 'empathic unsettlement' while speaking or writing about the discrimination and oppression of Palestinian citizens and non-citizens.

Nowhere in the books have we found a hint of a possibility, of an intention or a wishful thought to better the situation, grant the Palestinian citizens equal democratic rights or ease the pressure off occupied Palestine for the sake of peace, as could be expected in a democratic state educating its young on humanistic values. When peace is mentioned in history textbooks, it 'is always presented as a lesser evil, as giving up, as a forced solution, never as a chance for more prosperous life and closer connections with the neighbours' (Firer, 2004: 83).

Racist Representation of Palestinians in Israeli School Books

> Racism has historically been a banner to justify the enterprises of expansion, conquest, colonization and domination and has walked hand in hand with intolerance, injustice and violence. (Rigoberta Menchú Tum, Guatemalan Indigenous Leader and Nobel Peace Prize Laureate: 'The Problem of Racism on the Threshold of the 21st Century')

Although the UN committee on racism and discrimination of minorities or indigenous populations has not yet succeeded in including Israel among the racist countries[2], it is obvious from the present study that racist and discriminatory practices against Palestinians are presented as legitimate to Israeli students.

Many Israeli school books are often imbued with prejudgments and ethnic prejudice towards an 'enemy' that includes not only the subjugated and out-of-sight Palestinian non-citizens in the occupied territories and Gaza but also the Palestinian citizens of Israel, often termed by Israeli officials 'the enemy within' or 'fifth column.'

Rigoberta Menchú Tum, quoted above, talks about racism as a 'phenomenon that is supported by the belief of superiority in the face of difference, in the belief that one's own culture possesses values superior to those of other cultures' (ibid.).

The books studied here present Israeli-Jewish culture as superior to the Arab-Palestinian one, Israeli-Jewish concepts of progress as superior to Palestinian-Arab way of life and Israeli-Jewish behaviour as aligning with universal values. They use many forms of racist representation – both visual and verbal – and legitimate many forms of official discrimination listed long ago by the UN as unacceptable (Allport 1958: 51). Some of these are:

1) Unequal recognition before the law and general denial of rights to particular groups.
2) Inequality of personal security: Interference, arrest, disparagement and killing because of group membership. Note that when Israeli school books speak of safety and security they refer – as the political and the media discourses – to the safety of Jews only.
3) Inequality in freedom of movement and residence: the books present as normal and therefore legitimate the ghettoisation of the Arab population, forbidden travel of Palestinians, prohibited areas, and curfew restrictions.
4) Segregation: As we have seen even in geography texts and maps the Israeli population is divided ethnically and the segregation of Palestinians is presented as necessary and natural.
5) Inequality in the enjoyment of free choice of employment: The official inequality is not spelled out in the books but the fact that Palestinian citizens are never mentioned but as primitive farmers, nomads and terrorists reinforces it.
6) Inequality in the regulation and treatment of ownership, i.e. confiscation of land and the prohibition to build on their own land, which is expressed by the definition of Palestinian construction as 'illegal.'

7) Inequality of opportunity in education or the development of ability or talent.
8) Inequality of opportunity in sharing the benefits of culture: Palestinian culture is never mentioned and their cultural needs are never considered.
9) Inequality in services rendered such as housing, bus services, electricity and water as was plainly shown in chapter 2: The Geography of Hostility.
10) Inequality in the enjoyment of the right to nationality.
11) Inequality in the right to participate in government.
12) Inequality in access to public office.
13) Sumptuary laws and public libel of groups.

All these inequalities are presented in the books studied here as Given, and are never challenged.

Conclusion

Coffin (1997, 2006) argues that students learn from their history books not only the discourse of historians but also the discourse of politicians, lawyers and other manipulators of discourses. They learn to present interpretations as facts, to insert personal views into seemingly neutral representations, in short they learn the language of power. This imposition of the official 'truth' not only alienates them from disciplinary discourse and ways of inquiry but, as Ricoeur (2004: 448) warns,

> The prime danger lies in the handling of authorized, imposed, celebrated, commemorated history – of official history. The resource of narrative then becomes a trap, when higher powers take over the emplotment and impose a canonical narrative by means of intimidation or seduction, fear or flattery. A devious form of forgetting is at work here, resulting from stripping the social actors of their original power to recount their actions themselves. But this dispossession is not without complicity, which makes forgetting semi-passive semi-active behaviour [...] in short by a wanting-not-to-know.

This 'wanting-not-to-know' inculcated to Israeli youth through education,[3] is in fact 'wanting not to teach.' The state of Israel has never encouraged 'peace education' or official mixing between Jewish and Palestinian students. On the contrary, as Rabinowitz (2001: 65) makes clear '[the] plethora of opportunities notwithstanding, the topic of peace and co-existence never became part of the formal academic curriculum and never carried any academic credit in its own right.'[4]

As we have seen throughout the study, besides serving as a tool for instilling discriminatory ideas and racist attitudes, the representation of Palestinians in Israeli school books enhances ignorance, both of the real social and geopolitical situations and of geographical and historical discourse. Assuming that school students do not run to libraries to verify the facts and fill in the gaps in their school books and that most teachers were brought up on similar books, one must conclude that the past three generations of Israelis are, for the most part, not aware of the geopolitical or social realities of their country.

With such distorted pictures and skewed maps firmly fixed in their minds, Israeli Jewish students are drafted into the army, to carry out Israeli policy *vis-à-vis* the Palestinians, whose life-world is unknown to them and whose very existence they have been taught to resent and fear. This indoctrination or rather 'mind-infection' in Dawkins' terms, is achieved through the authority of scientific discourse, both verbal and visual, which is considered neutral, objective, unbiased and therefore representative of truth (Martin, 1993).

The negative representation of others, also found in some European countries regarding 'the Third World' and immigrants (see Van Leeuwen 1992 on Dutch school books) coaches students to hostility and contempt towards their immediate neighbors and environment and towards international accords and laws.

This is quite contradictory to the persistent Israeli claim, echoed by American and European politicians who endorse Israeli propaganda, that 'Palestinians teach their children to hate us and we teach Love thy neighbor.'[5]

Regarding the reasons for and eradication of discrimination the United Nations Expert Group Meeting on Managing Diversity in the Civil Service (2001) agreed on the following conclusions about the social causes of race prejudice, that reflect the Israeli reality:

> Social and economic causes of racial prejudice are particularly observed in settler societies wherein are found conditions of great disparity of power and property, in [...] which individuals are deprived of equal access to employment, housing, political participation, education, and the administration of justice [...]. Discrimination deprives a group of equal treatment and presents that group as a problem. The group then tends to be blamed for its own condition, leading to further elaboration of racist theory [...]

The United Nations Expert Group recommended some 'major techniques for coping with racism [which] involve changing those social situations which give rise to prejudice, preventing the prejudiced from acting in accordance with their beliefs, and combating the false beliefs themselves.'

They recognized 'that the basically important changes in the social structure that may lead to the elimination of racial prejudice may require decisions of a political nature. It is also recognised, however, that certain agencies of enlightenment, such as education and other means of social and economic advancement, mass media and law, can be immediately and effectively mobilised for the elimination of racial prejudice.'

The United Nations Expert Group gives special weight to education, arguing that,

> The school and other instruments for social and economic progress can be one of the most effective agents for the achievement of broadened understanding and the fulfilment of the potentialities of man. They can equally much be used for the perpetuation of discrimination and inequality. It is therefore essential that the resources for education and for social and economic action of all nations be employed in two ways: The schools should ensure that their curricula contain scientific

> understandings about race and human unity, and that invidious distinctions about peoples are not made in texts and classrooms. [...] Furthermore, in cases where, for historical reasons, certain groups have a lower average education and economic standing, it is the responsibility of the society to take corrective measures. These measures should ensure, so far as possible, that the limitations of poor environments are not passed on to the children. In view of the importance of teachers in any educational programme, special attention should be given to their training. Teachers should be made conscious of the degree to which they reflect the prejudices which may be current in their society. They should be encouraged to avoid these prejudices.

Unfortunately these recommendations have not reached either Israeli policy makers or educators and are not part of Israeli education or of the criteria for judging and authorizing school books in Israel. The lack of contact, enhanced by physical and mental barriers, between Israeli-Jewish and Israeli-Palestinian youth keeps these youngsters ignorant of each other's lives. The image of the Palestinians as potentially 'blood thirsty desperados, yearning for violent revenge, pushed to act against their own interests if they can only harm as many Israelis as they can' (Rabinowitz, 2001: 76) is still prevalent in textbooks as in the general discourse.

Israeli educational discourse as manifested in mainstream school books often present Palestinians' 'state of exception' as normative and their being Homini-Sacer namely people who are deprived of all human rights and are treated as 'bare life' (Agamben), people who lack, or are forcibly denied, all social or legal status, and whom anyone can do away with, as a necessity for Israel's security, as is evident from testimonies of soldiers.[6]

It would of course be presumptuous to believe school books are the main tool of indoctrination. However, as I hope this books has shown, Israeli school books reflect the social circumstances that produced them, and their discourse is nourished to a large extent by the political and military discourse of the state.

Suggestion for Further Study

The present study concentrated on the semiotic means used in school books to convey their messages, but it did not study the effect these books have on the students. So far, as Porat (2004) and Wertsch (2002) have shown 'textbooks do not seem to help redefine the cultural and historical perspectives that are shaped in concert with the wider socio-cultural context.' (Bekerman and Zembylas in press). As Bekerman and Zembylas further note: 'Textbooks and curricula are political tools but their influence is not necessarily greater than that of other mass media apparatus. Moreover, given the context in which they function–schools–they lose a force that in another context might have been noticed.' The conclusion of these studies and observations is, that text-books that are meant to change fixed ideas do not always succeed in doing so, but as Israeli youth's attitude towards Palestinian may prove, textbooks that seek to ingrain dominant ideas, biased and fraudulent as they may be, do succeed, as they are part of an all-encompassing promulgation of an anti-Arab myth.

A further study is needed in order to determine the role of school books in the formation of Israeli youth's consciousness as manifested in their behaviour both as soldiers and as citizens.

End-note:

At the end of every sentence you say in Hebrew sits an Arab with a Narguila.

Even if it starts in Siberia or in Hollywood with Hava-Naguila.

Meir Ariel 'A Song of Pain.'

PERMISSIONS

Three chapters of this book were published in shorter versions in academic journals.

Peled-Elhanan, N. (2009a) 'Layout as Punctuation of Semiosis: Some Examples from Israeli School Books', *Visual Communication* 8(1): 91–116.

Peled-Elhanan, N. (2009b) 'The Geography of Hostility and Exclusion', *Visual Literacy* 27(2): 179–208.

Peled-Elhanan, N. (2010) 'Legitimation of Massacres in Israeli School Books', was published in *Discourse and Society* 21(4). Pp.377–404.

I thank the journals for letting me reproduce the articles in this book.

I thank the publishers of the school books for letting me reproduce extracts.

NOTES

URLs were correct at the time of writing.

Preface

1. The word is half the speaker's and half the listener's. For the act of reading as personal meaning-making see also Iser, *The Act of Reading*, Barthes' *The Pleasure of the Text*, S/Z, Eco's *The Limits of Interpretation*, Bruner's *Acts of Meaning* to name but a few.

Introduction: A Jewish Ethnocracy in the Middle East

1. The study adopts Yiftachel's (2006) definition of ethnicity as 'cultural identity, based on belief in common ancestry at a specific place,' *Planning Theory* 5(3) p. 216.
2. For further discussion and bibliography regarding the role of Israeli Archeology in the creation of the Israeli national narrative of continuity see Sand, S. 2008: *When and How the Jewish People was Invented.*
3. *Haaretz*, 27 December 2008.
4. Walls, 2010 shows the changes in Swedish textbooks regarding the Israeli-Palestinian conflict and the Zionist influence on these books.
5. Fogleman, S., *Haaretz*, 29 July 2010: 'What happened to 130,000 Syrian citizens who lived in the Golan Heights in June 1967?'
6. See Bar-Tal and Nets-Zehngut 2008.
7. In a class of 20 students, when asked to define their identity two Israeli-born girls stated first and foremost that they were anti-Zionist. Two immigrant girls from former Soviet Union defined themselves personally. One said, 'I

am a woman, my name is Tania.' The other said: 'I am Sasha, feminist, social activist, trans-gender.'

8. See for example, 'Who Is a Jew? Court Ruling in Britain Raises Question' by Sara Shall, the *New York Times*, 7 November 2009. Also, Navot, Suzi, *The Constitutional Law of Israel*. Kluwer 2007, p.189; Uzi Rebhun, Chaim Isaac Waxman, *Jews in Israel: contemporary social and cultural patterns*, Brandies University Press 2004. (pp.296–297).
9. See for example, *Families fight 'racist' Israeli citizenship law,* BBC News, 9 March 2010.
10. The systematic razing of Palestinian presence on the land was discovered by historian Aharon Shay who revealed in an article published (in Hebrew) in the periodical Cathedra, (vol. 105, 2002) the existence of a cleansing unit founded by Ben Gurion in 1965. Regarding this unit and its project, Algazi (2007) explains: 'Its establishment was secret; the government decision to create it was never publicized. Its mission was cleansing the country, erasing systematically the remnants of the Palestinian villages lying abandoned since 1948 from the landscape. The Ministry of Foreign Affairs claimed that village ruins along the roads gave rise to unnecessary questions from tourists. [...] and Israel's Land Administration claimed that "levelling" the villages would spare Israel's Arab citizens anguish and the frustration of longing to return to their birth villages without being able to do so. The unit, which was headed by a former paratrooper officer, Hanan Davidson, erased over one hundred villages. [...] Archaeologists were required to conduct comprehensive surveys before the bulldozers entered the area. The Israel Archaeological Survey Society, established in 1964, received the funding for this from Israel's Land Administration. Surveying and demolishing, documenting and erasing went hand in hand. [...] The operation of "levelling" Palestinian villages was not confined to the Green Line, Israel's pre-1967 border. [...] Four days after the end of the 1967 war [...] the destruction operation, financed by Israel's Land Administration Bureau, was accelerated. The surveyors rushed to Yalou, Beit Nouba and Amwas, the three Palestinian villages in the Latrun area whose residents were driven out and their villages destroyed (Canada Park was built on these lands). The destruction of more than 100 villages in the Golan Heights was also carried out by Davidson's people in cooperation with the IDF.' http://www.kibush.co.il/show_file.asp?num=20936.
11. http://news.bbc.co.uk/2/hi/8163959.stm. Israeli textbooks to drop 'Nakba' 22 July 2009.
12. The Israel Democracy Institute http://www.idi.org.il/sites/english/OpEds/Pages/NakbaaLaw.aspx.

13. One of the most famous laments and the one that symbolizes the Exile of the children of Israel is, 'On the rivers of Babylon, there we sat and wept, remembering Zion' (Psalms 137). In that lament is also the phrase: 'If I forget thee O Jerusalem, may I forget my right hand.'
14. See Bar-Tal and Nets-Zehngut (2008) for the influence of fear on political and social decisions in Israel.
15. Israeli current minister of education believes that allowing the Palestinians to mourn their *Nakba* would be the 'moral bankruptcy' of Israel, and Zvulun Orlev, head of Educational Committee in the Knesset believes it would be the ruin of Israel as a Jewish state. (*Haaretz*, 1 May 2008).
16. Israeli school books are trade books, sold on the free market, and teachers may choose which book to use. However, they all need to be authorized by the Ministry of Education or at least be compatible with the national curriculum.
17. Published in: *Peace and Conflict: Journal of Peace Psychology*, 1532–7949, 14 (3), 2008, pp.233–258.
18. This was verified by reports from book stores regarding the most popular textbooks and by personal reports of teachers. Since teachers can choose from a variety of school books I asked major book stores to indicate which were the most popular books among teachers or the most asked-for by schools in the fields I studied.
19. Report of the committee for the examination of the history textbook *A World of Changes,* presided by Professor Yossef Gorni on 4 March 2001.
See Haaretz, July 13, 2001: "A few days after Limor Livnat was appointed minister of education, she banned a high-school history textbook called 'A World of Changes,' edited by Danny Yaakobi in consultation with seven scholars from four universities [...] Public criticism of the book was largely political: Its critics wanted a more patriotic textbook. [...] Apparently the Education Ministry continued to view the existing copies of the book as a serious hazard to the Zionist soul of the country's youth, as toxic material – so it decided to destroy them. The ministry's decision was cited in a letter written by the director of the curriculum planning and development department, Nava Segen, to one of the book's scientific consultants, Haim Saadon. The Jerusalem weekly Kol Ha'Ir, which carried a report by Neta Alexander on the subject last week, headlined it 'Where books are destroyed,' and accompanied it with a photograph from the textbook that is going to be destroyed – of the burning of books in Nazi Germany.
20. Kress 2003; Van Leeuwen 1992; Kress and Van Leeuwen 1995; 1996 among others.

21. 7 days – weekend supplement of Yediot Araronot daily journal, 2 July 2010. Interview with the principal of Hertzlia Gymnasium Zeev Degani.
22. *Haaretz* correspondents Yuval Goren, Yoav Stern and Mazal Mualem, 16 June 2009. On 23 July 2010 Aharonovish recommended amnesty to a policeman who killed a Palestinian and was sentenced by the Supreme Court – 2 days before – to 30 months in jail.
23. See Peled, Y. Adalah's Newsletter, Volume 6, October 2004: *The Or Commission Compared to the US Kerner Commission*. The conditions of political murderers of Jewish faith are much better than that of Palestinian political prisoners. While Jewish murderers are privileged with holidays, visits and amnesty, Palestinian prisoners who committed or attempted to commit the murder of Israelis do not have this privilege.
24. See for instance Kapeliuk: *Sabra and Shatila, Inquiry into a Massacre* published by the Association of Arab-American University Graduates. Belmont. MA. USA. (June 1984). The Christian fraction of Lebanon has been considered for a long time as an ally of Israel; this partnership culminated in the slaughter of Sabra and Shatila refugee camps in 1982 by the Christian phalanges, which the Israeli army enabled.
25. A student of mine in Tel Aviv University once said in class: 'We try to cultivate them, but they lock their women and daughters inside the house, beat them up and don't let them be educated'. When I pointed out to her that in the rows behind her there were about twenty Arab Muslim female students who could give her different information she said: 'I don't need that, I take Mid-Eastern Studies and I read articles'.
26. Interview with Zeev Galili, Yediot Aharonot, 22 November 1974.
27. A letter from Sholem to Rosenzweig 26 December 1929. In: *Od-Davar*. Tal-Aviv, Am Oved 1989. pp.59–60.
28. *The Jerusalem Post* 26 March 2008.
29. Arab-Palestinians and their supporters are never called 'victims' in Israeli media.
30. Or Heler, 16:55 20 June 2010. Nana10 News, Chanel 10, Israeli TV.
31. Yossi Melman, *Haaretz*, 17 July 2010.
32. For definitions of ethnic cleansing and its application to Palestine See Pappe, I. 2006, *The Ethnic Cleansing of Palestine*.
33. See Kress and Van Leeuwen 2002, Van Leeuwen 2010.
34. Olson (1989); Van Leeuwen (1992); Luke (1988, 1996); Veel and Coffin (1996); Wertsch (2002); Tyack (2003).
35. Swedish textbooks for instance are not controlled by the ministry of education and yet they all endorse the Zionist narrative for various reasons. See Walls, M. 2010.

36. My comments about teachers' reading are based on my 25 years of university and in-service instruction of school teachers.

1 The Representation of Palestinians in Israeli School Books

1. Non-Jews who are not Arab are often included in the 'Jewish' group, as will be shown in chapter 2.
2. Shamir, S. 1 March 2005, Haain Hashviit Israel Democracy Institute http://www.the7eye.org.il/Dailycolumn/pages/article5519.aspx. (Hebrew).
3. Cited in Akiva Eldar, www.haaretz.com 09 December 2004. Learning all the wrong facts: A study of Israeli and Palestinian textbooks shows how both sides tell the narrative of the conflict from their own perspective, ignoring the other side. http://www.haartez.com/hasen/pages/ShArtVty.jhtml?sw=akiva+eldar&itemNo=511984.
4. Or Kashti, http://www.haaretz.co.il/hasite/spages/1155708.html.
5. These categories are discussed in Van Leeuwen (2000:349).
6. See for instance, Yoav Stern *Haaretz*, 6 June 2010: Attempts to stop house demolition in Wadi Ara: it is not in Arab genes to build without a license.
7. One of the reactions published in a Labour online publication *Ofakim Hadashim* (New Horizons) on the 15 January 2007 written by right-wing journalist Yemini Ben-Dror, opens with the following words: 'Nowhere in the entire world is there a situation similar to ours. Many countries have minorities (some bigger and some smaller) but nowhere in the world is there a country that contains a minority that wishes to attach itself to its fellow ethnic group in a neighbouring country in order to destroy (or at least change) the ethnic character of the country in which it lives. Therefore, we must strive for complete separation between the ethnic movements, Jewish and Arab, without damaging the civil rights of Arab citizens and without relinquishing one iota the Zionist-Jewish character of the State of Israel.' (ofalcim.org.il/zope/home/he/authors/1113904789_auto?...).
8. For instance Zipi Livni in *Haaretz*, 27 December 2008.
9. Kahana, the founder of the separatist Jewish Defense League in Brooklyn, became the founder and leader of *Kach,* an ultra-right political party, which secured a seat in the Israeli Knesset in 1984 but was disqualified by the central election committee and the Supreme Court in 1988. Both bodies determined that the party spread illegal racist propaganda (Rabinowitz 2001).

10. Published by Adammeer, Association for human rights and prisoners' support. 1 March 2011 and Betselem, Israeli information centre for human rights in the occupied territories, February 2011.
11. A non-Jew hired to perform necessary work on the Sabath.
12. An interesting note to be made here is that Begin actually said the war was an alternative to 'Another Treblinka' but the writers chose to substitute Treblinka with Auschwitz, probably because Auschwitz is one of the major *lieux de memoire* in Israeli collective memory. Pre-army students are taken to Auschwitz every year as part of their initiation procedure – and it has long become the symbol of anti Semitism and Jewish extermination, even for people who hardly read or know anything about the Holocaust. The authors may have assumed that most students know at least the connotation of the word Auschwitz and changed Begin's words in order to make the message clearer.
13. According to Shlaim, A, (2001:32) 'There were many reasons for the Palestinian exodus, including the early departure of the Palestinian leaders when the going got tough, but the most important reason was Jewish military pressure. [...] By the end of 1948 the number of Palestinian refugees had swollen to around 700,000.' (*The Iron Wall: Israel and the Arab World*, (2nd Ed.) W.W. Norton & Company, New York/ London).
14. The exact facts of the ethnic cleansing of Palestine are not mentioned in any of the school books; according to Zochrot, 530 cities and villages were cleansed. 74 per cent of them (392 settlements) by the Jewish soldiers; 25 per cent as a result of Israeli threats and only 1 per cent (5 villages) were 'abandoned' due to orders from Arab leaders (Zochrot 2008: *How to say Nakba in Hebrew?*). http://www.nakbainhebrew.org/en.
15. Lydda (Lod) and Ramlah – ten miles south-east of Tel Aviv – were cleansed in Operation Danny of 10–14 July 1948, which resulted in a massacre at Lydda and the forcible transfer of the entire population of the townships of Ramlah and Lydda to Jordan.
16. This argument is also found in Shlaim (2001: 32): 'Plan D was not a political blueprint for the expulsion of Palestine's Arabs: it was a military plan with military and territorial objectives. However, by ordering the capture of Arab cities and the destruction of villages, it both permitted and justified the forcible expulsion of Arab civilians'.
17. The 'lodging' of Jewish immigrants on the 'abandoned' Palestinian lands was made possible by the 'retroactive transfer' of the Palestinian refugees and the 1950 law of Absentees' Properties, though none of the books mention it. The law states that the refugees are not to be allowed to return to their homes, to reclaim their property, or to seek compensation. An official

body called 'The Custodian' was authorized to sell absentees' land (defined in Clause 1[b] of the Law) to the Development Agency, a government body created specifically for the acquisition of these lands. This agency then sold it on to the Jewish National Fund which 'leases' the lands only to Jews and to non-Jews who are not Arab. (Piterberg, 2001).

18. Shahar Ilan, *Haaretz* http://www.haaretz.com/hasen/spages/1021288.html.
19. The village Nabi Samuel near Jerusalem is being cleansed as I write (http://www.mahsanmilim.com// Tamar Goldschmidt and Aya Kaniuk, 6 June 2010). Similarly the village El-Arakib in the Negev is being destroyed time and again for real-estate reasons (for the 15th time on the 10 February 2011). Houses in east Jerusalem, in Sheikh Jarakh, Silwan and Issawiya, are being evicted daily.
20. Shahar Ilan, *Haaretz* http://www.haaretz.com/hasen/spages/1021288.html.
21. The last example of this was the visit of prominent Israeli-Palestinian persons in Libya in April 2010.

2 The Geography of Hostility and Exclusion: A Multimodal Analysis

1. Textbooks of Independent Orthodox and state-religious streams were not included.
2. Reisigl and Wodak (2001: 28).
3. See for instance Or Kashti (*Haaretz,* 12 August 2009): Israel aids its needy Jewish students more than their Arab counterparts. The average per-student allocation in Arab junior high schools amounts to only 20 per cent of the average in Jewish junior highs.
4. This segregation is now legalized by a law that allows the Jewish National Fund to refrain from leasing land to Arab citizens and the Screening Committees Law approved on the 23 March 2011. The laws are a response to the Supreme Court 2004 ruling in favor of the Arab citizen Adel Kaadan, who wanted in 1995 to buy land in the outpost of Katzir and was refused on the ground that the land is reserved for army veterans (Supreme Court File 8060/03) and to the Supreme Court's ruling in 2007 in favour of the Zvidat family from Sakhnin who were rejected by the screening committee of Rakefet – (built on confiscated Sakhnin land) – who wanted to lease land in the nearby outpost, after being denied a permit to build on their own land. (Jaki Juri. Haaretz, 14 February 2007). Now the law allows settlements to reject people who are judged by the screening committees as unfit and the

no land can be leased without the permission of the screening committees (Ynet news 17.06.08, http://www.haaretz.co.il/hasite/spages/1195587.html).

5. There are at least 7 different sorts of Arab villages in Israel (Grossman and Katz 1993), each characterized by topographic conditions, type of land and crops.
6. One example is the ongoing destruction of the Bedouin village El-Arakib in the Negev, in order to plant a forest on their land. See for instance http://www.haaretz.com/print-edition/news/police-destroy-dozens-of-buildings-in-unrecognized-bedouin-village-in-negev-1.304443.
7. http:/www.mfa.gov.il/MFA/facts about Israel/Israel in maps#threats& topography. 1 January 2004.
8. The outposts or 'Mitzpim' are small ex-urban settlements, established during the late 1970s and early 1980s in the Galilee, ranging between 30 to 1,000 households, scattered between the Arab villages (Yiftachel, 2006: 33).
9. *How to lie with maps* (p.95) shows a similar map, issued by the Jewish National Fund in Canada in 1973, when Israel was twice its present size as it was still occupying the Sinai Peninsula. In this map Israel is a white spot squeezed between two dark Muslim blocks, and the title proclaims: 'Visual proof of Arab lies about Israel's "aggression".'
10. These terms are taken from Van Leeuwen (1992: 45), who used the terminology of television and film.
11. A million Palestinian refugees is not an accurate figure but the figure given by the book. Israel admits there are 3 million, UNRWA claims there are 3.5 million, and the Palestinians claim there are 5 million refugees, 1.5 million in Gaza Strip.
12. This statement stands in contrast to statements in history textbooks (i.e. *The 20th*:214) which assert that the Jewish refugees from Arab countries were actually deceived and treated badly by the state of Israel and their problems are still far from being resolved. However it serves the Israeli claim that it should be absolved of all responsibility for the Palestinian refugees for it had Jewish refugees from Arab countries to absorb.
13. Kress and Van Leeuwen (1996, 1995) explain that the polarization of left and right, top and bottom has ideological meaning. In English the left side would mean the Given or agreed-upon part of the message while the right side would include the new information; in Hebrew, the Given, known and uncontested information would be on the right and the New of the left. However, in all representations the bottom part of the page is reserved for the real or down-to-earth information while the top part is reserved for that which is presented as Ideal or abstract.

3 Layout as Carrier of Meaning: Explicit and Implicit Messages Transmitted Through Layout

1. Kress (2000), Van Leeuwen (1992, 1996, 2001, 2005, 2005a); Van Leeuwen and Selander (1995), Van Leeuwen and Kress (1995), Kress and Van Leeuwen (1996).
2. All emphases are mine unless indicated otherwise.
3. Jews – as explained in Israeli school books – had never been allowed to own land in most of the countries of their 'exile' of 2000 years, and had to recur to 'despised' professions such as money loaners, pawnbrokers and peddlers. Gordon, the 'prophet' of socialist Zionism, preached to leave this 'parasitic' way of life and live a '*whole and fulfilled life of work with our own hands*' which, he maintained, would be '*the only way to our resurrection*' (*The Age of Horror and Hope*, p.43).
4. A 'prolepsis' according to Genette (1972:106–107) is the insertion, in a literary work, of events that are posterior to the ones the text reports.
5. On 31 July 2007 one house in Ein H'ud was connected to electricity power. There are more than 100 'unrecognized villages' in Israel.
6. As a rule, this pulped book treats the Palestinians and the Jews as two equal parties that inhabit the contested land. For instance it calls the 1948 war a civil war and not the War of Independence as it is usually called in Israel.
7. In fact Galil Maimon did not participate in the attack but came later to rescue the children. The omission of this fact from the text may be another rhetorical means to enhance the criticism the caption is meant to convey.
8. Account according to Coffin (1997/2006) is a report which contains interpretation or judgmental explanation and therefore is structured not only chronologically but also rhetorically.

4 Processes of Legitimation in Reports about Massacres

1. *No Rattling of Sabers: Israeli War Poetry 1940–1990.* Translated from Hebrew by Esther Raisen. Austin: The Center for Middle Eastern Studies and The University of Texas Press, (1996: 140). Courtesy of University of Texas Press.
2. Merriam Webster online.
3. Lior Zlatin. *Davar.* 8 April 1993. Quoted in Blum-Kulka 2000.
4. See also: Amir, E., 'Not a Dozen but a Hundred and Ten', *Haaretz*, 22 May 2009.
5. Segev, T. (27.10.2006), *Back to Kaffer Kassem.* Available at: http://www.haaretz.co.il/hasite/pages/ShArtPE.jhtml?itemNo=779296&contrassID=2&subContrassID=13&sbSubContrassID=0; Karpel, D., Interview with Benyamin Kol, *Haaretz*, 8 October 2008; Rosenthal (2000).

6. It was after Tawfiq Touby, a Palestinian Knesset member from the communist party, divulged the event on the 23 November 1956 after visiting the village and interviewing the wounded. Toobbi wrote among other things: 'The direct perpetrators of the crime are not the only guilty ones, but mainly those who are responsible for the policy of persecution and oppression of the Arab population.' [...] http://www.tarabut.info/he/articles/article/tawfik-touby.
7. Sources include Segev, T., *Back to Kaffer Kassem*. Available at: http://www.haaretz.co.il/hasite/pages/ShArtPE.jhtml?itemNo=779296&contrassID=2&subContrassID=13&sbSubContrassID=0; Karpel, D., Interview with Benyamin Kol, *Haaretz*, 8 October 2008; and Rosenthal (2000).
8. Bar-Navi (1998) writes that the sentence 'was sweetened' and the soldiers were released after a short while. Naveh et al. write they were released after a year. None of the books mentions the fact that their commanding officer was fined for 2 pounds.
9. Yiftachel, O. (Un) Settling colonial presents, *Political Geography* (2007) vol. 26(1): 43–52.
10. See for instance Or Kashti, 11 March 2010: 'Half of Israeli youth against equal rights to Arab citizens. The majority denies Arabs' right to be elected to the Knesset.' http://www.haaretz.co.il/hasite/spages/1155708.html.
11. The most recent example is the law that permits screening committees to reject candidates who do not adhere to the settlement's cultural or religious life. Another law is the one allowing universities to grant priority in dorm allocation to army veterans, namely to Jews. Both laws were enacted in reaction to a court ruling that denounced these norms; the laws overrode the court ruling and legalized the norms.
12. For instance, as reported by Uri Blau in *Haaretz*, 28 November 2008, the chief of staff and IDF generals constantly find ways to deceive the Supreme Court and violate its ruling against extrajudicial assassinations. The former commander of the occupied territories General Yair Naveh is quoted saying upon *Haaretz*'s revelation: 'Leave me alone with the Supreme Court, I want the "wanted" one to be killed right away without messing around'. Thousands of documents regarding this command were given to the journalist Blau by the ex-soldier Anat Kam who was a secretary in the chief of staff's office during her military service. Kam is now standing trial for treason. http://www.timesonline.co.uk/tol/news/world/middle_east/article7086417.ece.
13. For instance, the instant killing of Ziad Jilani on 11 June 2010 by border guards who suspected him of intentionally trying to run over people with his car; the suspicion was found out as a wrong assumption. See http://www.haaretz.co.il/hasite/spages/1175712.html.

14. Both the UN Committee against Racism and Amnesty found the Law of Citizenship tainted with worrying racism. http://www.amnesty.org/en/report/info/MDE15/037/2005 http://news.bbc.co.uk/2/hi/middle_east/3152651.stm.
15. On 20 September 2007, MK Yuval Steinitz, head of the Knesset committee for security and foreign affairs, declared on Israeli radio that he supported shooting civilians in areas from which Kassam missiles are launched. Answering the legal advisor to the government who had warned against committing war crimes, he said: 'Israel's deterrent capacity rests upon the principle of fire for fire and horror for horror and those who denounce that forsake the security of Israeli citizens'. Available at: steinitz.likudnik.co.il. Also, following the killings in the religious college Merkaz Harav in Jerusalem, and in support of the decision of Israeli defense minister Barak to demolish the home of the killer's family, the ex-chief Rabbi of Israel, Rabbi Elyahu said as reported in *Haaretz*, 4 April 2008: 'The Gemara says that if the Gentiles take silver from Israel they should return gold, anything they take they should return double. But in this case it cannot be because 1000 Arabs are not worth 1 Jewish student.' Such declarations were made by officers during the raid on Gaza in 2009, according to soldiers' testimonies to Breaking the Silence. See: Occupation of the Territories, Israeli soldier testimonies 2000–10, Breakingthesilence.org.
16. On 15 March 2008, actor Shlomo Vishinsky told Israeli TV that the army spokesman had called to notify him that the IDF had avenged the death of his son, killed in action in Gaza, by assassinating his killer's 'dispatchers'. Later, the national radio wanted to know if the assassination gave him any consolation. Both my own sons, who were soldiers at the time of their sister's murder by a Palestinian suicider from the West Bank, were egged on by their commanders to avenge her death by committing 'reprisals' in Lebanon. They refused.
17. See for Instance Jewish Encyclopedia http://www.daat.ac.il/encyclopedia/value.asp?id1=1645.
18. This effect stated as an historical fact is actually a quote from an article written in the popular daily newspaper Yediot Aharonot by the commander of this massacre, Ariel Sharon, 39 years after the slaughter, on 18 October 1992. The article was called 'the operation that has restored the dignity of the IDF.'
19. One of the only three who ever returned alive from Petra was 19-year-old Meir Har-Zion, who later became the fiercest warrior of Unit 101 and a mythological hero in his lifetime, admired by his commander Sharon, by the Chief of Staff Dayan and by the Prime Minister Ben Gurion as an invincible fighter. Har-Zion features in the photograph, standing first from the left.

See Morris, Benny (1993) Israel's Border Wars, 1949–1956. Arab Infiltration, Israeli Retaliation, and the countdown to the Suez War. Oxford University Press, ISBN 0 19 827850 0. p.239.

20. Melinky's order was to have 'at least 10 bodies in every village in order to better enforce the curfew,' as one of the junior commanding officers – Benyamin Kol – told Dalya Karpel from *Haaretz* more than 50 years after the slaughter (8 October 2008). When asked what about women and children, or workers coming in late from the fields, Melinky answered in Arabic: 'May Allah have mercy on them,' which is equivalent to 'May they rest in peace.' When asked, 'What about the wounded?' he replied: 'There will be no wounded.' http://www.haaretz.co.il/hasite/pages/ShArtPE.jhtml?itemNo=779296&contrassID=2&subContrassID=13&sbSubContrassID=0.

    Such instructions are not unusual. Former Chief of staff and present minister of Transport, Shaul Mofaz, has allegedly required IDF commanders in a meeting held on 6 May 2001 a score of 70 Palestinian bodies a day (Akiva Eldar, *Haaretz*, 2 September 2008).

21. The only books that admit there was such an order are Domka et al. (2009), Naveh et al. (2009) and the civil studies book: *Being Citizens in Israel*, which is now being seriously revised.
22. The most known defender of the thesis that there was no massacre in Dier Yassin is historian Uri Milstein, See: Milstein, Uri (1996). *History of the War of Independence: Out of crisis came decision.* Vol. 4. Sacks, A., trans. New York: University Press of America. (pp.376–396). Milstein, Uri (2007) *Blood Libel: The True Story of the Massacre of Dier Yassin.* Survival Institute Publishers. Israel.
23. This particular event is not discussed in this chapter because it did not involve the killing of Palestinians but of Jews. However, the rhetoric is identical.
24. Boymel (2002:156) explains that the military government was abolished only after the 1967 war, when Israel felt more secure and the pretext of the Arab citizens being 'an enemy from within' was weakened. Another major factor was the movement of labor from the Palestinian occupied territories into Israel, which became the new security threat and the focus of military control. Also, by that time Israel had realized that the military government's chief goal – to 'encourage' a self-transfer of Palestinians to Jordan – would not be achieved. The final and most decisive factor was the retirement of Ben Gurion from office in 1963 and his replacement by Levi Eshkol who had never supported the idea of the military government.
25. Boymel, Y. (2002). The Military Government on the Israeli Arabs and its Cancellation, 1948–1968. in: *Hamizrach Hachadash* (The New Orient), Vol.43. pp.133–156.

26. Tzafrir Goldberg (one of the writers), personal communication.
27. Or Kashti, *Haaretz*, 16 November 2009.
28. Or Kashti, *Haaretz*, 1 September 2010, http://www.haaretz.co.il/hasite/spages/1187466.html.
29. As this book is coming to its end, the incoming head of the National Security Council, Major–General (res.) Ya'acov Amidror defined the order to fight with caution as a manifestly unlawful order. 'The idea is to kill as many bastards from the other side. We should win, full stop.'

    He added that soldiers have to kill whomsoever is on their way to complete their mission. http://www.haaretz.co.il/hasite/spages/1218121.html.
30. As is expressed in the law – endorsed by the Israeli parliamentary committee for legislation and constitution on 23 February 2010, to withdraw budgets from municipalities that allow the commemoration of Palestinian catastrophe in 1948. http://www.ynet.co.il/articles/0,7340,L-3852834,00.html.
31. Television interview, 25 January 2008.

Conclusions

1. This popular shared narrative is well expressed in a reaction to my work by an Israeli journalist Ben-Dror Yemini who wrote in NRG (Maariv on line) on 27 December 2008: 'She writes about the "slaughter of Palestinians" though she knows Israel has never committed a massacre or anything close to a massacre, in more than 40 years of occupation'.

   An illustration of the danger of endorsing the 'other's narrative' can be my own misinterpretation of Israeli state discourse: On the morning of the Israeli raid on Gaza, 28 December 2008, Minister of Defense Barak said on television, 'Those who hurt civilians will pay,' and I misunderstood his words as an order to his own soldiers not to obey manifestly unlawful orders and not to harm Palestinian civilians. However, as I found out later, this statement was part of the rationalizing and legitimating discourse that allowed aggression against Palestinian civilians in Gaza.
2. See *Haaretz*, 1 January 2009 for an account about the Durban Conference on Racism http://www.haaretz.com/news/delegates-unanimously-adopt-durban-ii-anti-racism-declaration-1.266846.
3. See for instance the interview with former minister of education Shulamit Aloni. http://www.axisoflogic.com/artman/publish/article_6869.shtml.
4. Rabinowitz mentions three shifts in the negative attitude of different Israeli governments along the years, for instance, 'In the late 1980s and early 1990s, when under Yitzhak Shamir's Likud government, which had the Ministry

of Education dominated by the National Religious Party, state sponsorship of the co-existence project became narrower in scope and more restrictive ideologically'.

The second shift came with the ascent to power of Binyamin Netanyahu's right-wing government in 1996, which brought about a steep decline in budget allocation for co-existence projects, followed by a sharp reduction in activities. In 1993 there was a very short-lived Ministry of Education's Unit for Democracy and Co-existence which was later changed to the unit of Value Education in a Jewish democratic state.

5. Minister of Foreign Affairs Zipi Livni during the Israeli raid on Gaza, *Haaretz*, 30 December 2008.
6. See Breaking the Silence – Testimonies from Gaza. http://news.bbc.co.uk/2/shared/bsp/pdfs/14_07_09_breaking_the_silence_pdf.

REFERENCES

The School Books

Geography

Aharony. Y., and Sagi T. (2003). *The Geography of the Land of Israel: A Geography Textbook for Grades 11–12.* Tel Aviv: Lilach Publishers.

Fine, T., Segev, M., and Lavi, R. (2002). *Israel: The Man and the Space: Selected Chapters in Geography.* Tel Aviv: The Centre for Educational Technologies Publishers.

Rap, E., and Fine, T. (1996/1998). *People in Space: A Geography Textbook for 9th Grade.* Tel Aviv: The Centre for Educational Technologies Publishers.

Rap, E., and Shilony-Tzvieli, I. (1998). *Settlements in Space: Chapters in the Geography of Settlements in the World.* Tel Aviv: The Centre for Educational Technologies Publishers.

Segev, M., and Fine, Z. (2007). *People and Settlements.* Tel-Aviv: The Centre for Educational Technologies.

Vaadya, D., Ulman, H., and Mimoni, Z. (1994/1996). *The Mediterranean Countries for 5th Grade.* Tel Aviv: Maalot Publishers.

History

Avieli-Tabibian, K. (1999). *Journey into the Past: Chapters in History for Grades 8–10.* Tel Aviv: The Centre for Educational Technologies.

Avieli-Tabibian, K. (2001). *The Age of Horror and Hope: Chapters in History for Grades 10–12.* Tel Aviv: The Centre for Educational Technologies.

Bar-Navi, E. (1998). *The 20th Century: A History of the People of Israel in the Last Generations for Grades 10–12.* Tel Aviv: Sifrei Tel Aviv.

Bar-Navi, E., and Naveh, E. (1999). *Modern Times Part II: The History of the People of Israel for Grades10–12.* Tel Aviv: Sifrei Tel Aviv.

Blank, N. (2006). *The Face of the 20th Century*. Tel Aviv: Yoel Geva.

Domka, E., Urbach, H., and Goldberg, Z. (2009). *Nationality: Building a State in the Middle East*. Jerusalem: Zalman Shazar Centre.

Eldar, T., and Yafe, L. (1998). *From Conservatism to Progress: A History Textbook for Grade 8*. Tel Aviv: The Ministry of Education and Maalot Publishers.

Inbar, S. (2004). *50 Years of Wars and Hopes*. Tel Aviv: Lilach Publishers.

Naveh, E. (1994). *The 20th Century: The Century that Changed the Order of the World*. Israel: Tel Aviv Books, Mapa Publishers.

Naveh, E., Vered, N., and Shahar, D. (2009). *Nationality in Israel and the Nations: Building a State in the Middle East*. Tel Aviv: Rehes.

Yaakoby, D., et al. (1999). *A World of Changes: A History Book for 9th Grade*. Tel Aviv: The Curriculum Centre in the Ministry of Education/Maalot.

Civic studies

Aden, H., Ashkenazi, V., and Alperson, B. (2001). *Being Citizens in Israel: A Jewish Democratic State*. Jerusalem: Maalot Publishers and the Ministry of Education.

General Bibliography

Agamben, G. (1987). *Homo Sacer: Sovereign Power and Bare Life*. Meridian: Crossing Aesthetics.

Allport, G. W. (1958). *The Nature of Prejudice*. New York: Doubleday Anchor.

Antaki, C. (1994). *Explaining and Arguing: The Social Organization of Accounts*. London: Sage.

Arnheim, R. A. (1988). *The Power of the Centre: A Study of Composition in the Visual Arts*. Berkeley: University of California Press.

Bakhtin, M. M. (1984). *Problems of Dostoevsky's Poetics*. Edited and translated by Caryl Emerson. Minneapolis: University of Minnesota Press.

—— (1986). *Speech Genres and Other Late Essays*. Trans. by Vern W. McGee. Austin, TX: University of Texas Press.

Bar-Gal, Y. (1993a). *Moledet and Geography in a Hundred Years of Zionist Education*. Tel Aviv: Am Oved Publishers.

—— (1993b). 'Boundaries as a Topic in Geographic Education: The Case of Israel,' *Political Geography*, 12(5), 421–435.

—— (1996). 'Ideological Propaganda in Maps and Geographical Education.' In van der Schee, J., and Trimp, H., *Innovation in Geographical Education: Netherlands Geographical Studies*, IGU, Commission on Geographical Education, Hague, 67–79.

—— (2000). 'Values and ideologies in place descriptions: The Israeli Case,' *Erdkunde: Archive for Scientific Geography*, 54, 168–176.

—— (2003). *Geographic Politics and Geographic Education: A Talk*. Conference of the Geographic Society, Bar-Illan University, Tel Aviv.

—— (2004). 'Unity–Transformation–Unity–Dissolution: Metamorphoses in the Country's Landscape.' In Ayal, A., *Our Landscape: Notes on Landscape Painting in Israel*, Haifa: Art Gallery, Haifa University, 29–33.

Bar-Tal, D. (2000). 'From intractable conflict through conflict resolution to reconciliation: Psychological analysis,' *Political Psychology*, 21, 351–365.

—— (2007). 'Sociopsychological foundations of intractable conflicts,' *American Behavioral Scientist*, 50, 1430–1453.

Bar-Tal, D., and Nets-Zehngut, R. (2008). 'Emotions in Conflict: Correlates of Fear and Hope in the Israeli-Jewish Society,' *Peace and Conflict: Journal of Peace Psychology*, 1532–7949, 14(3), 233–258.

Barthes, R. (1957). *Mythologies*. Paris: Editions de Seuil.

—— (1967a). 'Le Discours de l'histoire.' In *Le Bruissement de la langue*. Paris: Editions du Seuil.

—— (1967b). 'L'effet du reel.' In *Le Bruissement de la langue*. Paris: Editions du Seuil.

—— (1977). *Image, Music, Text.* London: Fontana.

—— (1969). *Sur Racine*. Paris: Editions du Seuil.

—— (1980). 'La chambre Claire.' In *Oeuvres Complètes*, Volume V. Paris: Editions du Seuil.

Baudrillard, J. (1983). *Simulations*. USA: Semiotext(e).

Bekerman, Z., and Zembylas, M. (in press). *Identity, Memory, Reconciliation and Beyond*. Cambridge University Press.

Boymel, Y. (2003). 'The Military Government on the Israeli Arabs and its Cancellation, 1948–1968,' *Hamizrah Hahadash* (the New Orient), 43, 133–156.

Begin, M. (1951). *The Revolt: Story of the Irgun*. New York: Henri Schuman.

Bernstein, B. (1996). *Pedagogy, Symbolic Control and Identity: Theory, Research, Critique.* London: Taylor and Francis Publishers.

Blum-Kulka, S. (2000). 'Hegemonic, polysemic or subversive discourse? News and History.' In Swarzwald, O., Blum-Kulka, S., and Olshtain, E., (eds), *The Rafael Nir Book*. Jerusalem: Carmel.

Boggs, S. W. (1947). 'Cartohypnosis,' *Scientific Monthly*, 64, 469–476.

Byrne, D. (1999). *Social Exclusion*. London: Open University Press.

Cazden, C. (2001). *Classroom Discourse: The Language of Teaching and Learning.* Portsmouth, NH: Heineman.

Chiffrin, D. (1988). *Discourse Markers*. Cambridge: Cambridge University Press.

Coffin, C. (1997). 'Constructing and Giving Value to the Past.' In Christie, F., and Martin, J. R., (eds), *Genres and the Institutions*. London: Continuum.

—— (2006). *Historical Discourse*. London: Continuum.

Confino, A. (2007a). 'Before the Locked Gate: The History and Memory of the1967 War,' *Haaretz* (Sfarim: Book Review Supplement), 6 June 2007: 20–21. http://www.haaretz.co.il/hasite/pages/ShArtSR.jhtml?objNo=60104&returnParam=Y&itemNo=866884&objNo=60104&returnParam=Y.

Confino, A. (2007b). 'Changing Eternity with a Historical Modesty: History and Memory in Israel and Palestine,' *Haaretz* (Sfarim: Book Review Supplement), 18 April 12007: 10–11. http://www.haaretz.co.il/hasite/spages/849473.html.

De Beaugrande, R. (1997). *New Foundations for a Science of Text and Discourse: Cognition, Communication and the Freedom of Access to Knowledge and Society through Discourse,* Volume LXI. Advances in Discourse Processes. New Jersey: Ablex Publishers.

Dray, W. H. (1957). *Laws and Explanations in History*. London: Oxford University Press.

Essed, P. (1991). *Understanding Everyday Racism: An interdisciplinary theory,* Volume 2. Sage Series on Race and Ethnic Relations. London: Sage.

Fairclough, N. (2003). *Analyzing Discourse: Textual Analysis for Social Research.* London: Routledge.

Finlayson, J.G. (2005). *Habermas: A Very Short Introduction.* Oxford. Oxford University Press.

Firer, R. (1985). *The Agents of Zionist Education*. Tel Aviv: Hakibutz HaMeuhad and Sifriyat Poalim.

—— (2004). 'The Presentation of the Israeli-Palestinian Conflict in Israeli History and Civics Textbooks.' In Firer, R., and Adwan, S., *The Israeli-Palestinian Conflict in Israeli History and Civics Textbooks of both Nations.* Hannover: Georg-Eckert-Institute fur internationale Schulbuchforschung, Verlag Hahnsche Buchhandlung.

Gellner, E. (1983) *Nations and Nationalism*. Ithaca, NY: Cornell University Press.

Genette, G. (1972). *Figures III, Collection Poétique*. Paris: Editions du Seuil.

—— (1982). *Palimpseste: La littérature au second degré.* Paris: Editions du Seuil.

Grice, P. (1989). 'Logic and Conversation.' In Grice, P., *Studies in the Way of Words*. Harvard, MA: Harvard University Press, 1–138.

Grossman, D., and Katz, Y. (1993). 'Patterns of Rural Settlements in the Land of Israel.' In Salomon, I., and Kark R., (eds), *Studies in the Geography of Israel*, Volume 14. Jerusalem: Israel Exploration Society, the Department of Geography, The Hebrew University of Jerusalem.

Groupe µ. (1992). *Traité du Signe visuel: Pour une rhétorique de l'image.* Paris: Editions de Seuil.

Habermas, J. (1975). *Legitimation Crisis.* Translated by McCarthy, T. Boston, MA: Beacon Press.

Hagiladi, N., and Kassem, F. (2007). *The War of Independence/The Nakba.* Jerusalem: The Van-Leer Institute and Al-Quds University.

Halliday, M. A. K. (1978). *Language as Social Semiotic: The Social Interpretation of Language and Meaning*. London: Arnold.

—— (1985). *An Introduction to Functional Grammar.* (First edition). London: Arnold.

Halbwachs, Maurice, *On collective memory*, Chicago (IL), The University of Chicago Press, 1992.

Henrikson, A. K. (1994). 'The Power and Politics of Maps.' In Demko, G. J., and Wood, W. B., (eds), *Reordering the World: Geopolitical Perspective on the 21st century.* San Francisco: Westview Press, 50–70.

Hodge, R., and Kress, G. (1993). *Language as Ideology.* London: Routledge.

Hicks, D. (1980). 'Images of the World: An Introduction to Bias in Teaching Materials,' *Accidental Paper No. 2.* Centre for Multicultural Education. London: Institute of Education.

Hroch, M. (1985). *Social Preconditions of National Revival in Europe: A Comparative Analysis of the Social Composition of Patriotic Groups among the Smaller European Nations.* New York: Cambridge University Press.

Jenkins, K. (1991). *Re-thinking History.* London: Routledge.

Kress, G. (1989). *Linguistic Processes in Sociocultural Practice.* Oxford: Oxford University Press.

—— (1993) 'Against Arbitrariness: The Social Production of the Sign as a Foundational Issue in Critical Discourse Analysis,' *Discourse in Society*, 4(2), 169–91.

—— (1996). 'Text and Grammar as Explanation.' In Meinhof, U., and Richardson, K., (eds), *Text, Discourse and Context: Presentations of Poverty in Britain.* Real Language Series. London: Longman.

—— (2000) 'Text as the Punctuation of Semiosis.' In Meinhof, U. H., and Smith, J., (eds), *Intertextuality and the Media*. Manchester: Manchester University Press.

—— (2003). *Literacy in the New Media Age.* London, Routledge.

Kress, G., and Van Leeuwen, T. (1995). 'Critical Layout Analysis,' *International Schulbuch Forschung*, 17. Braunschweig: Zeitschrift des George-Eckert-Instituts, 25–43.

—— (1996/2006). *Reading Images: The Grammar of Visual Design.* London: Routledge.

—— (2002). 'Colour as a Semiotic Mode: Notes for a Grammar of Colour,' *Visual Communication*, 1. London and New York: Sage Publications, 343–369.

Lemke, J. (1998). 'Metamedia Literacy: Transforming Meanings and Media.' In Reinking, D., Labbo, L., McKenna, M., and Kiefer, R., (eds), *Handbook of Literacy and Technology: Transformations in a Post-Typographic World.* Hillsdale, NJ: Erlbaum, 283–301.

La Capra, D. (2001). *Writing Shoa, Writing Trauma.* Baltimore, MD: Johns Hopkins University Press.

Luke, A. (1988). *Literacy, Textbooks and Ideology.* London: Falmer Press.

—— (1996). 'Genres of Power: Literacy Education and the Production of Power.' In Hasan, R., and Williams, G., (eds), *Literacy in Society.* New York: Longman.

Lyotard, J. F. (1984). *The Postmodern Condition.* Manchester: Manchester University Press.

—— (1988). *The Differend: Phrases in Dispute.* Minneapolis, MN: University of Minnesota Press.

—— (1992). *The Postmodern Explained: Correspondence 1982–1985*. Minneapolis, MN: University of Minnesota Press.

Martin, J. R., and White, P. R. R. (2005). *The Language of Evaluation: Appraisal in English.* Basingstoke: Palgrave Macmillan.

Martin Rojo, L., and Van Dijk, T.A. (1997). '"There was a problem, and it was solved!" Legitimating the Expulsion of "Illegal" Immigrants in Spanish Parliamentary Discourse,' *Discourse and Society*, 8(4), 523–67.

Monmonier, M. (1996). *How to Lie With Maps.* Chicago: University of Chicago Press.

Morgan, J. (2003). 'Investigating Images.' In Rogers, A., and Viles, H. A., (eds), *The Student's Companion to Geography* (second edition). Malden, MA: Blackwell Publishing Ltd., 253–260.

Morris, B. (2000). *The Birth of the Palestinian Refugee Problem Revisited.* Cambridge: Cambridge University Press.

Nasser, R., and Nasser, I. (2008). 'Textbooks as a Vehicle for Segregation and Domination: State Efforts to Shape Palestinian Israelis' Identities as Citizens,' *Journal of Curriculum Studies*, 40(5), 627–650.

Nitzan, T. (2006). The Limits of Occupation: The Rarity of Military Rape in the Context of the Israeli-Palestinian Conflict. Unpublished M.A. thesis in Anthropology.

Noth, W. (1995). *Handbook of Semiotics*. Indianapolis, IN: Indiana University Press.

Nora, P. (1996). *Rethinking the French Past: Realms of Memory. Volume 1: Conflicts and Divisions*. New York: Columbia University Press.

—— (1984–1992). *Les Lieux de mémoire.* (Gallimard) abridged translation, *Realms of Memory*. New York: Columbia University Press.

Novick, P. (1999) *The holocaust in American Life.* boston. Houghton Mifflin company

Ogbu, J., and Matute-Bianchi, M. E. (1986). 'Understanding Sociocultural Factors: Knowledge, Identity, and School Adjustment.' In *Beyond Language: Social and Cultural Factors in Schooling Language Minority Students.* Sacramento: California State Department of Education, 73–142. Cited in Cazden 2001: 163.

Olson, D. R. (1989). 'On the Language and Authority of Textbooks.' In de Castell, S., (ed), *Language, Authority and Criticism: Reading on the School Textbooks.* London: Falmer Press, 233–4.

Oren, N., and Bar-Tal, D. (2007). 'The Detrimental Dynamics of Delegitimization in Intractable Conflicts: The Israeli-Palestinian Case,' *International Journal of Intercultural Relations*, 31, 111–126.

Oxford, S., Dorling, D., and Harris, R. (2003). 'Cartography and visualization.' In Rogers, A., and Viles, H. A., (eds), *The Student's Companion to Geography* (second edition). Malden, MA: Blackwell Publishing Ltd., 151–157.

Page, B. (2003). 'Critical Geography and the study of Development. Showers of Blessings?' In Rogers, A., and Viles, H. A., (eds), *The Student's Companion to Geography* (second edition). Malden, MA: Blackwell Publishing Ltd., 97–103.

Panofsky, E. (1974). *Meaning in the Visual Arts*. Princeton: Princeton University Press.

Pappé, I. (2006). *The Ethnic Cleansing of Palestine.* London and New York: Oneworld Publications.

Piterberg G. (2001). 'ERASURES,' *New Left Review*, 10, July-August 2001. London.

Podeh, E. (2000). 'History and Memory in the Israeli Educational System: The Portrayal of the Arab-Israeli Conflict in History Textbooks (1948–2000),' *History and Memory*, 12(1), 65–100.

—— (2002). *The Arab-Israeli Conflict in Israeli History Textbooks, 1948–2000.* Westport, CT: Bergin and Garvey (Greenwood).

Porat, D. (2006). 'The Nation Revised: Teaching the Jewish Past in the Zionist Present (1890–1913),' *Jewish Social Studies*, 13(1), 59–86.

Rabinowitz, D. (2001). 'Natives with Jackets and Degrees: Othering, Objectification and the Role of Palestinians in the Co-existence Field in Israel,' *Social Anthropology* 9(1), 65–80.

Ricoeur, P. (1983). *Time and Narrative, Volume 1.* Chicago, IL: Chicago University Press.

—— (2004). *Memory, History, Forgetting.* Chicago, IL: Chicago University Press.

Rosenthal, R. (2000). *Kaffer Kassem: Events and Myths.* Tel Aviv: Hakibbutz Hameuchad.

Reisigl, M., and Wodak, R. (2001). *Discourse and Discrimination: Rhetorics of Racism and anti-Semitism.* London and New York: Routledge.

Samoyault, T. (2003). *L'intertextualité: Mémoires de la litérature.* Paris: Armand Colin.

Shamir, S. (2005, 2009). 'How the Media Confuse between Palestinians and Philistinians and Why is it Important,' *Haayin Ha-Shviit,* 1 March 2005; *Haaretz*, 18 April 2009.

Shohat, E. (1988). 'Sephardim in Israel: Zionism from the Standpoint of its Jewish Victims,' *Social Text*, 19/20.

Smooha, S. (1997). 'Ethnic Democracy: Israel as an Archetype,' *Israel Studies*, 2(2), 198–241.

Shlaim, A. (2001). *The Iron Wall: Israel and the Arab World.* (Second edition) W.W. Norton and Company: New York and London.

Stock. B. (1990). *Listening for the Text: On the Uses of the Past.* Philadelphia: University of Pennsylvania Press.

Thompson, J. B. (1987). 'Language and Ideology: A Framework for Analysis,' *The Sociological Review*, 35, 516–535.

Tyack, D. (2003). 'Patriotic Literacy: History Textbooks in the Nineteenth Century.' In *Seeking Common Ground: Public Schools in a Diverse Society.* Harvard, MA: Harvard University Press, 38–67.

Van Dijk, T. A. (1997). *Ideology: A Multidisciplinary Approach.* London: Sage.

Van Leeuwen, T. (1992). 'The Schoolbook as a Multimodal Text,' *International Schulbuch Forschung,* 14(1), 35–58. Frankfurt: Diesterweg.

—— (1996). 'The Representation of Social Actors.' In Caldas-Coulthard, C. R., and Coulthard, M., (eds), *Texts and Practices: Readings in Critical Discourse Analysis.* London: Routledge.

—— (2000). 'Visual Racism.' In Reisigl, M., and Wodak, R., (eds), *The Semiotics of Racism.* Vienna: Passagen Verlag, 333–50.

—— (2001). 'Semiotics and Iconography.' In Van Leeuwen, T., and Jewitt, C., (eds), *The Handbook of Visual Analysis.* London and New York: Sage Publications, 92–119.

—— (2005a). 'Multimodality, Genre and Design.' In Norris, S., and Jones, R. H., *Discourse in Action.* London: Routledge, 73–95.

—— (2005). *Introducing Social Semiotics.* New York: Routledge.

—— (2005b). *Introducing Social Semiotics.* London. Routledge.

—— (2007). 'Legitimation in Discourse and Communication,' *Discourse and Communication* 1(1), 91–112.

—— (2008). *Discourse and Practice: New Tools for Discourse Analysis* (Oxford Studies in Linguistics). Oxford: Oxford University Press.

Van Leeuwen, T., and Jaworski, A. (2002). 'The Discourses of War Photography,' *Journal of Language and Politics*, 1(2), 255–275.

Van Leeuwen, T., and Selander, S. (1995). 'Picturing our "Heritage" in the Pedagogic Text: Layout and Illustrations in an Australian and a Swedish History Textbook,' *Journal of Curriculum Studies,* 27(5), 501–522.

Van Leeuwen, T., and Wodak, R. (1999). 'Legitimizing Immigration Control: A Discourse-Historical Analysis,' *Discourse Studies*, 1(1), 83–118.

Veel, R., and Coffin, C. (1996). 'On Learning to Think Like an Historian.' In Hasan, R., and Williams, G., (eds), *Literacy in Society.* New York: Longman.

Walls, M. (2010). *Framing the Israel/Palestine Conflict in Swedish History School Textbooks.* Unpublished PhD dissertation at University of Gothenburg, Sweden. School of Global Studies and Center for Educational Science and Teacher Research.

Waltzer, M. (1987). *Interpretation and Social Criticism.* Harvard, MA: Harvard University Press.

Wertsch, J. V. (1991). *Voices of the Mind: A Sociocultural Approach to Mediated Action.* Harvard, MA: Cambridge University Press.

—— (1994). 'Struggling With the Past: Some Dynamics of Historical Representation.' In Voss, J. F., and Carretero, M., (eds), *Cognitive and Instructional Processes in History and the Social Sciences.* Hillsdale: Erlbaum, 323–38.

—— (2002). *Voices of Collective Remembering.* Cambridge: Cambridge University Press.

White, H. (1973). *Metahistory: The Historical Imagination in Nineteenth-Century Europe.* Baltimore, MD: Johns Hopkins University Press.

—— (1978). 'Interpretation in History.' In White, H., *Tropics of Discourse: Essays in Cultural Criticism.* Baltimore, MD: Johns Hopkins University Press.

Wodak, R., and Reisigl, M. (2001). *Discourse and Discrimination: Rhetorics of Racism and Anti-Semitism*. London: Routledge.

Wineburg, S. (2001). *Historical Thinking and Other Unnatural Acts: Charting the Future of Teaching the Past*. Philadelphia, PA: Temple University Press.

Woodrow, R. (1999). 'Erwin Panofsky's Iconology.' http//www.newcastle.edu.au/discipline/fine-art/theory/analysis/panofsky.htm

Yiftachel, O. (2006). *Ethnocracy: Land and Identity Politics in Israel/Palestine*. Philadelphia, PA: University of Pennsylvania Press.

Yona, Y. (2005). *In Virtue of Difference: The Multicultural Project in Israel*. Israel: The Van-Leer Institute in Jerusalem and Ha-kibbutz Ha-Meuhad Publishers.

Zach, N. (1996). *No Rattling of Sabers: Israeli War Poetry 1940–1990*. (Translated by Raisen, E.) Austin, TX: The Center for Middle Eastern Studies and the University of Texas Press.

Zertal, E. (2004). *Death and the Nation*. Tel Aviv: Dvir Publishers.

Zerubavel, Y. (2002). 'The "Mythological Sabra" and Jewish Past: Trauma, Memory, and Contested Identities,' *Israel Studies*, 7 (2), 115–144.

Žižek, S. (1989). *Violence*. New York: Picador.

INDEX